STORM
STORIES OF SURVIVAL
FROM LAND AND SEA

STORM

STORIES OF SURVIVAL
FROM LAND AND SEA

EDITED BY CLINT WILLIS

Thunder's Mouth Press and
Balliett & Fitzgerald Inc.

New York

An Adrenaline Book®

Published by
Thunder's Mouth Press
A Division of Avalon Publishing Group Incorporated
841 Broadway, 4th Floor
New York, NY 10003

and

Balliett & Fitzgerald Inc.
66 West Broadway, Suite 602
New York, NY 10007

Distributed by Publishers Group West

Book design: Sue Canavan

frontispiece photo: courtesy of the Collection of Dr. Herbert Kroehl, NGDC.

Manufactured in the United States of America

ISBN: 1-56025-300-2

Library of Congress Card Number: 00-108282

For Susan Kohaut

contents

p h o t o g r a p h s

introduction

I associate storms and other big weather with death—with the kind of force that makes me wonder about time and the nature of things. I grew up in south Louisiana, which, among other things, is a good place for hurricanes. My godfather, a man named Neill, worked in New Orleans, but commuted there from a sleepy beachfront community on the Mississippi Gulf Coast. My parents and my brother and sister and I spent a weekend with Neill and his family early in the summer of 1969 when I was eleven years old.

Neill was an engineer, and at one time was much in demand as a restorer of antebellum homes and buildings in small Mississippi towns like Natchez and Hattiesburg. He had just finished some major improvements to his own home, a big white house that had been in his wife's family since before the Civil War. He was proud of the house, which stood about 100 yards up the beach from the Gulf of Mexico. I remember that Neill had built a guest cottage, where we stayed, and had installed in the main house a series of display cabinets for his china collection. Way upstairs somewhere he led my father and me to a nook that interested me more: I remember Neill standing in it showing us his library, which in my partly shuttered recollection is dominated by the westerns of Louis L'Amour.

Saturday afternoon we put on bathing suits and pulled up crab nets from the pier, a tall wooden structure that extended far out into the water. We waded into the Gulf, which, partly thanks to some barrier islands, was calm and warm and amazingly shallow for long distances out from the shore. You could keep your feet for what I remember as a quarter of a mile or more. Late in the day, the teenagers took Neill's boat and went water-skiing, and I tagged along. I remember skimming on skis over schools of fish whose movement dappled the surface of the water in all directions; if you fell you would tumble among them, which worried me but was thrilling. Neill's young son Layton drove the boat.

Later that summer Hurricane Camille, one of only two Force 5 hurricanes ever to come ashore in the United States, came along and washed the pier and the house and the china collection entirely away. When I heard this I didn't want to believe it. The house was too big and it mattered too much to Neill. And I had liked it there; yet this storm had decided that none of us could ever go back to that house, those rooms.

Neill built another house on the same spot, using modern specifications and materials to make it more storm-proof. But other things changed. His children grew up. His marriage ended, and the new house stayed with his former wife. Late in life, Neill made a very happy second marriage and built another home, this one in the Blue Ridge Mountains. He took to living there in the summer.

I saw Neill for the last time when he was old and grief-stricken. His son Layton had died suddenly, and I had traveled to New Orleans for the funeral. Neill himself died a year or so later at his home in the mountains; he was reading the Sunday travel section of the *New York Times* when it happened. When I heard the news, I remembered what I felt like when I was eleven years old and my mother told me that the storm had blown away Neill's house and his china collection and his books and the pier where we got splinters in our feet pulling up the crab nets.

Anyway, weather for me is linked to death and to other ideas that have to do with the passing of time and the way that moments of happiness or unhappiness enter a life, surprising a person and often abiding with a person for years and years—maybe until that person's life is over.

When hurricanes came to town during my childhood, my family would drop our routine and start buying things: tape for windows, groceries that could survive a power outage, batteries for the radio, maybe an extra flashlight. We'd fill up the bathtub with water and sleep on the floor in the living room. Some of our neighbors had to move to school gymnasiums and other public buildings that were built on higher ground, but we got to stay put, waiting for the coming of darkness— the wind and the water that in my experience always came at night.

Those nights come back to me as perfect parties. I remember my parents and the three children all on the floor in the dark—the electric power in our neighborhood long gone—watching the wind bend two giant sycamores that stood next to each other in our front yard. We buzzed and chattered at the excitement of being together in it. I had seen big trees on the ground after storms, so I knew that one of the big oak trees on the side of the house could come through the roof and crush us. Still, watching the wind do its work I felt happier and safer than I felt on still summer nights alone in my room.

I think that my happiness came from the pleasure of sharing with my family a profound insight, and from the pleasure of the insight itself. We loved the storms for their power—not so much their brute force as their power to come and go, carrying everything they wanted with them. The storms revealed to us a world more powerful, more important, and in some ways more appealing than our world of convention, which at times seemed mindless or even cruel: a somewhat confusing mix of soft drinks and hard liquor, courtesy and bigotry, old houses and new cars, and politicians who were astonishingly corrupt and sometimes wildly amusing.

Those storms were evidence to me, at least, that people didn't decide everything. No one told the weather what to do; it could come along and sweep us and our things away at any time. And if weather could surprise us, maybe other things could too; maybe things could change in the most fundamental ways. Change was frightening and sad, but might bring new revelations and new thrills. On balance, I liked the idea that things could change.

Maybe the five of us watching the wind in the trees saw the storm's power as something we could own. We are part of things, and our energy informs the weather in some way. The heat that escapes our bodies rises and stirs up the sky; the water in us comes from the rain and goes back to it on our breath. When I visited northern New Mexico this summer I saw skies that defy my description: black rain walking across the distant desert sky to the south; red clouds back-lit by flickering sheet lightning to the east; discrete, enormous bands of light shot through the sky from the setting sun—all of it at once, all of it oblivious to me, but all of it connected to a larger impulse that I share.

I wonder if that impulse is the impulse to show off. Why not show off? Why not show ourselves in all our glory? Anyone who has ever been outside in a storm knows that the rest of nature isn't shy. In that way weather offers a kind of permission to exercise power as well as a reminder that our power is a force for change and that change is coming whether we like it or not.

Some of this helps explain to me why many people go out looking for bad weather or go to places where they're likely to encounter it. These stories have more to say about that. They also tell us something about what happens when people find that weather or when it finds them.

The people who encounter and survive a big storm generally have a story to tell, and it's often a good one. If nothing else, they're here to remind us of what the weather has to say about things—in particular, about how unsteady things are and how little we can do about it. When we hear or read such a story, we're left to ponder how we feel about all of that.

I still mostly like it. If I glance up from my work right now, I look out of my window at Portland Harbor, but I can't see much. It is raining hard enough for me to hear it. Mist obscures the sun and Peaks

Island; there's no way to tell if the ferry is running right now. The water has absorbed the fog's ash-white hue so that there is no line between them. A single vessel—a fishing boat—is crossing the harbor. I don't know where it's been or where it's going, but I watch until it's gone.

—Clint Willis

from Dark Wind
by Gordon Chaplin

Gordon Chaplin (born 1945) and Susan Atkinson in 1992 sailed to the Marshall Islands in the Central Pacific. There, the couple found themselves in the path of a typhoon. They considered their options, and decided to ride their storm out on board their boat, moored off Wotho Island.

We were watching the sky, where the storm would come from. In the morning, hazy cumulus clouds shot past, alternating with searing blasts of white sunlight. The air glowed with humidity, and quick, luminous terns rode the damp currents like trout. Our skins were shiny and sticky and we were always a little short of breath.

"I feel like a frog," Susan said. "I smell like a frog."

"How does a frog feel?"

"Permanently damp."

"How does one smell?"

"Aquatic. Fertile. Kind of like a pond in summer."

"We're in the same boat," I said, sniffing.

"Luckily," she said. "I better not kiss you, you might turn back into a prince."

By midafternoon the clouds had thickened and turned gray. The air currents had settled down and were moving with steady force across the surface of the lagoon. The formerly electric blue element now matched the air in color, except for small, luminous whitecaps that stood out as strongly as the terns had a few hours earlier.

The wind was pouting through the gray coconut palms of Wotho Island, making them writhe like water plants in a strong current. Kids played excitedly on the grayish-yellow beach. We saw the minister in his white long-sleeved shirt come out of his cinder-block house, look at the sky, look out across the 300 feet of clear, warm, choppy water that separated him from our vessel, and wave. That morning, after we'd gone ashore and Susan was off with her girls, he'd said she'd be welcome to spend the night in the church—along with himself, his wife, and his congregation. He knew better than to invite the captain.

I told Susan about it as we were walking down to the dinghy. "Give it some thought," I'd joked, knowing that she wouldn't. "If anything ever happened to you, I wouldn't want to be the one to have to tell Ashley and Page."

The moment didn't seem important. The storm was going to miss us, we were sure it was. And there was a lot of work to do to get the boat ready. I needed her help.

It wasn't as if we were far from land. I could row her in later, after the work had been done.

If things looked bad.

If she wanted to go.

If I thought she should go.

We were stripping the *Lord Jim* of everything that might catch the wind: sails, sheets, awnings, dock lines, fenders, the boarding ladder. We stowed everything below but the life raft and four large plastic bags of trash and garbage up on the wheelhouse roof.

The bags had been accumulating since Hawaii and some of the garbage was pretty ripe, but Susan had refused to let me bury it under the palms of the deserted island where we'd been anchored. Our first argument since coming to paradise.

The bulky brown bundles were in a different place when I came up from the cabin after stowing a load of gear—aft of the cockpit, in a little eddy of wind that curled around the wheelhouse and blew the smell back inside it. They rose high over the cockpit combing, hid the dock lines, and made it hard to get to the dinghy.

"I moved them down there so they wouldn't blow off," she said.

I opened my mouth, thought better of it, closed it—and opened it again. "They'll blow off anyway. Look at them."

She never turned. "Fine. If they blow off, they were meant to blow off. At least it won't be us doing it."

I threw up my hands and thought, *She has no idea how bad it could be.* But later, when I'd had a chance to think about it a lot more, I realized that she might have had a better idea than I. Worrying about the garbage was her way to cut the storm down to size.

It was nothing short of miraculous to everyone who knew us that we'd managed to survive so much time together alone on a small boat. We'd had our spats—that morning, when she'd been unable to remove the mizzen, I'd suggested that after three years of living aboard she might have learned how. "You never showed me how," she'd shot back. "You never show me anything because you want to keep me helpless."

Helpless! First I'd laughed in amazement, and then I'd apologized. Yes, she was small of stature (about five foot four), but she'd been fired from at least one job for feminist militancy, had kicked an armed mugger out of her car, had thrown her husband out of their house for philandering, and almost jumped ship in Costa Rica. I admit I pushed her out of a dinghy once, but that was nothing compared to the Silent Treatment, her favorite weapon.

Sooner or later, though, we'd rediscover how much we loved what we were doing and how much we needed each other to make it work. Our love for each other flourished on the boat as nowhere else. All the extraneous elements were gone. There was just us between the sky and the water, and our tasks were clearly delineated: to help each other survive and make it over a new horizon to the next port.

• • •

The rushing grayness all around us was deepening into dusk as I put on my mask, snorkel, and fins and jumped overboard to check the anchors. The wind now was well over 20 knots, but we still had a good lee from the nearby island and the water wasn't too rough. It was as warm as the air or warmer, comfortable and reassuring. Angelfish and wrasses were playing near the bottom, glowing like jewels in the dim light.

Both the 45-pound CQR plow on the three-eighths-inch chain rode and the 40-pound Danforth on the three-quarter-inch nylon were well buried in soft mud, a great holding bottom. If the wind shifted, and it probably would, the boat had room to swing 360 degrees without coming close to coral.

The water felt so luxurious I didn't want to come out into the wind. I floated on my back, kicking slowly, enjoying its movement past my skin. The *Lord Jim* lay nicely to the two rodes, and Susan watched me from the wheelhouse. I took a few deep breaths, jackknifed my body to raise my feet in the air, and slid down toward the bottom 20 feet away. I moved slowly, so the fish wouldn't be alarmed, and headed back to the boat underwater about a foot from the bottom.

The 6 p.m. weatherfax from Honolulu came over clearly. Typhoon Gay was about 120 miles east-northeast and moving west-northwest at 7 knots. Maximum winds were 80 knots. When we tuned in WWVH, the powerful radio station in Kauai, Hawaii, that broadcasts time signals twenty-four hours a day for navigational purposes and emergency weather reports every hour at exactly forty-eight minutes after the hour, their report coincided with the weatherfax. Things looked good.

Four days earlier, when we'd first thought about leaving Wotho for Ponape, 480 miles southeast in the Carolines, an ominous low-pressure area had been hanging over the open water we had to cross. We waited another day; the low-pressure area divided like an amoeba. One of the new nuclei began to drift up to the northeast, in our general direction.

Toward the end of the day it had become a tropical depression, with winds around 30 knots.

The next day it had reached the islands a few hundred miles eastward and intensified to a tropical storm, with winds up to 60 knots. We assumed it would now follow the usual storm track northwest and decided to wait until it was safely out of the area. But instead of moving out, it zigzagged north and south and continued to intensify.

When it finally resumed the storm track sometime in the middle of the night, it had become Typhoon Gay. Waiting it out still seemed best; our anchorage was protected to the north and east by the island and the curve of the reef. The track would take it more than 60 miles to the north of us. Winds at Wotho shouldn't be much stronger than the last storm's, where our two-anchor system had been more than adequate. There were no other boats around to break loose and drift into us. If we sailed south away from the storm, the winds would be less strong but we'd be in open ocean—at night.

Stripping the boat had made a big change in the way she rode. "I bet the wind's over thirty knots now, and she's perky and buoyant as can be," I said. "Just like you."

Susan was wearing a dark green tank top, over a black bra, and the pink jogging shorts she'd bought in Hawaii for our daily run in the park near Keehi Marine. Her hair was loose and windblown.

We were alone in the still-grayish darkness, although on shore we could now see the flickering kerosene lamps of the village and the single battery-powered electric light at the community center. No matter what, the night was going to be long and dark, and without her, after all those other nights we'd been through together, I would have felt only half there.

"I'm glad you're not ashore." I put my arms around her. "Really glad." Her body was warm and soft and smelled of sun and suntan lotion; her hair tickled my cheek. When I looked down at her, her eyes were closed.

"I am too," she said, a bit absently. "Listen, I really should call

Ashley and Page. Page has probably been tracking this thing. She tracks all of them."

I groaned. We were out of range of High Seas Radio in San Francisco and had to place our calls now through Sydney Radio in Australia. Even in the best of weather the routine was long, complicated, excruciating. "Couldn't we call them all after the storm?" I said. "Please?"

She finally agreed. We uncorked a bottle of cold California Gewürztraminer from the refrigerator, poured ourselves glasses, looked at each other, toasted, and drank. The rising wind in the shrouds made a little trilling sound every once in a while, like a songbird, and the faint but somehow reassuring smell of the garbage curled through the cabin.

"Well," I said, "I guess tomorrow we'll know what we should have done, won't we?"

We heated up two cans of extra-hot Hormel chili while the wind rose steadily and backed into the north, so we were no longer protected by the island. By 9 p.m. the sustained force seemed to be approaching 50 knots (not that easy to judge in the dark with no anemometer) with gusts over 60—stronger than anything we'd been through before. The 9:48 weather on WWVH hadn't been updated, so we assumed there hadn't been any major changes in the storm's direction or intensity.

We called the village radio and asked them what they'd heard. They said the storm was due to pass at around midnight or a little later. We drew its projected course on our chart and figured that the wind might get a little stronger, but not much. I went up on the bow to check the anchor lines, adjust the antichafe guard on the nylon one, and let a little out so that as the boat swung farther into the north the strain on both rodes would remain the same.

As soon as I got out there, it seemed, the wind picked up. It whistled in my teeth and blew a tune through my nose. Looking directly into it was difficult. My shorts flapped painfully against my legs. When I got back I checked with Susan to see if I'd imagined the change, and she said I hadn't.

• • •

At about 10 p.m. we started the big Perkins diesel, which hadn't failed us yet. The idea was to warm it up and get it ready to use later, if necessary, to take strain off the anchor rodes by motoring slowly ahead.

As usual, one touch of the starter was enough. The needles jumped in the dials and gradually settled into their accustomed places: temperature 80 degrees centigrade, oil pressure 50 psi, RPM 900, transmission pressure 140 psi, starboard alternator charging at about 20 amps. Under the floorboards, the engine was warm and purring.

When I went down in the cabin to take a leak (the wind was too strong to do it over the side anymore), there was a faint smell of decay. I assumed it was from the garbage bags back on the stern but noticed that instead of getting weaker as I moved forward toward the head, it got stronger. I realized it was coming from two gleaming black-spotted tiger cowrie shells we had found a couple of days earlier, alive, in shallow water just short of the drop-off on the barrier reef. I'd found one and, later, Susan had found the other.

At the time, I hadn't realized that shells in some cultures are considered bad talismans. But when I found my shell, glowing eerily in the darkness of its crevice, I'd felt an odd current that was not the joy of discovery. Still, I hadn't resisted taking it back to the boat and showing it to Susan. As she took its smooth, dark heaviness into her hands she had that same wide-pupiled look she had when we made landfall in Hawaii and dropped anchor here.

We let the animal in my shell gradually die and deliquesce until it could be washed out in salt water. The smell was so horrendous that we tried a different approach when she found hers, boiling it briefly to kill and harden the animal and then picking it out with a fishhook. Her way was more humane and the smell wasn't as bad, but the boiling had caused slight chipping and discoloration.

The two shells were now side by side in a sea-railed pocket on the drop-leaf teak salon table. It was too late to throw them overboard; the animals had already died. They were just beautiful skeletons now, and Susan had always been on good terms with skeletons. She collected bones of all kinds, went out of her way to visit cemeteries, and had once put together a photographic essay on the death markers along the Transpeninsular Highway of Baja California. She'd want to keep hers, and it would be wrong to heave mine even though it was the smellier.

No, the two shells should stay together, in death as in life.

The boat was beginning to pitch uneasily in the short chop when I came back up to the wheelhouse. Susan, holding on to the grab rails with her small, strong hands, was looking out the window at the one light still visible on shore: the generator-powered electric light in the community center. All the kerosene lanterns were gone now, and the boat could have been floating in outer space. Susan's face was lit from below by the amber numerals on the depth finder, the pale green glow of the GPS, and the lamps in each of the engine dials. Neither of us spoke.

In that same illumination I could see the face of my watch; a little after 11 p.m. We'd been in darkness for five hours and had at least seven more to go before dawn.

Land people, most of them anyway, tend to sleep through the night. It's different on a boat at sea. The watches continue, no matter what time it is. You sleep a few hours at night and a few hours during the day.

In our usual voyaging schedule, the last watch of the night carried over into daylight and Susan took that, while both of mine were in darkness. On long passages I seemed to be awake at night more than during the day, becoming a creature of the night—a small, vulnerable one. I was well acquainted with the stars, the Southern Cross, the moon (in all its phases), the feel but not the look of big ocean swells. It was a fearsome beauty.

Squalls always seemed to come at night. Cold, sharp, horizontally moving raindrops would rattle against the black windows of the wheelhouse, and the sails would begin to boom like shotguns. I'd cut the automatic pilot, trim the sheets, and try to find the wind, which would be shifting wildly through all points of the compass. Confused, choppy seas would broadside the hull, break into the cockpit, and make me worry about the thin glass in the wheelhouse. The seas would be invisible as always, except for the white foam running down their fronts, but they'd sound like sliding rocks.

Ships always passed at night, too, moving at more than 20 knots, so fast they could be on us twenty-five minutes after their lights appeared on the horizon. And once again I'd marvel at how, in the middle of nowhere, two boats on two different courses originating on opposite sides of a vast ocean could pass so terrifyingly close.

I've read a lot of rhapsodies on the joys of night sailing in the trades. Personally, I was always very glad to see the sun come up, to have survived yet another twelve hours of uncertainty, punctuated by not a few of those waking nightmares, snatches of disembodied conversation, lights and huge waves that didn't exist. When dolphins streaked through that darkness like glowing comets, with unearthly breathing and startling churnings and splashes, I'd tell myself they were the spirits of my dead father enjoying themselves and wishing me well on this voyage. But I never believed it.

The sustained force of the wind now seemed over 60 knots, with occasional gusts that felt well over 80. But how could you judge? It was a dark wind, while the storm in Honduras—our only standard of comparison—had been a daytime one. Does being able to see what you're faced with make it worse or better? You'd think better, except that sometimes at sea, when the sun comes up and illuminates the waves you've been taking for granted all night, they look terrifying. All I can say for sure is that this warm, damp, heavy entity sometimes felt a little stronger than anything we'd experienced before, and sometimes quite a bit stronger.

"*Lord Jim*, how are you doing?" asked Wotho Radio. Usually it was the mayor himself who talked to us, but the mayor was away at the President's Invitational Billfishing Tournament at Kwajalein atoll, about fifty miles southeast. The speaker's English was better than the acting mayor's, whom we'd met earlier in the day, so we couldn't put a face to the voice. It would have been nice to have been able to. "We're doing okay so far," I said. "Have you heard anything new?"

Nothing new. The storm center was still due sometime after midnight, it was still headed west-northwest, and the present latitude was about 11 degrees. It still should pass well to the north.

"Are you sure you don't want to come ashore?" Wotho Radio asked.

It was the voice of experience talking, and we should have listened. Maybe Susan did listen and wanted to go, but she didn't tell me. I didn't ask her. I couldn't make out her expression in the dim light. I wanted her to stay. I was confident in our technology and even more confident that as long as we stayed together everything would be all right.

We couldn't have rowed ashore, of course. The inflatable dinghy would have been blown downwind like a balloon. But swimming ashore in the warm, cozy water would have been easy. It was only 300 feet to the protected beach. I could have swum in with Susan and then swum back. Or I could have stayed ashore with her and let the *Lord Jim* fend for herself.

"We'll hang on here," I said, trying to make out Susan's face. "But your light is very helpful. It lets us know where we are."

"Okay, roger, roger. Wotho Radio standing by."

The idea of abandoning ship—our home, our career, our life—was unthinkable to me, at least at that point. We weren't in trouble, not even close. There were many things we could do if it got worse, but how much worse could it get? I was prepared to take a chance, and I assumed Susan was too.

I went forward to check the anchors again and, as before, the wind seemed to pick up immediately. I could feel the features on my face changing under it into a wind-tunnel grimace—my lips pulled back over my teeth, my eyes squeezed shut, my cheeks flapping.

I had let out all hundred feet of the nylon rode and needed more, so I tied one of the braided orlon dock lines to it with a double fisherman's bend and fitted another polyethylene chafe guard on the other side of the knot. The wind blew through my fingers and made them clumsy as I paid the line out through the bowsprit roller and snubbed it. On the other bowsprit roller the anchor chain, held with a chain hook attached to a 15-foot length of springy one-inch nylon rope to absorb the jerks, still had some belly left in it.

I was cold and breathless by the time I got back to the wheelhouse. Susan handed me a towel. "It doesn't seem to like me going out there, does it?" I joked. I was always complaining that she took things too personally, even the weather. "That last gust was a good eighty knots, didn't you think?"

She nodded without smiling back.

"Maybe we ought to try putting it in gear," I said. "Take the strain off the lines." My hand was shaking slightly as I pushed the Morse control lever forward and watched the RPMs climb to 1,000, the slowest possible motoring speed. "I'll have to go up again and see what's happening."

She put a warm hand on my arm. "Oh, wear your harness. Please!"

It was the first time she'd sounded fearful; maybe she was wishing she was safely onshore. It should have worried me. "We're at *anchor*, Susan." Grinning. "We're not out in the middle of the ocean. If I fall overboard I can climb back on. Actually, it would be really nice to be in the water." I meant it. The air was filled with cold 80-mph raindrops that stung like buckshot. The water, as I imagined it, would be comforting, almost motherly.

This time there was no question: as soon as I left the wheelhouse the wind gusted to the highest velocity yet. I could tell by the weight of it on my body. I had to crouch and shield my eyes. Through the tears, I could see that the engine had caused us to run up dangerously on the anchor rodes and at the same time fall off to port.

I let the wind carry me back to the wheelhouse and took the engine out of gear. Towel again. "Hope we didn't piss off the storm god," I said, with the old casual reassuring grin. I leaned out the wheelhouse door and shouted, "Sorry! For Christ's sake, we're *s . . . o . . . o . . . o . . . o . . . r . . . r . . . y!*"

Maybe if I'd known then what I know now, I wouldn't have shouted so cockily. Maybe. Though the WWVH weather broadcasts told us otherwise, by dusk the storm had actually turned 20 degrees to the southwest and was now headed right at us, with an intensifying wind speed of between 85 and 105 knots.

We were targeted.

The storm god hates technology. For the first time in the four years we'd owned the boat, the depth finder began to malfunction. It would register the correct depth of eighteen feet for a little while, but then the number would be replaced by a line across the screen, meaning that its range had been exceeded or that it was actually sitting on the bottom. The line would be replaced by arbitrary numbers, and then—at increasing intervals—the real ones would come on again. This was unsettling, because a change in depth would be the best way to tell if we were dragging.

Another way would be by the light onshore. But what if the light onshore went out?

A third way could be by means of the GPS, which was accurate to a quarter mile. I programmed a way point that corresponded to the spot where we were anchored so that later, if we seemed to be dragging, we could check our actual position against it.

By this time, Susan had taken up a position on the floor of the wheelhouse near the closed door leading out to the cockpit, the most protected space on board. I was on the settee next to the radio and weatherfax. The boat rolled and pitched sharply, and the noises around us had deepened in tone from a screaming to a deep thrumming vibration. Talk was difficult; there didn't seem to be much to say anyway. The wind outside blew our thoughts away, even though inside the air was calm.

I wondered idly whether the large wheelhouse windows would blow in. The big diesel pulsed. We hung on and waited for the clock to move, and it had never moved more slowly.

Sometime after midnight, I saw that the light onshore was no longer there, although I thought I could still see the loom of the island. There was a chance we could be dragging.

"I better go check the anchors again," I said.

"Oh, God, don't go out there."

I grinned and said something flip, even though I understood very well what she was worried about. To go out would make the storm worse. At the time, I didn't wonder how bad things would have to get before the insouciance she hated so much gave way to tenderness and sympathy.

I tugged the wheelhouse door open. "Well, anyway, the garbage is still on board."

Susan didn't answer. I turned to see why not (in the darkness I couldn't make out her expression), almost went back, almost put my arms around her, but instead I went out and closed the door behind me.

Standing upright on deck now was impossible, so I hauled myself forward from handhold to handhold in the crouch of a man who has had too much to drink—the old Hurricane Walk.

The anchors were holding, but the nylon rode was tight as a piano string and the thick nylon spring line on the anchor chain was stretching more than a foot with every heave of the boat. As it stretched, it chafed against the sharp edge of the bulwark next to the bowsprit. The belly in the chain was gone.

I considered letting out more chain but that would have meant a complicated series of maneuvers. Susan would have to add power from the engine to take the strain off the rodes. When the strain was off, I'd have to reach down with my hand and release the steel bar that locked into the cogs of the windlass and held it immovable.

As Susan cut back the power and the chain paid out, I'd have to control it with the windlass brake while slacking the nylon rode with my other hand. When they were both out enough, I'd have to snub them (the chain with the windlass brake and the nylon with the cleat) and attach the chain hook again. If the brake slipped while I was releasing or engaging the locking bar and the strain of the boat suddenly came back on the chain, I could easily lose a finger or a hand.

I decided not to try, to wait it out and hope for the best. How much worse could it get? We had a third 45-pound CQR plow anchor to throw in an emergency. But for the first time, I began to feel a hint of passivity, a slight inclination to say to myself, "It's gone too far; it's out of my hands."

Back in the cockpit, I saw that our ten-foot inflatable dinghy, which had served us faithfully and well since we'd bought the boat, was floating upside down behind us. As I watched, the wind blew it right side up again; then for a while it left the water completely and streamed out behind us at the end of its painter like a kite. I grabbed the line and shortened it up until the dinghy was snubbed against the hull, but the chafing was worse that way. I tried to haul the whole thing into the cockpit but didn't have the strength.

Finally, I just let it go, feeling that curious passivity gain a little. And, thinking about it later, I realized that the garbage must have blown away by then or it would have been in my way.

For the first time, Susan and I didn't talk about whether the wind had picked up while I was outside. "I don't think the spring line is going to hold much longer," I said, as she handed me the towel, pushing it into my hand as she'd been trained to pass a scalpel to a surgeon in an operating theater. When I tried to check our position against the way point I'd programmed into the GPS, I noticed some unfamiliar symbols next to the numerals. The numerals didn't change when I punched the keys, they didn't respond. There was some malfunction in it, too.

Normally, I would have opened the chart table, taken out the GPS manual, and painstakingly gone through it to find out what the numerals signified. But I didn't. I just didn't seem to have it in me. I sat down on the settee to rest for a minute, and the feeling of inertia gained another notch.

Susan was back in her protected position by the wheelhouse door, staring at me. We were witnessing a performance. What next? Nothing we had been through before in our lives had prepared us for this, but we stayed calm because we had each other. Because everything was going to work out. And because at that moment there was nothing else to do.

Except jump overboard and swim for shore. It would have been easy. But even now, I was pretty sure that the wind wasn't going to get much stronger, that if the spring line broke the chain would hold, that if the chain broke, the emergency anchor on another 200-foot three-quarter-inch nylon rode could replace it. If it didn't we could beach the boat under power, make her fast to some palm trees, and repair the damage when the storm had passed. The big propeller gave so much thrust I still didn't want to put it in gear and risk overriding the rodes.

"Jesus," Susan said, as a banshee gust once again stretched the limits of what we could imagine. Her eyes looked black. There was a heavy, dense thud and the hull lurched backward off the wind for an instant and came up again. "There goes the spring line," I said, on my way out the door. Up on the bow, the anchor chain was rigid as a steel rod. The lunatic wind blew my brain clean. There was nothing to do but let the force carry me back to the cockpit.

My head stayed empty—*too empty to put the engine in gear*—as we sat in the wheelhouse and waited for the chain to break. Or not. The passive feeling gained a few more notches. Five or ten minutes later the chain did break, with the same dense thud. The hull lurched backward again but did not seem to bring up.

Blessed action. The tonic of movement, of carrying out a plan. Susan was at the wheel, applying enough power to move the boat up parallel to the anchor we were still attached to. I was out on the foredeck again, struggling with the emergency anchor. The plan was: when we got into position I'd drop it, and we'd fall back again on the two rodes. I waved my arm, motioning her forward, but the boat had turned far enough broadside to the wind for the high deckhouse to catch its full force. We were blown over at a 45-degree angle and held there, as if the 8,800 pounds of ballast in the keel didn't exist.

We had entered the realm of the storm god. The performance had turned into a demonstration. We were his, now. He set the rules. He made the plans. He wrote the script.

Up on the bow, though, I was so busy reacting that I didn't have time to think. Everything seemed as natural as anything else, as in a dream.

The heavy anchor, the coil of rode, and I slid down the steeply inclined deck to leeward and brought up against the bulwark. I worked slowly and methodically to get things cleared away; the hull now broke the wind so I felt comfortable, as if I could work there forever.

Reality now being beyond question, it didn't surprise me in the least that our little waterproof flashlight, which I'd used on all previous ventures forward, was dimming out. And neither did it come as a great shock, when I finally got the anchor over the side and began to pay out the rode, that there was no strain at the other end. It wasn't holding.

Neither was there much strain on the other rode, when I tested it. Maybe we were still drifting down on it, after having powered upwind to drop the emergency.

Anyway, the job was done. When I stood up to work my way aft, the wind caught me and for a second I was flying. I landed on my knees on our newly nonskidded deck and skidded over the sharp little nubbles, pushed by solid air, wondering how much skin and flesh would be left but, clambering into the tilted cockpit, too busy to look.

"Head her up in the wind!" I yelled at Susan. She was clinging to the wheel to stop herself from slipping down the floor. I closed the wheelhouse door and latched it, and suddenly the enveloping nightmare outside turned stagy and unreal, like a movie from the thirties. I felt her warm, dry body against me as I turned the wheel into the wind and applied power.

We couldn't hear the engine but the tachometer registered 2,200 RPM, full power. It made no difference at all. The boat stayed broadside to the wind, held by it at 45 degrees from the vertical and drifting to leeward, not moving forward or heading up. The depth finder continued to malfunction, but I knew there were coral heads near us and expected one or both of the anchors to snag and pull the bow around. We had shipped no water, and once the bow was back in the wind the boat could straighten up again.

It was as if the anchors didn't exist. We continued to drift to leeward, and now I noticed the engine temperature was into the danger zone, well over boiling. No surprise: it was all part of what was happening. I shut it down, rather than run the risk of ruining it forever; both the propeller and the cooling system intake must have been out of the water.

My watch read 1:10 a.m. I noticed the clasp had been damaged as I'd wrestled with the anchor, so I took it off and carefully put it next to my glasses on the ledge under the wheelhouse windows. It was an old Rolex Oyster diving watch my father had given me when I was eighteen, and I didn't want to lose it. "Well," I said to Susan, "you better call Wotho on the radio and tell them we're drifting"—I checked the compass—"south, out of control."

She called, but (no surprise) there was no answer. Then she said, "Do you think we better get our life jackets on?"

I shrugged and grinned, a strange reflex, but there it was. I'd done all I could. Life jackets were her area of responsibility, her decision. To me they'd always been a little like the EPIRB: a harbinger, a Jonah. An admission of defeat.

"Well, do you?" She sounded angry.

"I guess we should," I said.

The life jackets were inflatable Mae West–type **U**-shaped vests. You put your head through the upside-down **U**. The two ends of it were attached to a web belt that you fastened around your waist with a jam buckle. You inflated it by blowing into a tube past a one-way valve. We put them on and stood there on the tilted wheelhouse floor, looking at each other. If anything, seeing Susan in the jacket made things even less real than before.

"I guess we shouldn't blow them up completely right now," I said. "We need to be able to maneuver."

She put her mouth to the tube and blew hers up about two-thirds of the way. When I tried to blow mine up, nothing happened. "Do you have to twist it or something?" I asked. "No air is going in."

"No you don't have to twist it," she said impatiently. "Just blow."

I blew as hard as I could, felt the one-way valve give reluctantly and the vest inflate. I stopped when it was one-third full.

We drifted downwind in silence for a while. Inside the wheelhouse it was still warm and dry. Someone in Kwajalein was speaking English on the radio, about supplies he'd be delivering somewhere the next day. His call sign was "Mr. Bill."

"Sooner or later we're going to hit the reef," I said. "Or an island. I don't know how much time we have, but we've got to think about what we're going to need." My mind felt sluggish. We both seemed slow, in movement and thought, as if we were in a dream.

Gradually we assembled the emergency items that Susan had prepared: a grab bag of flares, another flashlight, a pocket knife, a compass, a signal mirror, a large polyethylene waterproof container with a first-aid kit and drugs, emergency rations, fishing line and hooks, ship's and personal papers, my swim fins, the EPIRB.

"You better put your watch and glasses in the waterproof container," Susan said.

It was an impressive, foresighted idea, but I never got around to implementing it. I was trying to coax my sluggish mind to think of more immediate things we'd need. *Wet suits?* We each had a three-millimeter-thick full-body surfing wet suit that would help buoy us up, protect us from the coral, and keep us warm, but they were in the forepeak locker, and the forepeak was full of stuff from on deck. I started down to get them anyway but Susan begged me not to. She was worried about a propane gas explosion, and indeed the red light of the gas sensor had been on for some time. But more than anything, anything in the world at that moment, she didn't want me to leave her alone.

Looking around the wheelhouse and the cockpit for more accessible things, I noticed the pile of dock lines formerly hidden by the bags of garbage. I selected a fifteen-foot three-quarter-inch line and tied the ends around our waists, using bowlines, a knot that doesn't slip tighter or jam. "Now you don't have to worry," I said, "I'll never leave you." I do believe I was grinning when I said it. "Is it tight enough?"

She pulled at it. "I don't think so."

I undid it and tied it again. I didn't want it too tight in case it snagged on something and she needed to get out of it. "How's that?"

She raised her eyes, looked me full in the face for a full count of five (I remember every count), and nodded.

We finally grounded with the kind of jarring lurch that usually makes a sailor's heart dive overboard, but all I felt was a strange relief. "Well, there's the reef." I nodded wisely. At last something had happened the way we'd thought it would.

The wheelhouse was still warm and cozy. Electronic equipment glowed blue, green, amber, and red. The radio crackled with snatches of talk. And the quarter-inch safety-glass windows still safely sealed us in.

Our keel bounced at shorter and shorter intervals but never completely settled, as the surf picked it up and dropped it over and over again on the coral. I turned on the roof-mounted searchlight and spun it around, looking for land. There was nothing in sight but howling, undifferentiated blackness. The light made it worse.

Eventually, we slid open the heavy teak wheelhouse door and worked our way out into the real world. We were still removed, not really with it, like newborn babies. The tilted hull rose over our heads and broke the unimaginable force of the wind. To leeward a strange white element that was a mixture of water, air, and rocks hissed and rushed. Invisible surf from the lagoon pounded the exposed bottom of the hull at our backs while unseen waves coming across the reef from the open ocean occasionally broke directly into the cockpit and threw us around. There was one thing, though, that we knew for sure. The water was warmer than the air.

Side by side, clutching the things we'd gathered together, we sat on the uptilted cockpit thwart, our feet braced on the downtilted one. All the literature said to stick with the boat until the last minute. There was no question of inflating the life raft—it would have vanished immediately. Our best chance was that the hull might work its way higher and higher onto the shallow reef until it was solid. Meanwhile, the searchlight continued to play on nothingness, unless you called that white fire-hosing element rushing at the leeward edge of the cockpit something.

The boat was already breaking up. When I went into the wheelhouse to look for the diving knife (still connected by our fifteen-foot rope) I saw the leeward windows, closest to the elements, had shattered. The teakwood components of the wheelhouse had started to split off jaggedly from the fiberglass of the hull. Down in the cabin, the red warning light of the propane gas sensor pulsed. Water, mixed no doubt with acid from our new Surrette Type D batteries, was over a corner of the floorboards and climbing up the settee toward our new blue canvas seat covers.

The knife was nowhere to be found. I reeled myself back along the rope to the small wet person alone in the cockpit, sat down next to her again, and put my arm around her. Automatically she leaned forward to clear her hair. She always did that, because she hated to have it pulled.

The last wave held us underwater for too long. It was time to go, and quite easy. We let the soft, almost blood-temperature element carry us clear of the foundering hull.

We were holding hands. The searchlight, now only a few feet up, shone away from us into blackness. The wind was easier, with only our heads in it. The noise was somewhere in the background. We were breathing the element, and it seemed breathable.

Drifting downwind from the hull, Susan's voice came more like a thought. "Where are we?"

I heard my matter-of-fact answer. "I don't know." The searchlight was extinguished, leaving us in darkness. The boat was gone. I blew on the tube to inflate my vest the rest of the way but no air would go in. A wave from the lagoon broke over us, tearing her hand out of mine, scraping my back against the reef. It was not sharp coral here, but weed-covered smooth rock. That was lucky.

Three-foot waves began breaking over us about every fifteen seconds. In the darkness we couldn't see them coming. They were big enough to roll us over and disorient us, to hold us underwater for a few seconds, to scrape us against the rocks but not to smash us. I held

Susan around the waist with one arm and with the other held on to my partially inflated life vest.

Its belt had come undone and the U-shaped part had slipped off my head. In the darkness, I couldn't make out how to put it back on. The valve was still stuck. All the things we had brought with us had disappeared by this time, or I would have put on my fins. They would have made swimming twice as easy.

In some of the waves we couldn't hold on to each other. We'd catch our breath, get oriented, get a new grip. Another wave would come and go. We'd start the process over. Then I lost contact with Susan completely. I pulled on the rope. There was no resistance; finally I felt the knot at my fingertips, the empty loop. Nothing was visible.

The energy I used up in the next three or four strokes equaled all the previous energy combined. But she was there, not far away. Quite near. My arm was back around her soft waist and her voice was back inside my head, almost like a thought. "I've come out of my jacket."

She was holding on to it now, like I was holding on to mine. Her wet round head, mouth open and facing up, was in silhouette—against what? Against blackness, and yet I could see it clearly, the first thing I'd been able to see since we'd left the boat. Between waves, I tried to fit the loop back over her shoulders, under her arms. And failed.

We were in deeper water, no more rocks under our feet. Had we drifted out over the reef into the open ocean? Her voice again. *"Hold me up."* An arm around my neck, a hug, an embrace, like so many times before.

"Not the neck, pet. Not the neck." Obediently, she took her arm away. Her back was to me, my arm was around her waist. A few more waves rolled through and I yelled, "Hold on to your jacket. Hold on to the rope. Are you all right? You have to tell me if you're not all night."

She was making an oddly reassuring noise, *"Oh, oh, oh, oh."* I knew it well. It was the noise she made when she was scared—as we rowed our tiny inflatable dinghy closer and closer to a sleeping whale or when a car shot out in front of us on the highway without warning. When she made that noise, I knew, there wasn't any real danger. When the danger was real—when our car actually left the road on a rainy, foggy night in upstate New York and flew through the air into a ten-foot-deep culvert; when the seventy-foot shrimp boat broke loose in the last storm in Honduras and began to drift down on us; when the Cessna 172 I was trying to land began to porpoise down the runway—there had been no noise from her at all.

I knew how she hated and feared being rolled in the waves even on a good day, but as long as she made that noise there couldn't be any problem. Things would work out. We were together.

We were underwater again. I opened my eyes and saw her clearly, as if she were outlined in black fire. She was relaxed. There was a little smile on her lips and her eyes were half closed. Her long hair spread out in the water. The top of her head was about a foot under the surface, and when I put my hand under her chin and tried to push up, another wave was there.

She moved farther away from me below the surface and the black light around her was extinguished. I reached out and felt her hair—the soft, fine ends. The tips of my fingers could still feel it as the tickly bubbles and warm currents of the next wave curled around me, wrapped me up, and did what they wanted with me.

I can feel it now.

The voice started talking in the womblike dark water sometime after I lost Susan. I was dog-paddling with one hand, holding the limp life vest with the other. I seemed to be in the open ocean now, with infinity in all directions, but whether or not I was on the surface was unclear. I could feel myself breathing something—air, water, or both. The storm seemed vague. *You blew it,* the voice said, and I felt myself crying, but it didn't seem to matter very much. *She's gone.* I would soon be gone myself. Maybe I already was gone. Is this what drowning feels like?

If it is, then drowning is mostly a process of waiting. Waiting for it all to be over with and wondering every once in a while how you'd know. No revelations, no home movies of your life, no regrets. No strong concerns, either about Susan or myself. A lonely way to die, but then what isn't? "What is the answer?" Gertrude Stein was asked as she slipped away, and she answered, "What is the question?" Neither the voice nor the womblike element that I floated in offered anything profound. I did have a feeling, though, that when I died I'd be able to see again.

Our story was almost complete. It was going to have an honorable end—and in a way, a happy one. We weren't going to die in each other's arms, but we were going to die in the same storm, in the same element, probably just about at the same time. Death was not going to put us asunder, the storm had done that; it was going to join us together again for good.

So the feel of sand under my slowly kicking feet was out of place, unbelievable. Sand instead of coral could mean a beach. A beach could mean an island. The story was being botched, I felt dimly, but there was nothing I could do about it; when I lost Susan I lost all control. My body wanted to survive, and each time my toes touched the sand I felt them dig in and push as hard as they could. They touched more and more often—they knew what they were doing.

I knew I was on land when I felt myself leave the water on hands and knees, felt the screaming air sandpaper my body raw, felt my arms and legs move me up, over a small ledge and partially out of the blast. The land was shaking. The air boomed. I pulled my knees up to my chin, wrapped my arms around my head, and lay there. *So you made it*, the voice said. *Nice going.*

Someone was laughing, a booming, roaring, awful laugh. I burrowed into the dense, thorny brush in front of me until I was too tired to move.

Sometime in the darkness the eye of the storm passed through, and in the half hour or so of calm I stumbled along the invisible beach calling for her until the wind screamed me down. Coming in from the southeast instead of the northwest, it seemed if anything stronger than before. The island vibrated in a deep base register, and big heavy things seemed to be flying over my head and into the water.

At first light, I began searching the parts of the beach that were pro-tected enough to stand on (the wind had dropped a little from its full force). Now I could see, though fuzzily without my glasses, where everything had happened. I had washed ashore at the northern end of a long, thin, low island, part of the uninhabited chain that encircled Wotho lagoon. A spit of sand led out into open water, a kind of channel in the reef with large, curling brown waves indicating a fair depth and current. Barely visible through the rain, blown sand, spume, and the blur of nearsightedness was a small rock ledge a few hundred yards away on the other side of the channel.

The *Lord Jim* must have hit near the rocky ledge. After we abandoned her, we'd been swept into the rough channel. There was no sign of the boat. Everything was brownish-whitish-gray, the color of the wind blowing the tops off the dirty waves and mixing them with air. The things that had been roaring through the air over my head were the tops of palm trees. They were in the surf, washing up and down the beach along with other detritus. *How do you like it now, gentlemen?* the voice asked.

Each time I searched the beach, a figure was there, cottony and vague, like everything else appeared without my glasses. The first few times I ran toward it, fearing I'd die before I got there. It would recede ahead of me, fade out, or turn into something else. But even when I couldn't see it, I felt it was there. I began to dread it, but desperately needed it at the same time.

I couldn't imagine Susan herself—where she might be if she wasn't on that beach. What she was thinking? It came to me later, as if trans-mitted by some celestial EPIRB: *Where is he? God, where did he go?*

I lost count of how many times I walked the two miles of coastline, searched through the high mounds of debris and dense thickets all the way to the other side, but the last few times there was nothing new, nothing more to come ashore. The narrative of shipwreck was starkly told by what was there, almost everything from the boat that wasn't bolted on and some things that were.

Nothing of Susan's was on the beach but—as if she'd arranged it before departing—I quickly and easily found all the things I needed to survive. There was the waterproof emergency container, which would have had my glasses and watch in it if I'd listened to her, but which did have the other things she'd stocked it with: beef jerky for protein and gumballs for quick energy, various antibiotic and pain pills for the coral cuts on my feet and legs; the ship's papers and our passports, which the authorities would need when I reported what had happened. There was her precious Class I EPIRB, still blinking away and transmitting its special coded message via satellite to the nearest U.S. Coast Guard station—probably Honolulu, more than two thousand miles to the northeast. Scattered up and down were most of the foam rubber cushions in their new canvas covers. I could lie on the foam and zip myself up in a cover like a sleeping bag for protection from the rain. And completely buried in sand except for one arm was my black full-body wet suit.

I uncovered it gently, and as I did so suddenly I was back in the boat's wheelhouse, drifting downwind out of control, about to go down to the forepeak and get our wet suits and hearing her say, *"No. Please don't leave me."*

But this time I did go down. I got the wet suits and we put them on in the wheelhouse. Their buoyancy kept us afloat after we'd abandoned ship, and the three-millimeter foam protected us nicely from the coral and kept us warm both in the water and after we'd crawled out on the beach and under the bushes. They were what saved us.

The scene had the reality of a drug hallucination. It was to be the first of many replays, each with its own new twist and each having a happy ending. They're still happening.

from Sheer Will
by Michael Groom

Australian mountaineer Michael Groom (born 1959) in 1987 lost a third of each foot to frostbite on Kangchenjunga. He returned to the high mountains, and was a guide on the 1996 New Zealand Everest expedition that put six people on the summit—and then lost four of them to a sudden storm. Here he offers a professional climber's perspective on those widely documented events.

I found myself joining a commercial expedition to Mount Everest in the spring of 1996 when Rob Hall needed another guide. Guiding clients up mountains has been an occupation for the last century, most notably when Edward Whymper employed two Swiss guides to make the first ascent of the Matterhorn in 1865. Unfortunately this ascent ended when four of their party fell to their deaths. In recent times some degree of criticism has been aimed at commercial expeditions for poor service and unsafe practices, or at guides who drag inexperienced climbers willing to pay large sums of money to the summit of their whimsical dreams. The situation also raises the question: Where does a guide's responsibility for a client stop in a life-or-death situation? I gave it considerable thought as I mulled over Rob's offer, but could not find a confident answer.

The days of sponsored expeditions are well and truly over and the large sums of money needed to mount an expedition to any of the world's highest mountains have to come from somewhere. Any climber with the experience and motivation to attempt Mount Everest must also have a network of like-minded climbing friends, all with disposable incomes and plenty of time, not only for the climb but for the planning stages as well. Anyone lacking any of these requirements is forced to look at other options. One is to look for a private expedition willing to sell off positions on their permit. This sometimes means a number of smaller teams operating under the one expedition permit, often with little overall planning, a mishmash of experience levels and to the detriment of such things as safety, food and equipment. Such expeditions can become a risk to other teams on the mountain, as well as to themselves. Of course, it can work well, as I have experienced, but it is far better for someone who does not have the network of resources and a high level of experience to join a professionally run (commercial) expedition.

In the world of commercial expeditions Rob Hall had an aura of respectability that was hard to match. I had become friends with him on the K2 climb and had enjoyed his generous hospitality at various base camps in the world's greater mountain ranges. Rob had shown me the impressive list of climbing résumés, but the final incentive came when a friend of mine, John Taske, was accepted on the climb as a paying member. In fact a few of the climbers had more experience than some of the members of the non-commercial expeditions I had been on in the past. I would be the third guide along with Rob and Andy Harris, a professional guide, whom I had not met but who, by all accounts, was an excellent guide and a likeable fellow. I would need no introduction to the quality of an expedition Rob organised and, as I had witnessed on many occasions, there would be no shortage of good food, worldwide satellite phone and fax communications, and the best equipment money could buy. It would be sheer luxury compared with my previous expeditions. As a guide I would be using oxygen, a foreign experience for me, so much so that I was embarrassed to admit I could not screw a regulator onto an oxygen bottle. Rob had to show me in the privacy of our mess tent. To compare an ascent of Everest using oxygen to one without was an interesting experiment.

I had been in Nepal for most of March co-guiding a trek to a couple of smaller peaks that unfortunately became a non-event due to a heavy snowfall. I left the trek a couple of days early, in the capable hands of my co-leader Mike Wood, to be in time to meet the Everest team in Kathmandu. The bus trip back from the foothills of the Himalayas was a dusty and exhausting ride, and to test my patience further I had difficulty finding a hotel room when I arrived. Looking worn and grubby means you are a less likely victim of streetside salesmanship, so it was with considerable ease that I made my way through the backstreet alleys to the barber. My barber friend knows me well from many visits and I have always felt comfortable in his rickety chair, even though we can only exchange a few words of greeting. I had only just submitted to his razor, when John Taske bounced in to have his pre-expedition haircut. He had climbed with me a couple of times in Nepal and Tibet and had a million and one questions about the pending climb and regaled me with gossip from home. I could only afford the occasional response, as the barber did battle with my two-week growth.

On my way back from the barber I called in to Rob's hotel to announce my arrival. It was then that I met the first of our eight members, Stuart Hutchison. I took an immediate liking to the tall, handsome Canadian who was working in the USA as a cardiologist. His considerable mountaineering experience had seen him on Broad Peak, Denali, K2 and the North Face of Everest.

Food fantasies are a common torture on climbing expeditions and why climbers persist in tormenting themselves by talking about food they cannot have until they return to civilisation, I do not know. On this expedition there would be no such problems. Helen Wilton, our BC manager, took great pride in overseeing the preparation of every lavish meal and she had a shopping list of fresh vegetables, meat, bread and the occasional beer brought in on a weekly basis. As this was my first luxury expedition, I was determined to make the most of the food, but I met tough competition from Lou Kasischke, a US attorney with numerous ascents of the world's smaller but better known mountains to his credit. He liked his food as much as his climbing; as he had a big engine to run it was usually Lou who won the silent battle over the last piece of tomato or dollop of chocolate mousse.

With the spring climbing season in full swing a record number of teams had gathered at the southern side of the mountain. It represented an enormous social scene which I normally enjoy but on a much smaller scale. Catching up with old friends and making new ones is part of the social activities at BC. But with any community of between 100 to 150 people there are inflated reputations, egos, one-upmanship and the inevitable false rumours. These elements I deplore in such a fine setting and purposely avoided them by keeping to myself.

BC had more home comforts than I was used to. A hot shower on call was just one of the many luxuries. It only made it difficult to leave and start up the hill. These comforts were thanks to Rob's meticulous planning and Helen, who took care of everything each time we came off the mountain. Caroline MacKenzie was our qualified doctor and at any given time of the day she could be seen treating someone, often from other teams. Her specialty, to use another doctor's expression, was coughs, colds and sore holes.

I had now been away from home for two months and I took full advantage of the phone and fax on a daily basis. This alone made being apart for so long a little more bearable. Little did we know what a key role our small phone would play towards the end of the climb.

Beck Weathers, a pathologist from Texas, and I had something in common—we liked to start the day with an early breakfast. Often it would be only Beck and I enjoying an early bite together in the BC mess tent. Without doubt Beck had the gift of the gab and my only opportunity to change the subject would come when someone else entered the mess tent. His unmistakable southern accent could often be heard on the mountain while he climbed—a considerable talent at altitude.

I first met Doug Hansen the year before when Veikka and I shared the same BC area while attempting to climb Lhotse. It was his second opportunity to attempt Everest with Rob. He had previously reached the

South Summit but was forced to turn around due to bad weather. This time he was determined to climb the last 80 metres.

Jon Krakauer was a journalist on assignment for an American outdoor magazine. With considerable climbing experience at lower altitudes, his brief was to cover the increase in popularity of commercial expeditions to the world's highest mountains. Jon certainly had a way with words as his sign on our BC toilet shows. YO! Dude! If you are not a member of The New Zealand Everest Expedition *Please* don't use this toilet. We are a way serious bunch of shitters, and will have no trouble filling this thing up without your contribution. Thanks, The Big Cheese.

Despite popular public belief that Everest has become a giant rubbish dump, modern-day climbers have taken it upon themselves to clean up the rubbish left behind by expeditions who believed no-one would be following in their footsteps. Everest is cleaner now than it has been for a long time. Every expedition is obliged to take out what it takes onto the mountains, otherwise heavy fines are enforced. In the case of our expedition we included the removal of human waste from BC.

Rounding out our team of eight clients were Frank Fischbeck and Yasuko Namba. Frank was a middle-aged Hong Kong publisher who seemed to be very much at ease with climbing Everest. He had attempted it 3 times before. I liked his reserved manner and after sharing a tent with him at C1 I discovered he was a real gentleman.

Yasuko Namba was a Japanese woman of featherweight build and gritty determination. She was the hardest to get to know. Although everyone tried to draw her into a conversation she responded with limited English. At times I felt for her, hoping she wasn't a raving extrovert bursting to have a conversation with someone.

The heavy work for our team settled on the shoulders of the strongest Sherpas around. The team of Lhakpa Chiri, Kami, Arita, Norbu, and Chuldrum were led by Ang Dorje. Over the next four weeks our group of individuals grew to become a harmonious team.

• • •

Scott Fischer's American expedition and ours had decided to team up for a combined effort in the belief that we would make a powerful force in trail-breaking to the summit. We met to finalise a date both teams could work towards for a summit attempt. As we discussed the next five or six days, it seemed increasingly likely that 10 May was the big day. As it happened, Rob and I considered the 10th to be our lucky date. Rob had summited Everest twice on that day, and I had summited a collection of the world's highest mountains on that day too.

Frank Fischbeck and I were the last to arrive at C4 late in the afternoon of 9 May, having spent most of the day climbing up from C3. It was windy on the South Col with light snow falling; this did not surprise me, nor was it cause for concern for our summit attempt beginning at 11:30 p.m. Although the day had started off under exhausting conditions weighed down with a heavy pack of personal gear plus rope and oxygen bottles, once I started to breathe bottled oxygen from midday onwards, the climb became a cruise. I experienced little of the stress I was used to when climbing without it, and I could see how climbers who become dependent on bottled oxygen can run off the rails when the supply abruptly runs out.

Arita, the designated cook at C4, shared a tent with Chuldum to prepare the basic noodle soup and cups of tea. It was far easier for them to do this and pass the mugs of hot drinks from door to door than each tent try to do their own. Ang Dorje, Lhakpa, Chiri, Kami, Norbu and Chuldum would accompany us to the summit.

The calm that I was hoping for arrived a couple of hours before our departure. Rob asked me to lead. We aimed to keep our eight climbers, three guides and five Sherpas within a distance of 100 metres from front to back. Ang Dorje, our head Sherpa, explored the climbing route ahead of us. Scott Fischer's group of a similar size would leave fifteen to twenty minutes after us. Frank had been considering an early failure for the last 24 hours but I had urged him to at least make a start for the summit in the hope that he might find some new lease of energy and motivation as I had done on previous attempts. Frank's gut feeling told him that today was not the day. He turned back early in the night, too tired to continue, but the rest plodded on in the light of a half moon and the occasional flurries of snow.

Certain landmarks prompted memories of my 1993 ascent and the debilitating cold which at the time froze any thought of reaching the summit. Now with oxygen I was comfortably warm and progress was relatively easy. At some stage, surrounded by many of the summits I had climbed, I marvelled at the luck which the 10th had brought me. On the eastern horizon was Kangchenjunga, climbed on 10 October 1987; then Everest, climbed on 10 May 1993; around the corner, Cho Oyu, climbed on 10 May 1990; and now, with the coming of dawn, 10 May 1996 was shaping up to be another great day. I quickly reprimanded myself for using luck to climb on. So brilliantly clear was the dawn that I stopped frequently to take in the view, something I was rarely able to do in 1993 when I could barely find the energy to take the next step.

This climbing was fun, and when we broke out into sunshine on the crest of the South East Ridge, I must confess feeling so confident that I put the summit 'in the bag.' We changed our oxygen cylinders and the sun was so warm I could change mine with bare hands.

Rob's arrival on the ridge meant we were together again as a team. Everyone had coped well with the pre-dawn hours, which psychologically can be the toughest, and after a long rest we set off for the steepest part of the climb to the South Summit. It was such a great day that it was almost deceitful in its promise of continuing good weather.

Summit fever. I have seen it in others on many occasions and have experienced it personally on my earlier climbs. Sometimes it can be the boost needed for that final push to the summit but often it can be a dangerous state with fatal consequences. Yasuko had told me she was well known in Japan and hoped to emulate her countrywoman, Junko Tabei, the first woman and the only Japanese woman to have climbed Mount Everest. I could see signs of summit fever in Yasuko's eyes and actions. I worried that her overwhelming desire to climb this mountain could end up killing her if she ran her race before her time. I purposely climbed in front of her to impose a more suitable pace.

The oxygen mask and goggles cover most of your face and hide your true feelings and expressions. All morning I had been bothered by bad stomach cramps. They were growing so bad, I was regularly doubled over in pain. To everyone else it would have looked like the normal resting position for high-altitude climbing, leaning heavily on your ice axe for support. It was becoming a threat to my position as a guide and my summit chances. Some members of the Fischer group, including the guide, Neal Beadleman, had passed us while we changed our oxygen cylinders. At the base of a steep rise leading directly to the South Summit we caught up to Neal who was about to fix a rope to this difficult section. I intended to help uncoil the rope for Neal and belay him but a sudden attack of stomach cramps stopped me in my tracks. Bent over in pain I seriously contemplated heading down. 'Tie this end to something solid will you,' yelled Neal as he tossed the end of the rope. It fell across my back as I was fearing losing control of my bowels. Impatient at my seemingly unhelpful attitude Ang Dorge snatched up the rope from my back and secured it to something solid. Fifteen minutes later I started up the rope that Neal had just fixed. I was feeling marginally better. It was 10.00 a.m. when I arrived at the South Summit. Jon was not far behind and while I waited I passed on the good news of our progress and position to Helen and Caroline who were monitoring our radio calls at BC now 3.2 kilometres below us. I remarked to Jon that we had only 80 metres to go; in fact, we could almost see the summit. I was barely able to control my temptation to push on. Rob, however, wanted us to regroup at the South Summit and assess the situation from there. Yasuko arrived next, followed by Andy, with Rob and Doug not far behind, but the steep unrelenting climb to the South Summit had taken its toll. Two hundred metres below us Stuart, John and Lou had reached their highest point at around 8600 metres before descending with one of our Sherpas. I felt sad for my friend John but he had climbed as far as he could and that is all one can hope for. I hoped he could salvage some satisfaction from this fantastic day we were experiencing. At this stage I don't remember any comment on Beck. He had, however, succumbed to problems with his sight and Rob had instructed him to stay near where we first changed our oxygen bottles until we returned. The attrition rate for both teams had been very high by the time we reached the South Summit. As the remaining members of both teams regrouped there, they became well and truly mixed together and it was difficult to tell who was who behind the oxygen mask and goggles.

The standing arrangement was that both teams of Sherpas would swap leads in fixing the sections of rope on the trickier sections. This system had not worked with Ang Dorge doing most of the trail breaking and Neal fixing the odd piece of rope. The Sherpa from the Fischer group had not materialised so at the South Summit Ang Dorge, and rightly so, considered he had done his share and refused to do any more. The question now seemed to be who was going to relent and do that little bit more. The sections to fix were not overly difficult with only a couple of short sections between us and the summit and I felt inclined to fix them myself, but Rob had given me instructions not to get involved. He would rather I stayed with our group. Precious minutes ticked by at the accountable rate of 2 litres of oxygen per minute. A rest of fifteen minutes was acceptable, given the time of day, but it was now starting to extend past that. I fought an internal battle: Should I ignore Rob's instructions not to fix ropes and for the team to regroup at the South Summit by heading for the summit now? The wind was also playing heavily on my mind, it had increased in strength making it difficult to decide if we should go up or down. Repeated calls on the radio to Rob for help to answer my dilemma were met with silence. No doubt he was climbing in the transmission shadow cast by the South Summit. Finally the problem was solved when Neal and Anatoli, two guides from the American team, decided to fix the ropes themselves.

Another call to Rob revealed he was just below the South Summit and he said those of us waiting should go on up to the summit. I had been watching Jon who reminded me a little of myself, although I never really got to know him. For an American he was quiet, almost reserved. It seemed he preferred to listen and think about an ongoing conversation, contributing a little only if he had to. During our forced delay on the South Summit Jon and, to a lesser degree, Andy could not hide their eagerness to continue. I knew the feeling well from 1993, but this year I had none of that driving ambition. Andy, with his usual thoughtfulness for others, suggested Jon and I should go on ahead but I knew the importance of an Everest summit for Andy and told him to go instead. The two of them would make short work of the distance to the summit; besides, he had some rope which might be useful above the Hillary Step. This would leave me to discuss with Rob my concern about the rest of us continuing. Yasuko had slowed dramatically, leaving me to wonder if she had the strength and speed to reach the summit before our turn around time of 1:00 p.m. Doug was certainly dragging the chain too. Rob remained out of radio contact.

The wind on the South Summit continued to increase but was certainly very mild compared to the wind on the summit ridge of Kangchenjunga. I was checking the oxygen supply in Yasuko's bottle when Rob arrived. 'Where are the others?' he asked.

Had he forgotten our chat just a few minutes earlier or had I misunderstood him? I pointed in the direction of the Hillary Step and offered no explanation for letting Andy and Jon go ahead, preferring instead to change the subject.

'What about this wind?' I asked. He considered my question carefully before he answered.

'It'll be all right, provided it doesn't get any worse. Why don't you and Yasuko go to the summit, while I wait for Doug. He's not far behind.'

The corniced and narrow ridge connecting the South Summit to the Hillary Step seemed more difficult this year than I remembered it, perhaps because there was less snow, so we took our time over this airy traverse. Every foot placement had to be spot on and backed up with our ice axes driven as deeply as possible into the hard-packed snow. Yasuko had regained her gritty determination and by the time we had overcome the final obstacle of the Step itself, Andy and Jon were returning from the summit. Meeting them on the narrows of the summit ridge created a delicate passing manoeuvre and Andy wanted to make our meeting even more memorable by greeting me with the 'high five'. He was justifiably pleased with his summit and he knew we were only minutes away from ours. His parting words were lost in the confines of his oxygen mask.

Yasuko and I went on to summit at around 2:15 p.m., just ahead of some members of the other team. The view did not compare with the morning's but it was still better than in 1993. The usual low-level cloud for this time of the day had flooded the valleys as the warm air of the plains rose to meet the cold air of the mountains. Yasuko's spirited arrival at the summit meant she had now reached the highest points on all the seven continents. I was pleased for her but personally felt little emotion. The summit had come too easily this time with the use of oxygen, and even though Everest was the highest point in the world, it felt like just another summit. I was not even interested in taking photos, but Yasuko was, so I tried to capture the moment for her: a panoramic shot of her sitting on the summit and a second filling the frame with her delighted smile.

Rob arrived on the summit as we were packing up, and he said that Doug was not too far behind. I gained some pleasure from this unrewarding achievement by shaking Rob's hand. In the short time we had known each other I had always enjoyed our partnership in the mountains and we had become good friends. I had purposely left the pleasure of speaking to Helen and Caroline for Rob as I knew that this moment was one of the highlights for Helen in her role as BC manager. No doubt they had already received a call from Andy and Jon and were waiting for the final summit tally so they could contact our family and friends. Once Rob had broadcast the good news, Yasuko and I started down as it was becoming quite crowded on the summit with five or six of the other team arriving. Rob would follow with Doug. As Rob predicted, we met Doug not far below the summit just above the Hillary Step. I slapped Doug's shoulder in encouragement and said the summit was 80 metres up the gently sloping ridge. It would come into view around the next corner and from there there would be no stopping him. It has been reported that Doug didn't reach the summit until after 4:00 p.m. This meant that Rob would have waited on the summit for another one and a half hours and presumably for a lot of that time watching Doug shuffle agonisingly slowly towards the summit.

Yasuko handled the descent to the South Summit with much more ease than the ascent. I was not so lucky. Halfway down the abseil of the Hillary Step I was caught with an acute urge to have a pee. Looking down to the fly of my climbing-suit, I saw the long cord attached to the zipper was tangled in a mixture of harness straps and buckles. Bent over double I waited in vain for the urgency to pass. I would have to abseil to the bottom of the Step and untie as quickly as possible. But in my haste I lost control and a pleasantly warm flood trickled down the inside of both legs, mainly to the left boot. I realised my left foot was the warmest it had been all day. I suffered none of the embarrassment of my childhood pants-wetting days, but I did worry that any icicles dangling from the crutch of my climbing-suit might raise Yasuko's curiosity! Thanks to modern-day fabrics, nothing could be seen.

Every second step squelched to the sound of a boot full of urine; I may have found this amusing, if it were not for finding Jon slumped on the ridge beneath the Hillary Step. He was in a very distressed state, having run out of oxygen—a crippling event at such altitude, made even more critical for Jon when Andy told him there was no more. This comment by Andy signalled that he was also affected by oxygen deprivation. I unplugged my bottle and connected it to Jon's hose. The benefit was almost instantaneous and the three of us continued to join Andy on the South Summit. Here I easily located our eight bright orange cylinders that we had stashed for our return. It would have been easy for Andy, in oxygen debt and in the euphoria of a post-Everest summit, to mistake full cylinders for empty as there is little noticeable difference in weight. However, I knew that Andy was behaving irrationally and I was keen to get him back on oxygen as soon as possible. I expected the same remarkable return to normality as I had seen from Jon just a half hour earlier.

At any other place in the world these full cylinders may have been looked upon as scrap metal or useless pieces of junk, but at the second highest summit in the world, they were priceless and they represented a return ticket to the real world below. I carefully distributed the cylinders to Andy, Jon and Yasuko as if they were newborn babies. This left four full ones in the stash for Rob, Doug and two of our Sherpas, Ang Dorje and Norbu, who were now accompanying Rob. My priority for attention was for Andy, I wanted to turn Andy's flow rate up to the maximum of 4 litres a minute for five minutes so he could recover, but I was distracted by Yasuko who fumbled with her cylinder dangerously close to the edge. Her tiny hands had difficulty grasping the cylinders so I helped her change. After this I was distracted again from helping Andy by Jon who wanted me to check the flow rate on his regulator which should have been on 2 litres a minute but was on 4 litres, which explained why he had run out prematurely. By now Andy had his mask on and things seemed to be under control. I still wanted to check with him but I had now been without oxygen for some time and felt it was important for me to get back on the Os.

Many months after this climb someone asked me how I could function without bottled oxygen while everyone around me couldn't. I put this down to the fact that I had done so much climbing above 8000 metres without bottled oxygen that my system could cope better than theirs when the oxygen was gone. I also, therefore, didn't have the emotional dependency on oxygen. This was the first time I had used oxygen above 8000 metres; for the others it was their first time above 8000 metres.

With everyone appearing to be comfortable with their new bottle of oxygen I stood up to see Rob's lanky figure standing patiently at the top of the Hillary Step waiting for someone to clear the ropes. Doug was standing there too, leaning heavily on his ice axe and no doubt Ang Dorje and Norbu weren't too far away. They were in for a long wait as five or six of the Fischer group were in the process of abseiling the Hillary Step. I waved to Rob, who acknowledged with the thumbs-up signal—this visual contact between the guides was common and a short wave of the hand had meant the situation surrounding them was under control. We could have easily used our radios to do this, but we were constantly out of breath, and when we had a clear sighting of each other, a simple hand signal was all that was needed. Satisfied everything was in control, I turned to Andy and said, 'Let's get out of here. Rob and Doug are just above the Hillary Step and they are going OK.'

'Go ahead. I'll follow you in a minute,' said Andy, who seemed to be in no hurry to move. Again I should have checked on him more closely but now there seemed to be nothing outwardly unusual about his behaviour.

Yasuko and Jon followed me off the South summit and we lost height quickly and so our line of sight to Andy, Doug and Rob. Just 70 metres above the point on the South East Ridge where we had exited from the gullies that dropped to C4, the radio inside my climbing-suit came to life with Rob's voice. I let Jon and Yasuko continue while I listened intently. He wanted to know where the spare oxygen bottles had been left on the South Summit. Before I could transmit, Andy, from wherever he was at the time, replied that there were none left on the South Summit. This I knew to be incorrect as I had personally checked and stacked the remaining four full bottles in a conspicuous place on the South Summit. I replied quickly. 'Rob, listen to me. This is Michael. I have left four bottles for you at the South Summit. Do you understand?' There was no reply. Repeated transmissions failed, only Andy's and Rob's confusing conversations could be heard. On many occasions earlier in the expedition I had spent idle minutes chatting on my radio but now, when I needed it most, it failed me. I tried BC, then C2 and finally C4, but there was no response. After more calls Caroline at BC picked up my signal and said she would pass on my message on her clear line of transmission to Rob. Content that everything was under control, I caught up to Yasuko and Jon and we continued descending with one of the Americans from Fischer's team, who was trying an unorthodox passing move in an uncontrolled tumble off to our left. From where I stood he looked out of control and in no hurry to regain it, preferring instead to slide happily towards the edge and into Tibet.

He stopped abruptly in an explosion of white from a thick bed of snow 30 metres below us with no sign of injury. Jon was anxious to keep moving, so I told him and Yasuko to go ahead while I helped the American. They had only just left on their way down the gullies to C4, when on my way over to the stunned American, I picked up Rob's call again for oxygen. I did not understand why there was still so much confusion. I waited with my gloved finger poised over the call button ready to steal some time in between the now desperate calls between Rob, Andy and BC. It was obvious that my radio was not working properly, as conversations dropped in and out. It was not the batteries, as I had changed them the day before. Whether it was my position on the mountain or something more technical than that, I couldn't tell. After persistent tries in between their conversations I eventually got through to Rob. I once again repeated the position of the oxygen bottles. I reassured him they were there. He seemed, however, quite convinced they weren't. He begged for help and I replied that I was on my way back up. It would take hours to get to him. I yelled to the American that the trail he needed to be on was over near me and then started to climb. It was 4:30 p.m.

I had climbed 100 metres. There was a light wind and snow fell softly settling on my shoulders. Above me I saw two people descending fast and for a few minutes I felt relieved as I believed them to be Rob and Doug—they must have found the oxygen and everything was okay. It wasn't. Our Sherpas, Ang Dorje and Norbu, materialised out of the falling snow. I asked if they had seen Rob, Doug or Andy, but they hadn't seen them since the South Summit.

'What about the oxygen? Is it still on the South Summit?'

Ang Dorje replied, 'Yes. Two cylinders are still there. We have two full ones with us.' His response only confirmed what I ready knew and I wished it could be as simple as that for Rob. I had left four bottles up there. Ang Dorje and Norbu now had two of those four. Rob and Doug only needed the remaining two. I couldn't understand why they had not found them. I asked Ang Dorje where he had collected their two bottles.

'Same place as this morning,' he replied.

I grabbed my radio. Thankfully it worked and I told Rob exactly where the bottles were. This time Rob did not seem so stressed and his immediate problem seemed to be solved. He only had to traverse 30 or 40 metres to the stash of oxygen on the South Summit, whereas I would need to climb up 200 metres to get the cylinders. If Rob now knew where the cylinders were, I saw no sense in continuing up, so I followed Ang Dorje and Norbu in their hasty descent. The fact that they had been with Rob and had come down indicated that things weren't as desperate as I thought they might have been. On reflection, I believe my call to Rob came at a moment when things were coming slightly back under control for him. There was a calmness in his voice and perhaps Andy, who was closer to Rob than me, had returned to the South Summit to help. He was certainly more lucid. However, it was never going to be quite that simple. Rob and Doug had been without oxygen for far too long and the three of them were still extremely high at a depressingly late hour of the day.

It continued to snow. Lower down the ridge the American who had passed us with such haste was amazingly only just getting to his feet after all this time and moving again, veering dangerously close to the wrong side of the mountain in a series of drunken flops into the snow, one of which could end up over the edge into Tibet. I detoured off my path to get close enough to speak with him. I could see that his oxygen mask had slipped off beneath his chin and clumps of ice hung from his eyebrows and chin. Lying half-buried in the snow, he was giggling—a result of oxygen debt to the brain. I told him to pull his oxygen mask over his mouth. In a fatherly sort of manner I then coaxed him closer and closer to the ridge crest, and as I did so I was interrupted by calls from BC. Every attempt to respond failed and from then on I heard no further talk on the air waves.

With the American now following me closely, we continued down the ridge a little way until we reached the exit point into the gullies that led down to C4. 'Now, see those two climbers down there in red? Just follow them,' I said pointing to Jon and Yasuko still visible in the gully below. He stepped off the ridge in such a haphazard manner, I wondered whether he cared if he lived or died. Concerned about his judgement, I decided to stick with him. All this time Beck Weathers had gone unnoticed standing beside me.

'Is that you, Mike?' The Texan accent startled me. Beck was camouflaged perfectly in a light sprinkling of fresh snow. He must have been standing still for some time, judging by the amount of snow that had settled on him. He looked like a tatty scarecrow, his bulky down suit pushing his arms awkwardly out to the sides.

'What are you doing here, Beck? I thought you would have been well and truly back at C4 by now.'

'I can't see, Mike. I have been waiting for you to come down.' He didn't have to say any more. I knew we were in trouble when I looked into his blank and unfocused eyes.

'How bad is it, Beck? Can you see anything at all?'

'Everything is a blur. I can't seem to focus,' said Beck in a remarkably calm voice, considering our position.

'Okay, Beck. We'll see how you go on this first bit, which is fairly easy. I have a rope if you can't manage. Follow me if you can.'

A year or so earlier Beck had had radial keratotomy to improve his failing vision. The sudden drop in barometric pressure, however, severely impaired his now delicate eyes.

Within the first few metres I knew I had a difficult task on my hands to get us both down alive as Beck fell over twice on easy ground. I pulled a rope from my pack and hastily tied it to Beck's harness because from here on the gully became much steeper and more difficult to negotiate. Just 2 metres of tight rope separated us, and just one wrong move separated us from certain death. I directed our progress from behind: 'Left! Right! Stop!' were the only words I used for the next couple of hours as Beck often balanced dangerously close to walking over the edge with many a step into thin air. I tried to predict his falls by bracing myself and driving my axe deep into the snow. This worked well, considering my disadvantage in weight—64 kilograms to Beck's 80 plus. On several occasions, however, caught on bare rock slabs, I was pulled forwards, my crampons scraping across the rock, and only just managed to stop Beck from toppling over the edge. There was no doubt that I was more nervous than Beck, for he could not see the exposure below us. I knew if there was any lapse in my concentration, Beck would pull us both over the edge. For one instant I thought of my friend, Lobsang, who had fallen from around here in 1993. I quickly put it out of my mind.

For hours I shouted my instructions to Beck as we weaved our way down through the endless rock and ice gullies. It was just on dark when we stumbled thankfully onto the easy snow slopes that led to C4, but they were stiff steep enough for Beck to sit and slide while I lowered him. I stopped for a few seconds to get a bearing on C4; we now looked across to it rather than down on top of it. Under normal conditions it would have taken half an hour, but for us it would be at least an hour. Here a few members of the Fischer group caught up with us, the only one that I knew being Neal Beidleman.

By now Beck was exhausted. It was still snowing and in the last few minutes of light I got my visual direction on C4. If we kept our bearing, we would walk straight into it, but the distractions were many as I shouldered a good deal of Beck's weight to try to make any sort of progress. The falling snow now had a sting to it brought about by a steadily increasing wind, and with Beck's regular requests for a rest I soon lost any sense of C4's position.

A few metres further on we came across Yasuko sitting in the snow. Neal had found her first and was removing her oxygen mask as her supply, like ours, had run out. No amount of persuasion could convince her that she had run out as she persisted in putting her mask back on, which only suffocated her more. Finally we ripped the straps from her mask and shoved it into her pack. Thankfully Neal and his group were able to descend with her, while I continued very slowly with Beck. Visibility was now down to a few metres as high winds lashed the upper slopes of Everest and with it came the energy-sapping cold. I was afraid we would lose sight of the others.

'Come on, Beck. We have to keep up with the others,' I yelled.

'Mike, I need to rest. Just a short rest,' he begged.

I relented, silently cursing with every second that passed. Beck was going nowhere without a rest. Meanwhile the others were moving further away from us.

Quickly the situation became critical: we lost sight of Neal's group and any shouting to contact them was carried off by the wind. Beck and I were alone. I had done everything I could to keep up with the others, but our pace was far too slow. I sat Beck down as the 70 to 80-kilometre-per-hour winds threatened to blow us off our feet and snow stung my eyes, temporarily blinding me. At best I could see 3 or 4 metres. I used my radio to call C4 but there was no reply on my useless piece of junk; nevertheless I continued my transmission in the hope that they could hear me. Even if they did respond it would have been difficult to hear them above the roar of the wind. We wanted a direction, a light, a voice, a familiar sound, anything to help guide us in.

It's not in my nature to beg, but that night I begged Beck to keep moving—every minute we delayed for a rest put another nail in our coffins. The wind was increasing rapidly and the temperature was dropping to an unbearable level. I shouldered Beck's weight for as long as I could, now ignoring his requests to stop in our relentless pursuit for shelter. Again I tried calling C4 on my radio; still there was no reply. A beam of light flashed in front of us; for a moment I thought it was help from C4, but as we came closer we found Neal and Yasuko who were as confused as we were. Neal was trying to regroup his team who had scattered in all directions. You didn't have to go far in these conditions to be totally lost. Slowly they regrouped and I allowed Beck to sit. I did not get involved in the yelling match about where C4 was—I was just as confused as the rest of them. My only contribution was a request that we all stay together and there was a unanimous agreement. Finally a direction was agreed upon and Neal led off hopefully; it was as good a direction as any. Beck leaned heavily on my shoulder—he could lean as much as he liked, so long as I could keep us both moving.

When I tripped over two old oxygen bottles, my spirits soared; we were obviously close to C4 and I told Beck this. Only a couple of head-

torches were working now, and their criss-crossing beams often silhouetted the distressing sight of clumsy figures struggling to stay upright. I
tried not to think that Beck and I would have looked equally pitiful.
Neal stopped to allow us to catch up, all the time encouraging his
team-mates to stay together and to keep moving. He asked if I had any
idea of the direction of C4, but I confessed that I didn't as the constant
attention to Beck and the white-out conditions had distracted any
sense of it. Others also voiced their opinion, but they often conflicted.
Today, looking back, I realise we had staggered depressingly close to C4
before veering away in the opposite direction.

I struggled with Beck but the dread of losing the others was enough
incentive to keep moving. I was tempted to try my radio again but the
fact that it had been malfunctioning made me think it was a waste of
time. We continued to chase the others in their search. Up front the
two leaders had come to an edge, their head-torches shining into a
black void. Between us and them lay four or five exhausted climbers;
some were kneeling, some had collapsed and were lying motionless in
the snow. The edge marked the most significant landmark we had
found in the last couple of hours, but was it the edge leading into
Nepal or was it the edge dropping into Tibet? No-one knew, although
there were some wild guesses. The situation was seriously grim now.
Beck had lost one of his gloves, leaving a bare hand exposed to the elements; I searched in the snow and rocks in the immediate area, but no
doubt the wind had carried it off, so I gave him mine and then checked
on Yasuko. She was still standing, still keen to push on, but she was
incoherent, unable to tell left from right. Now I had a chance to use my
radio. It worked! Stuart answered my call from C4. I asked him which
direction the wind was blowing from at C4, as it might help me get
some idea of where we were on the South Col. If I had been warm and
rested with a sea level supply of oxygen, I would have easily made use
of the small amount of information he was able to give me, but tonight
it made little sense at all. Once Stuart had picked up my call, he wasted
no time in coming out to look for us, banging metal and shining his
head-torch in wild arcs into the night sky to give us the best chance of

seeing him. But he could only travel a short distance from camp for fear of becoming hopelessly disoriented too. Stuart tried desperately to find us before having to return to his tent to recover from the cold. He came back out time and time again, but all to no avail.

I moved closer to the edge to look for any clues. There was nothing but a black hole where only the wind dared to go. It could easily have been the edge of the earth. I stepped back quickly; it was no place to stand braced against the gale. For a moment I paused, confused. I had to try to think of a new plan of action but that action was more or less decided for us, because lying on the rocks at our feet were the pitiful figures of three or four climbers who had been pushed beyond their limit with the torments of the cold and exhaustion. We desperately needed to find C4, but we were going nowhere, we had nowhere to go. Neal yelled to a couple of his team-mates who were still standing to lie low to try to shelter from the bitterly cold wind that was showing us no mercy. He asked if I agreed with his decision to shelter as best we could and I nodded my agreement. There were maybe twelve of us altogether and Yasuko lay down among the other climbers on the rock and ice, tucking her hands in between her legs and pulling her knees up to her stomach. My fingers had long since stopped performing any delicate tasks and had become useless attachments. I grabbed a handful of Beck's clothing and pulled him to the ground beside me, unapologetic for the way I was handling him. I didn't want to lose sight of him now, as I doubted I had the energy to repeat any unnecessary action. Up until now the uncertainty of whether or not I'd find C4 had remained a finely balanced question but now the broad expanse of the South Col as jet stream winds blasted across it brought crippling temperatures well below -40°C. Any sense of control over the elements was lost to me. I was trapped in a giant wind tunnel, that was equal to the most desolate place in the world.

I lay on my side in a small depression and pulled Beck in behind me to protect him from the wind. From this position he was able to put his frozen hands inside the chest pockets of my climbing-suit where I tried to rub some warmth into them. Although I had run out of oxygen some time before, I kept the mask on to protect my face from the cold. This prevented me from speaking clearly to anyone, but the wind made sure of that regardless. The wind was now unrelenting in its bid to drive the cold deeper into our bodies and for hours we shivered uncontrollably. I felt totally alone and, even though I had no intention of dying, my thoughts did turn negative from time to time. It did not bother me to think about it for I have had plenty of practice over the years. Unfortunately, freezing to death doesn't happen quickly; it torments your mind and body with a slow and painful suffering for hours before finally showing some mercy in allowing you to go to sleep, never to wake again. For long and wandering periods I thought of Judi, and of our hot and humid holiday in Fiji just a few months earlier, when a sudden and uncontrollable shiver made me lurch from my rocky resting place. With this sudden movement came a terrible stinging pain to my right ear. I had been using my pack as a pillow and my ear had become glued to it with ice. I rubbed the palm of my gloved hand up and down the length of my pack to feel if the top part of my ear was stuck to the pack, but I came to the drowsy conclusion that I couldn't care less; it would be just another body part lost to frostbite. Now that I was sitting up, I had a look around: it looked like doomsday, everyone seemed dead until I heard some moaning coming from the motionless bodies scattered around me. Someone was crying, someone else was begging not to be left to die like this. I saw Yasuko shaking from the cold but otherwise lying silently behind one of the Americans. It was a hopeless situation and I lay back down, the pain from my ear being just another discomfort in the whole miserable affair. I tried to pretend it was only a nightmare, that it would all go away.

I tried my radio again, first to C4, then to BC, but no-one responded. I turned my attention to Beck.

'Beck, how are you going?'

'I'm very cold but I'm OK,' said Beck. His distinctive Texan accent was slurred and only just recognisable above the roar of the wind. For me it was a small but comforting thought to know he was still alive because I did not know how much longer I could last protecting Beck from the full force of the gale. I could only hope that Yasuko was equally protected in her hollow. It was a long night and I was starting to surrender to the temptation of eternal sleep.

Throughout the night the roar of the wind brought numerous false alarms when we thought someone had found us, which sent our small group into an excitable frenzy only to be miserably disappointed. It was after midnight when the alarm was raised again. I think it was Neal who saw it first and I rose, fully expecting to be disappointed again. A gap had appeared in the cloud that was whipping across the Col and left a short but adequate sighting onto the south-east slopes of Everest. To get a better view I had to break away the ice that hung from my eyebrows and around the rim of my hood. From this unmistakable landmark we were able to gain some idea of where we were in relation to C4. We were too far east—closer to Tibet than Nepal.

Neal gathered those in his team that could still walk and headed off in the direction he thought C4 should be in.

I pulled Beck to his feet. Yasuko had managed to get to her feet with the other climbers. Beck had lost his glove again and as my head-torch had expired because of the cold, I had to search the ground with my hands. Luckily I found it stuck to Beck's cramponed boots, otherwise it would have surely blown away with the wind. Beck suggested that if he had his head-torch on, the beam might give him some direction to focus on. I shoved my frozen hands into his pack in search of it, but it was a fruitless effort as my hands had no feeling.

All this had consumed precious minutes and by the time we were ready to move, the others were out of sight. Yasuko had tried to go with them but had collapsed not far in front of us. She stood up again, swaying precariously on her feet as if she had been hit with a knockout punch. Staring stubbornly into the teeth of the storm brought no answers for her. There were three more bodies in our vicinity sitting in the snow. At first I thought they were dead, but one of them started crying. It was a female voice and again I heard the plea. 'Don't leave me. I don't want to die here,' she begged.

I ignored the pleas for help as I fought against the wind to gather in Yasuko before she wandered off into the night.

By this time Yasuko had collapsed again, so I pulled her back onto her feet and removed the rim of ice around her hood so she could see. By now the three Americans had moved off and disappeared. I stretched Beck's left arm around my shoulder and supported his weight as best I could, but I had become so incredibly weak in the last few hours that we swayed like two old drunks. Yasuko fell yet again. Leaving Beck to stand unsupported like a statue, I picked up Yasuko; this time as I stood her up, her arms moved in a swimming fashion, so I pulled them down to her side and held them there, yelling at her to follow Beck and me. 'Camp Four is not far away,' I said for encouragement, but I doubt she understood me. I still had no idea where C4 was.

The three of us began to move, leaning heavily into the full force of the gale. After a few metres Beck needed to rest. This time I was thankful as he was becoming far too heavy for me to support any longer. Yasuko stumbled and fell face down. I didn't dare let go of Beck as I knew I would not have the strength to lift him to his feet again.

'Come on, Yasuko. Keep moving. Follow me,' I yelled, but I expected little response from her. None of us was able to walk a straight line as we teetered on the edge of total exhaustion. Only the recent sighting of the upper slopes of Everest gave me some motivation to keep trying. Step by step we moved on if ever so slowly.

We had been out in the elements for twenty-six hours and I doubted we could last much longer. If the wind increased its intensity, it would bring the wind chill factor down to an unbearable level and this would finish us off quickly. Beck, Yasuko and I had stumbled just 15 metres when we encountered the three Americans again; two of them had fallen to the ground and the other was pleading with them to keep moving. Here Yasuko stumbled and fell. The American male and I both knew that we were not going to make it under these dreadful conditions and he asked if I could go and find C4 and bring back help. I hesitated, pretending for a second or two that I hadn't heard his request, but it seemed like our only chance for survival.

Yasuko was now lying motionless behind us; Beck stood, barely, and my fellow path-finder had his two companions lying semi-conscious in the rock and snow. I only agreed to go on the condition that all of them stayed put and did not separate. The American agreed and I slapped Beck hard across his shoulder to make sure I had his attention before I explained my request.

'Stay here with Yasuko. Don't let these people out of your sight.' I immediately felt stupid, as I had forgotten Beck could not see.

'OK,' mumbled Beck. I repeated my request to the more able-bodied American. It was even more important that he understood my instructions concerning Beck's and Yasuko's condition.

My frozen hands made it extremely difficult untying the rope that bound me to Beck. I was very reluctant to leave Beck and Yasuko behind while I went in search of help. The short piece of rope had forced Beck and me to work as a unit and now I felt I was giving up on him. On the other hand it was our only choice, if anyone was to survive. I propped Yasuko up against a rock. Of all of us she was probably the closest to death. I yelled my instructions to stay with Beck and the others directly into her face. She nodded agreement but she didn't stop nodding as I walked away—I doubted she had understood any of it.

I drew on the limits of my reserves to make some headway into the wind. I leaned heavily into the gale and protected my eyes from the high-velocity ice particles that had the sting of a thousand needles. It dawned on me that the people I had just left could well be the lucky ones. Perhaps the others who had left us about twenty minutes earlier had already found C4 and were sending back help; perhaps I would be the one who remained lost and alone; perhaps in the near-zero visibility I would walk over the edge, never to be seen again. I had no idea where I was going and every second rock looked like the outline of a tent.

My crampons skidded uncontrollably across the rocky terrain of the South Col; each stumble only confused my sense of direction even more. At some stage I stopped and stared at two head-torch lights bobbing and weaving high up on Everest, somewhere in the vicinity of the gullies that led down to C4. My immediate thought was that it was Rob and Doug making their way down, but on reflection I know it wasn't; I suspect I was longing for the lights to belong to them and therefore imagined it. In my lonely search I stopped to rest, believing I had been wandering for hours and that soon it would be morning. I even considered stopping altogether because I couldn't remember what I was searching for. By now I had lost all sense of urgency. I had forgotten about Beck, Yasuko and the others, the wind no longer bothered me and, worst of all, I felt comfortably warm. As far as my body temperature was concerned, I could not have been more seriously cold.

I wanted a nice place to sit and wait for morning. This special place couldn't be just anywhere; it had to be big enough for two of us. I sensed his powerful presence: Lobsang was with me now and we had a lot to talk about since we said goodbye on the summit ridge of Everest in 1993. As we looked for a place that would give us the best view of the sunrise, a sudden clearing in the turbulence of the wind-driven snow and ice extended my visibility to 40 or 50 metres.

'There it is!' I said to Lobsang. 'Over there!' I had just spotted the unmistakable outline of our wind-crushed tents at C4, and I suddenly remembered the reason I was here alone.

I don't know why but I went past the first tent, preferring instead to go to one in the middle of the huddle. There was a long moment of disbelief on both sides as I crouched outside the door belonging to Stuart and Jon. Did they know who the ice-encrusted apparition was? Or was I the one that was dreaming? I am not sure if I spilled out the speech that I had so carefully rehearsed in my mind during those crazy hours of wandering around on the Col. If I did say something, it probably sounded like a drunken slur. Whatever I said, I hoped I gave some accurate directions and instructions to help find Beck, Yasuko and the others.

I was convinced that as a result of whatever conversation took place between us, rescuers would be rounded up to help me get Beck and Yasuko back into camp. Somehow I was confronted with another closed tent door. Had Stuart closed the door on me to prevent the tent being filled with snow? Or had I just imagined my conversation? Or was this a different tent? If anything was clear to me at this moment, it was that I didn't have a clue where I was. I only remember kneeling outside the tent trying to unzip the door that I had thought was open. Stuart may have even directed me to my tent. It was a frustrating exercise in coordination, a skill I no longer had. If Stuart was playing a joke, it was a bad one. I yelled for help and Frank responded from inside the tent. I was trying to remember where the full oxygen bottles were to take back for Beck and Yasuko, but Frank operated with the efficiency of a battlefield medic and pulled me inside the tent. It was then I gave up trying. Frank swore at me and I thought he was abusing me for being late. Before I knew it I was being wrapped and buried in a sea of down sleeping-bags. The questions continued while he broke away the ice from around my face. If I answered them, I answered very few.

Everything seemed to be happening in slow motion, most likely because the cold had drained every ounce of energy. Speaking was difficult and confusing. I tried to sit up to answer a voice that I thought came from outside the tent—it was probably Stuart wanting to confirm directions for Beck and Yasuko—but I couldn't even find the strength to sit up. At some stage Frank went outside, leaving me in the hands of John, an anaesthetist by profession. I was not an easy patient for him that morning as I shook uncontrollably while he tried to keep an oxygen mask on my face. I settled down slowly, and in the belief that a search party had gone for the others.

The next thing I remember it was early morning on 11 May and high winds continued to batter our tent. I immediately looked for Yasuko, hoping to see her dark eyes peeping out from the bulk of her over-filled sleeping-bag, but there was nothing except a shambles of ice-encrusted gear littering our tent. John told me that Frank had gone to keep Lou company, as his tent-mates Beck, Doug, Andy and Rob were still missing. I asked what had happened to Beck and Yasuko—they should have been here by now—but John had no answer.

In the meantime I continued to drift in and out of reality, with one dreamlike conversation after another. The few real events I remember were John's persistent efforts to supply me with more and more drinks—

a difficult task of coordination and strength. However, in the back of my mind I was still aware of those unaccounted for. I tried to gather my wits and strength to get up to at least look for Beck and Yasuko but John, who could judge my condition better than me, said there was nothing I could do. I suspect he knew everything that could be done in these dreadful conditions was being attempted.

It is my understanding that after alerting Stuart he set out alone to find Beck and Yasuko but once again, like so many times before, he found himself in danger of becoming hopelessly lost in the blizzard conditions. The guide Anatoli, who was Neal's counterpart in the Fischer group and who had returned to C4 from the summit by late afternoon, was alerted by Neal's desperate arrival at C4 with a few surviving members of his team. In a long and sweeping search of the South Col Anatoli found no-one and returned to the tent. Undaunted by his fruitless search he set out again. This time he found the three Americans, and Beck and Yasuko who lay motionless he presumed they were dead.

At dawn Stuart and Lhakpa Chhiri went out in search of Beck and Yasuko. Later Lhakpa Chhiri and Ang Dorje made a determined but hopeless attempt to reach Rob, who was still trapped up at the South Summit. Too weak to move, Rob was known to be still alive due to his intermittent radio calls that had been picked up by BC and Jon and Stuart who had our spare radio.

Throughout the expedition I had felt uncomfortable about using the Sherpas to do the back-breaking work; their tireless efforts and cheerful attitude made me feel lazy and guilty. Without them our expedition would not have existed and they were as much a part of our team as anyone else. I found out that these rescue attempts were being made when I regained some degree of consciousness, and I was crushed by a heavy weight of guilt as I lay incapacitated in my tent. No amount of persuasion or money had made Stuart, Ang Dorje or Lhakpa Chhiri do what they were doing; it was their nature to do so.

I learnt later that the Fischer group had left C4 that morning in an effort to get to safer ground. How they made progress under those conditions, I do not know. Stuart and Jon had our only working radio in their tent and they kept Helen and Caroline at BC informed of our situation and of the high winds that continued at C4.

Jon thought he had last seen Andy Harris only a stone's throw from C4 just before 5:30 p.m. of 10 May, when Andy made a sudden turn to the right towards the Lhotse Face saying, as he disappeared, 'I'm going straight to BC.' Jon, however, has since changed his mind and thinks that, in the confusion of the moment, he saw someone else. An expedition that summited much later in May found Andy's ice axe at the South Summit. It is widely accepted that Andy was behaving abnormally from hypoxia and could easily have left the South Summit without his axe just as he believed there was no oxygen on the South Summit. However, I believe he returned to the South Summit to help Rob. This explains why Rob sounded in control of the situation when I made that final call to him from below the South Summit: Andy had returned to help. Sadly, we will never really know.

The struggle of someone wrestling his way into the tent woke me from my hazy existence. It was around midmorning, 11 May. I was alarmed at the sight of Stuart, exhausted and wind blown. Above the roar of the wind that continued to hammer our tents he yelled out that he had found Beck and Yasuko. He said that in the time it took for him to return to the tent, Yasuko would most likely be dead but Beck might yet be alive. To make things worse, he said they were close to an edge, perhaps the Kangshung Face—not where I remembered leaving them. It was a risky proposition for anyone to venture out to get Beck. Stuart asked me what I wanted to do.

I was coherent enough to understand what was going on and the implications of Stuart's question. Without doubt it was the most difficult question I have ever been asked. Lhakpa Chhiri and Ang Dorje had been beaten back by violent winds higher up; Stuart had done everything he could for Beck. Who among us had the strength to go out again and operate a rescue? Was it worth risking other lives to rescue someone who would most likely be dead when found or would die soon after? I couldn't ask another to go if I couldn't go myself. This was the ruthless way I had to look at it. My priorities had to shift to the surviving members of our team. It was crucial for me to regain some control of the situation and get our team out of C4 and descending as soon as possible, otherwise more would die. John's antidotal comment about decisions being made in the Vietnam war to save the lives of surviving soldiers by abandoning their less fortunate and critically injured teammates was only mildly comforting.

Around early afternoon there was a lull in the gale, which allowed a rescue party to reach C4: Pete Athans and Todd Burleson were members of an independent expedition. Their mission was two-fold, to lend assistance to us and to try and rescue Rob. They tried to coax me into getting the rest of my team down to a lower camp, preferably to C2 as soon as possible. It was the correct decision but it was not possible—I was barely able to sit up in my sleeping-bag or think clearly, let alone descend to C2; also Lou was snowblind. I nearly suggested that Pete and Todd take the remaining members down while I stayed, but Lou would most likely have to remain too and I did not know if I would improve enough by the morning to get myself moving and to help a blind person down. Both of us would need assistance, and we needed more time to recover to be able to help ourselves down. Time at this altitude, however, was also a killer. I asked Stuart to count the remaining full oxygen bottles. There were enough for the six remaining team members and our four Sherpas to survive one more night and descend the next day.

I explained our situation to Todd and Pete; considering the late hour of the day, I felt we would be moving too slowly with our disabilities to reach the safety of a lower camp before nightfall. I believed it was better for us get an early start the next morning. There was a risk, however, that the jet-stream winds might intensify and pin us down even longer at C4. I made the assumption that Lou and I would have recovered enough to be able to descend the next day without assistance and if the winds did increase, it would be up to the individual disabled climber to struggle down into the shelter of the Western Cwm without hindering the others. Pete and Todd reluctantly agreed to let us stay one more night and they set up a tent next to ours.

Around mid-afternoon Jon and Stuart brought the radio into my tent. They had been maintaining contact with Helen and Caroline at BC, who were relaying the information, most of it not good, to Madeleine, Rob's personal assistant at the office of his guiding company in New Zealand. It was not a clean and simple connection of two phones—all the guides had two-way radios which allowed us to speak to each other and to BC. At BC the incoming phone calls could be patched to the incoming two-way radio calls via the satellite phone. Madeleine then had the unenviable task of giving news of our individual team members to their families. I was warned by Jon that an earlier conversation with Rob, who was still trapped on the South Summit, had revealed that Doug had gone. No explanation was given, none was asked for; we all knew what it meant. When Rob came on line, all the radios between BC and C4 tuned into his channel. I managed to get through to him only once before I was cut off by another caller, and in a hopeless effort of persuasion to get him moving in our direction, I told him we were all waiting for him at C4 to come down. It was the last time I spoke to him and no amount of encouragement by anyone else could make Rob move. The radio conversation gave little hint of the real misery he was suffering. Why hadn't he made an effort to continue? Perhaps the answer lay in my own condition— exposure to the cold had sapped all my energy and the motivation to move. I thought of the time a couple of years earlier when Rob, Veikka and I had to fight our way down from the high camp on K2 in conditions similar to these. I was trying to think of what to say next when the radio crackled into life with the sound of Rob's wife, Jan, speaking via telephone from New Zealand. We listened for only a few seconds before turning off our radio. It was the last time I heard Rob's voice. Outside the deafening roar of the wind continued to trash our tents; inside a sad silence formed an uncomfortable barrier between us all. Rob was dying.

Murphy's Law prevailed. That night the terrible wind picked up in strength and it became the toughest night yet at C4. I placed my pack to the windward side of the tent and pushed hard with my feet to prevent the tent collapsing in on top of John and me. Much-needed sleep and rest were impossible under such conditions. Unlike earlier in the day I was now conscious and fully aware of our situation. My thoughts tended to wander between those who were missing or dead and our immediate danger. I already had all my gloves on to keep my frostbitten hands warm and had tucked my boots into my sleeping-bag in case the weather turned into a full-on storm and the tent ripped open or was ripped from its tie-down points and blown away with us in it. Whose tent would we go to, if ours exploded like a balloon? What would we do if all the tents ripped open? Fortunately though, I had experienced far more serious storms than this, and I knew what to expect. I guessed the temperature to be minus 30°C and the winds to be blowing at 70 to 80 kilometres per hour. They had the potential to return to their normal velocity of over 200 kilometres per hour at any moment. A shrapnel cloud of ice and rock could shred the tents in minutes. If this happened, it would be no good praying. The emergency actions for our team's survival filled my mind until the cold, grey hours of dawn and the eventual subsidence of the life-threatening gale to nothing more than a nuisance.

It was 6:00 a.m. on 12 May. The wind had punished us severely for daring to stay another night at C4. Our once-cosy tent was a shambles of displaced food, drinks and frozen pee-bottles. John lay shaking in his ice-coated sleeping-bag. I assumed he was cold from the amount of ice on his bag, so offered him my down vest, but the cold wasn't the problem—he said he was worried about our chances of getting out of this mess alive. I assured him we would be on the move to safer ground in less than an hour and to start packing.

'Bring only the essentials. Abandon everything else and leave room in your pack for a full bottle of oxygen,' I said.

Before I put on my boots, I checked my feet for frostbite. I could see the tell-tale signs appearing on both feet, and the left was far worse because it had been swimming in my urine that had since frozen. Thumbs and fingers on both hands had more advanced frostbite, with the tips of some turning a dark blue-purplish colour.

I dressed and ventured out to the other tents to pass on the same message. My instructions were simple: be ready by 7:00 a.m. with a full bottle of oxygen. In passing from tent to tent, I saw that the night had been tough on the others as well by their bewildered faces: the last forty-eight hours had not been a bad nightmare but reality. I took in the devastation of our hostile environment—torn and twisted tents were everywhere and for a few moments I couldn't help but think of the others who were still unaccounted for, and I knew there would be casualties from other teams as well. For the moment, though, I had to deal with the more immediate problems. I only looked towards the summit of Everest once that day; it was still lashed by jet-stream winds. Somewhere between the summit and me were Doug, Andy, Rob, Beck and Yasuko—all dead. I didn't look that way again.

The Hermit's Story
by Rick Bass

Rick Bass (born 1958) has written a dozen or so books of fiction and nonfiction. Bass often writes about what people find out about themselves and each other when they go outside. The results can be entrancing, as in this short story.

An ice storm, following seven days of snow; the vast fields and drifts of snow turning to sheets of glazed ice that shine and shimmer blue in the moonlight, as if the color is being fabricated not by the bending and absorption of light but by some chemical reaction within the glossy ice; as if the source of all blueness lies somewhere up here in the north—the core of it beneath one of those frozen fields; as if blue is a thing that emerges, in some parts of the world, from the soil itself, after the sun goes down.

Blue creeping up fissures and cracks from depths of several hundred feet; blue working its way up through the gleaming ribs of Ann's buried dogs; blue trailing like smoke from the dogs' empty eye sockets and nostrils—blue rising like smoke from chimneys until it reaches the surface and spreads laterally and becomes entombed, or trapped—but still alive, and smoky—within those moonstruck fields of ice.

Blue like a scent trapped in the ice, waiting for some soft release, some thawing, so that it can continue spreading.

It's Thanksgiving. Susan and I are over at Ann and Roger's house for dinner. The storm has knocked out all the power down in town—it's a clear, cold, starry night, and if you were to climb one of the mountains on snowshoes and look forty miles south toward where town lies, instead of seeing the usual small scatterings of light—like fallen stars, stars sunken to the bottom of a lake, but still glowing—you would see nothing but darkness—a bowl of silence and darkness in balance for once with the mountains up here, rather than opposing or complementing our darkness, our peace.

As it is, we do not climb up on snowshoes to look down at the dark town—the power lines dragged down by the clutches of ice—but can tell instead just by the way there is no faint glow over the mountains to the south that the power is out: that this Thanksgiving, life for those in town is the same as it always is for us in the mountains, and it is a good feeling, a familial one, coming on the holiday as it does—though doubtless too the townspeople are feeling less snug and cozy about it than we are.

We've got our lanterns and candles burning. A fire's going in the stove, as it will all winter long and into the spring. Ann's dogs are asleep in their straw nests, breathing in that same blue light that is being exhaled from the skeletons of their ancestors just beneath and all around them. There is the faint, good smell of cold-storage meat—slabs and slabs of it—coming from down in the basement, and we have just finished off an entire chocolate pie and three bottles of wine. Roger, who does not know how to read, is examining the empty bottles, trying to read some of the words on the labels. He recognizes the words *the* and *in* and *USA*. It may be that he will never learn to read—that he will be unable to—but we are in no rush, and—unlike his power lifting—he has all of his life in which to accomplish this. I for one believe that he will learn it.

Ann has a story for us. It's about one of the few clients she's ever had, a fellow named Gray Owl, up in Canada, who owned half a dozen speckled German shorthaired pointers and who hired Ann to train them all at once. It was twenty years ago, she says—her last good job.

She worked the dogs all summer and into the autumn, and finally had them ready for field trials. She took them back up to Gray Owl— way up in Saskatchewan—driving all day and night in her old truck, which was old even then, with dogs piled up on top of each other, sleeping and snoring: dogs on her lap, dogs on the seat, dogs on the floorboard. How strange it is to think that most of us can count on one hand the number of people we know who are doing what they most want to do for a living. They invariably have about them a kind of wildness and calmness both, possessing somewhat the grace of animals that are fitted intricately and polished into this world. An academic such as myself might refer to it as a kind of biological confidence. Certainly I think another word for it could be *peace*.

Ann was taking the dogs up there to show Gray Owl how to work them: how to take advantage of their newly found talents. She could be a sculptor or some other kind of artist, in that she speaks of her work as if the dogs are rough blocks of stone whose internal form exists already and is waiting only to be chiseled free and then released by her, beautiful, into the world.

Basically, in six months the dogs had been transformed from gangling, bouncing puppies into six raging geniuses, and she needed to show their owner how to control them, or rather, how to work with them. Which characteristics to nurture, which ones to discourage. With all dogs, Ann said, there was a tendency, upon their leaving her tutelage—unlike a work of art set in stone or paint—for a kind of chitinous encrustation to set in, a sort of oxidation, upon the dogs leaving her hands and being returned to someone less knowledgeable and passionate, less committed than she. It was as if there were a tendency in the world for the dogs' greatness to disappear back into the stone.

So she went up there to give both the dogs and Gray Owl a checkout session. She drove with the heater on and the window down; the cold Canadian air was invigorating, cleaner, farther north. She could smell the scent of the fir and spruce, and the damp alder and cottonwood leaves beneath the many feet of snow. We laughed at her when she said it, but she told us that up in Canada she could taste the fish in the streams as she drove alongside creeks and rivers.

She listened to the only radio station she could pick up as she drove, but it was a good one. She got to Gray Owl's around midnight. He had a little guest cabin but had not heated it for her, uncertain as to the day of her arrival, so she and the six dogs slept together on a cold mattress beneath mounds of elk hides: their last night together. She had brought a box of quail with which to work the dogs, and she built a small fire in the stove and set the box of quail next to it.

The quail muttered and cheeped all night and the stove popped and hissed and Ann and the dogs slept for twelve hours straight, as if submerged in another time, or as if everyone else in the world were submerged in time—encased in stone—and as if she and the dogs were pioneers, or survivors of some kind: upright and exploring the present, alive in the world, free of that strange chitin.

She spent a week up there, showing Gray Owl how his dogs worked. She said he scarcely recognized them afield, and that it took a few days just for him to get over his amazement. They worked the dogs both individually and, as Gray Owl came to understand and appreciate what Ann had crafted, in groups. They traveled across snowy hills on snowshoes, the sky the color of snow, so that often it was like moving through a dream, and except for the rasp of the snowshoes beneath them, and the pull of gravity, they might have believed they had ascended into some sky-place where all the world was snow.

They worked into the wind—north—whenever they could. Ann would carry birds in a pouch over her shoulder—much as a woman might carry a purse—and from time to time would fling a startled bird out into that dreary, icy snowscape—and the quail would fly off with great haste, a dark feathered buzz bomb disappearing quickly into the teeth of cold, and then Gray Owl and Ann and the dog, or dogs, would go find it, following it by scent only, as always.

Snot icicles would be hanging from the dogs' nostrils. They would always find the bird. The dog, or dogs, would point it, at which point Gray Owl or Ann would step forward and flush it—the beleaguered bird would leap into the sky again—and then once more they would push on after it, pursuing that bird toward the horizon as if driving it with a whip. Whenever the bird wheeled and flew downwind, they'd quarter away from it, then get a mile or so downwind from it and push it back north.

When the quail finally became too exhausted to fly, Ann would pick it up from beneath the dogs' noses as they held point staunchly, put the tired bird in her game bag and replace it with a fresh one, and off they'd go again. They carried their lunch in Gray Owl's day pack, as well as emergency supplies—a tent and some dry clothes—in case they should become lost, and around noon each day (they could rarely see the sun, only an eternal ice-white haze, so that they relied instead only on their rhythms within) they would stop and make a pot of tea on the sputtering little gas stove. Sometimes one or two of the quail would die from exposure, and they would cook that on the stove and eat it out there in the tundra, tossing the feathers up into the wind as if to launch one more flight and feeding the head, guts, and feet to the dogs.

Perhaps seen from above their tracks would have seemed aimless and wandering rather than with the purpose, the focus that was burning hot in both their and the dogs' hearts—perhaps someone viewing the tracks could have discerned the pattern, or perhaps not— but it did not matter, for their tracks—the patterns, direction, and tracing of them—were obscured by the drifting snow, sometimes within minutes after they were laid down.

Toward the end of the week, Ann said, they were finally running all six dogs at once, like a herd of silent wild horses through all that snow, and as she would be going home the next day, there was no need to conserve any of the birds she had brought, and she was turning them loose several at a time: birds flying in all directions; the dogs, as ever, tracking them to the ends of the earth.

It was almost a whiteout that last day, and it was hard to keep track of all the dogs. Ann was sweating from the exertion as well as the tension of trying to keep an eye on, and evaluate, each dog—the sweat was freezing on her in places, so that it was as if she were developing an ice skin. She jokingly told Gray Owl that next time she was going to try to find a client who lived in Arizona, or even South America. Gray Owl smiled and then told her that they were lost, but no matter, the storm would clear in a day or two.

They knew it was getting near dusk—there was a faint dulling to the sheer whiteness, a kind of increasing heaviness in the air, a new density to the faint light around them—and the dogs slipped in and out of sight, working just at the edges of their vision.

The temperature was dropping as the north wind increased—"No question about which way south is; we'll turn around and walk south for three hours, and if we don't find a road, we'll make camp," Gray Owl said—and now the dogs were coming back with frozen quail held gingerly in their mouths, for once the birds were dead, they were allowed to retrieve them, though the dogs must have been puzzled that there had been no shots. Ann said she fired a few rounds of the cap pistol into the air to make the dogs think she had hit those birds. Surely they believed she was a goddess.

They turned and headed south—Ann with a bag of frozen birds over her shoulder, and the dogs, knowing that the hunt was over now, all around them, once again like a team of horses in harness, though wild and prancy.

After an hour of increasing discomfort—Ann's and Gray Owl's hands and feet numb, and ice beginning to form on the dogs' paws, so that the dogs were having to high-step—they came in day's last light to the edge of a wide clearing: a terrain that was remarkable and soothing for its lack of hills. It was a frozen lake, which meant—said Gray Owl—they had drifted west (or perhaps east) by as much as ten miles.

Ann said that Gray Owl looked tired and old and guilty, as would any host who had caused his guest some unasked-for inconvenience. They knelt down and began massaging the dogs' paws and then lit the little stove and held each dog's foot, one at a time, over the tiny blue flame to help it thaw out.

Gray Owl walked out to the edge of the lake ice and kicked at it with his foot, hoping to find fresh water beneath for the dogs; if they ate too much snow, especially after working so hard, they'd get violent diarrhea and might then become too weak to continue home the next day, or the next, or whenever the storm quit.

Ann said she could barely see Gray Owl's outline through the swirling snow, even though he was less than twenty yards away. He kicked once at the sheet of ice, the vast plate of it, with his heel, then disappeared below the ice.

Ann wanted to believe that she had blinked and lost sight of him, or that a gust of snow had swept past and hidden him, but it had been too fast, too total: she knew that the lake had swallowed him. She was sorry for Gray Owl, she said, and worried for his dogs—afraid they would try to follow his scent down into the icy lake, and be lost as well—but what she was most upset about, she said—to be perfectly honest—was that Gray Owl had been wearing the little day pack with the tent and emergency rations. She had it in her mind to try to save Gray Owl, and to try to keep the dogs from going through the ice, but if he drowned, she was going to have to figure out how to try to get that day pack off of the drowned man and set up the wet tent in the blizzard on the snowy prairie and then crawl inside and survive. She would have to go into the water naked, so that when she came back out—if she came back out—she would have dry clothes to put on.

The dogs came galloping up, seeming as large as deer or elk in that dim landscape, against which there was nothing else to give them perspective, and Ann whoaed them right at the lake's edge, where they stopped immediately, as if they had suddenly been cast with a sheet of ice.

Ann knew they would stay there forever, or until she released them, and it troubled her to think that if she drowned, they too would die—that they would stand there motionless, as she had commanded them, for as long as they could, until at some point—days later, perhaps—they would lie down, trembling with exhaustion—they might lick at some snow, for moisture—but that then the snows would cover them, and still they would remain there, chins resting on their front paws, staring straight ahead and unseeing into the storm, wondering where the scent of her had gone.

Ann eased out onto the ice. She followed the tracks until she came to the jagged hole in the ice through which Gray Owl had plunged. She was almost half again lighter than he, but she could feel the ice crackling beneath her own feet. It sounded different too, in a way she could not place—it did not have the squeaky, percussive resonance of the lake-ice back home—and she wondered if Canadian ice froze differently or just sounded different.

She got down on all fours and crept closer to the hole. It was right at dusk. She peered down into the hole and dimly saw Gray Owl standing down there, waving his arms at her. He did not appear to be swimming. Slowly, she took one glove off and eased her bare hand down into the hole. She could find no water, and tentatively, she reached deeper.

Gray Owl's hand found hers and he pulled her down in. Ice broke as she fell, but he caught her in his arms. She could smell the wood smoke in his jacket from the alder he burned in his cabin. There was no water at all, and it was warm beneath the ice.

"This happens a lot more than people realize," he said. "It's not really a phenomenon; it's just what happens. A cold snap comes in October, freezes a skin of ice over the lake—it's got to be a shallow one, almost a marsh. Then a snowfall comes, insulating the ice. The lake drains in fall and winter—percolates down through the soil"—he stamped the spongy ground beneath them—"but the ice up top remains. And nobody ever knows any differently. People look out at the surface and think, *Aha, a frozen lake.*" Gray Owl laughed.

"Did you know it would be like this?" Ann asked.

"No," he said. "I was looking for water. I just got lucky."

Ann walked back to shore beneath the ice to fetch her stove and to release the dogs from their whoa command. The dry lake was only about eight feet deep, but it grew shallow quickly closer to shore, so that Ann had to crouch to keep from bumping her head on the overhead ice, and then crawl; and then there was only space to wriggle, and to emerge she had to break the ice above her by bumping and then battering it with her head and elbows, like the struggles of some embryonic hatchling; and when she stood up, waist-deep amid sparkling shards of ice—it was nighttime now—the dogs barked ferociously at her, but remained where she had ordered them to stay, and she was surprised at how far off course she was when she climbed out; she had traveled only twenty feet, but already the dogs were twice that far away from her. She knew humans had a poorly evolved, almost nonexistent sense of direction, but this error—over such a short distance—shocked her. It was as if there were in us a thing—an impulse, a catalyst—that denies our ever going straight to another thing. Like dogs working left and right into the wind, she thought, before converging on the scent.

Except that the dogs would not get lost, while she could easily imagine herself and Gray Owl getting lost beneath the lake, walking in circles forever, unable to find even the simplest of things: the shore.

She gathered the stove and dogs. She was tempted to try to go back in the way she had come out—it seemed so easy—but considered the consequences of getting lost in the other direction, and instead followed her original tracks out to where Gray Owl had first dropped through the ice. It was true night now, and the blizzard was still blowing hard, plastering snow and ice around her face like a mask. The dogs did not want to go down into the hole, so she lowered them to Gray Owl and then climbed gratefully back down into the warmth herself.

The air was a thing of its own—recognizable as air, and breathable, as such, but with a taste and odor, an essence, unlike any other air they'd ever breathed. It had a different density to it, so that smaller, shallower breaths were required; there was very much the feeling that if they breathed in too much of the strange, dense air, they would drown.

They wanted to explore the lake, and were thirsty, but it felt like a victory simply to be warm—or rather, not cold—and they were so exhausted that instead they made pallets out of the dead marsh grass that rustled around their ankles, and they slept curled up on the tiniest of hammocks, to keep from getting damp in the pockets and puddles of dampness that still lingered here and there.

All eight of them slept as if in a nest, heads and arms draped across other ribs and hips, and it was, said Ann, the best and deepest sleep she'd ever had—the sleep of hounds, the sleep of childhood—and how long they slept, she never knew, for she wasn't sure, later, how much of their subsequent time they spent wandering beneath the lake, and then up on the prairie, homeward again—but when they awoke, it was still night, or night once more, and clearing, with bright stars visible through the porthole, their point of embarkation; and even from beneath the ice, in certain places where, for whatever reasons—temperature, oxygen content, wind scour—the ice was clear rather than glazed, they could see the spangling of stars, though more dimly; and strangely, rather than seeming to distance them from the stars, this phenomenon seemed to pull them closer, as if they were up in the stars, traveling the Milky Way, or as if the stars were embedded in the ice.

It was very cold outside—up above—and there was a steady stream, a current like a river, of the night's colder, heavier air plunging down through their porthole, as if trying to fill the empty lake with that frozen air—but there was also the hot muck of the earth's massive respirations breathing out warmth and being trapped and protected beneath that ice, so that there were warm currents doing battle with the lone cold current.

The result was that it was breezy down there, and the dogs' noses twitched in their sleep as the images brought by these scents painted themselves across their sleeping brains in the language we call dreams but which, for the dogs, and perhaps for us, was reality: the scent of an owl *real*, not a dream; the scent of bear, cattail, willow, loon, *real*, even though they were sleeping, and even though those things were not visible, only over the next horizon.

The ice was contracting, groaning and cracking and squeaking up tighter, shrinking beneath the great cold—a concussive, grinding sound, as if giants were walking across the ice above—and it was this sound that had awakened them. They snuggled in warmer among the rattly dried yellowing grasses and listened to the tremendous clashings, as if they were safe beneath the sea and were watching waves of starlight sweeping across their hiding place; or as if they were in some place, some position, where they could watch mountains being born.

After a while the moon came up and washed out the stars. The light was blue and silver and seemed, Ann said, to be like a living thing. It filled the sheet of ice just above their heads with a shimmering cobalt light, which again rippled as if the ice were moving, rather than the earth itself, with the moon tracking it—and like deer drawn by gravity getting up in the night to feed for an hour or so before settling back in, Gray Owl and Ann and the dogs rose from their nests of straw and began to travel.

"You didn't—you know—*engage*?" Susan asks: a little mischievously, and a little proprietary, perhaps.

Ann shakes her head. "It was too cold," she says. I sneak a glance at Roger but cannot read his expression. Is he in love with her? Does she own his heart?

"But you would have, if it hadn't been so cold, right?" Susan asks, and Ann shrugs.

"He was an old man—in his fifties—and the dogs were around. But yeah, there was something about it that made me think of . . . those things," she says, careful and precise as ever.

"I would have done it anyway," Susan says. "Even if it was cold, and even if he was a hundred."

"We walked a long way," Ann says, eager to change the subject. "The air was damp down there, and whenever we'd get chilled, we'd stop and make a little fire out of a bundle of dry cattails." There were little pockets and puddles of swamp gas pooled here and there, she said, and sometimes a spark from the cattails would ignite one of those, and all around these little pockets of gas would light up like when you toss gas on a fire—these little explosions of brilliance, like flashbulbs, marsh pockets igniting like falling dominoes, or like children playing hopscotch—until a large-enough flash-pocket was reached— sometimes thirty or forty yards away from them, by this point—that the puff of flame would blow a chimney-hole through the ice, venting the other pockets, and the fires would crackle out, the scent of grass smoke sweet in their lungs, and they could feel gusts of warmth from the little flickering fires, and currents of the colder, heavier air sliding down through the new vent-holes and pooling around their ankles. The moonlight would strafe down through those rents in the ice, and shards of moon-ice would be glittering and spinning like diamond-motes in those newly vented columns of moonlight; and they pushed on, still lost, but so alive.

The mini-explosions were fun, but they frightened the dogs, and so Ann and Gray Owl lit twisted bundles of cattails and used them for torches to light their way, rather than building warming fires, though occasionally they would still pass through a pocket of methane and a stray ember would fall from their torches, and the whole chain of fire and light would begin again, culminating once more with a vent-hole being blown open and shards of glittering ice tumbling down into their lair . . .

What would it have looked like, seen from above—the orange blur-rings of their wandering trail beneath the ice; and what would the sheet of lake-ice itself have looked like that night—throbbing with the ice-bound, subterranean blue and orange light of moon and fire? But again, there was no one to view the spectacle: only the travelers them-selves, and they had no perspective, no vantage or loft from which to view or judge themselves. They were simply pushing on from one fire to the next, carrying their tiny torches. The beauty in front of them was enough.

They knew they were getting near a shore—the southern shore, they hoped, as they followed the glazed moon's lure above—when the dogs began to encounter shore birds that had somehow found their way beneath the ice through small fissures and rifts and were taking refuge in the cattails. Small winter birds—juncos, nuthatches, chickadees—skittered away from the smoky approach of their torches; only a few late-migrating (or winter-trapped) snipe held tight and steadfast, and the dogs began to race ahead of Gray Owl and Ann, working these familiar scents—blue and silver ghost-shadows of dog-muscle weaving ahead through slants of moonlight.

The dogs emitted the odor of adrenaline when they worked, Ann said—a scent like damp fresh-cut green hay—and with nowhere to vent, the odor was dense and thick around them, so that Ann wondered if it too might be flammable, like the methane—if in the dogs' passions they might literally immolate themselves.

They followed the dogs closely with their torches. The ceiling was low—about eight feet, as if in a regular room—so that the tips of their torches' flames seared the ice above them, leaving a drip behind them and transforming the milky, almost opaque cobalt and orange ice behind them, wherever they passed, into wandering ribbons of clear ice, translucent to the sky—a script of flame, or buried flame, ice-bound flame—and they hurried to keep up with the dogs.

Now the dogs had the snipe surrounded, as Ann told it, and one by one the dogs went on point, each dog freezing as it pointed to the birds' hiding places, and it was the strangest scene yet, Ann said, seeming surely underwater; and Gray Owl moved in to flush the birds, which launched themselves with vigor against the roof of the ice above, fluttering like bats; but the snipe were too small, not powerful enough to break through those frozen four inches of water (though they could fly four thousand miles to South America each year and then back to Canada six months later—is freedom a lateral component, or a vertical one?), and as Gray Owl kicked at the clumps of frost-bent cattails where the snipe were hiding and they burst into flight, only to hit their heads on the ice above them, they came tumbling back down, raining limp and unconscious back to their soft grassy nests.

The dogs began retrieving them, carrying them gingerly, delicately—not preferring the taste of snipe, which ate only earthworms—and Ann and Gray Owl gathered the tiny birds from the dogs, placed them in their pockets, and continued on to the shore, chasing that moon, the ceiling lowering to six feet, then four, then to a crawlspace, and after they had bashed their way out (with elbows, fists, and forearms) and stepped back out into the frigid air, they tucked the still-unconscious snipe into little crooks in branches, up against the trunks of trees and off the ground, out of harm's way, and passed on, south—as if late in their own migration—while the snipe rested, warm and terrified and heart-fluttering, but saved, for now, against the trunks of those trees.

Long after Ann and Gray Owl and the pack of dogs had passed through, the birds would awaken, their bright dark eyes luminous in the moonlight, and the first sight they would see would be the frozen marsh before them, with its chain of still-steaming vent-holes stretching back across all the way to the other shore. Perhaps these were birds that had been unable to migrate owing to injuries, or some genetic absence. Perhaps they had tried to migrate in the past but had found either their winter habitat destroyed or the path down there so fragmented and fraught with danger that it made more sense—to these few birds—to ignore the tuggings of the stars and seasons and instead to try to carve out new lives, new ways of being, even in such a stark and severe landscape: or rather, in a stark and severe period—knowing that lushness and bounty were still retained within that landscape. That it was only a phase; that better days would come. That in fact (the snipe knowing these things with their blood, ten-million-years-in-the-world), the austere times were the very thing, the very imbalance, that would summon the resurrection of that frozen richness within the soil—if indeed that richness, that magic, that hope, did still exist beneath the ice and snow. Spring would come like its own green fire, if only the injured ones could hold on.

And what would the snipe think or remember, upon reawakening and finding themselves still in that desolate position, desolate place and time, but still alive, and with hope?

Would it seem to them that a thing like grace had passed through, as they slept—that a slender winding river of it had passed through and rewarded them for their faith and endurance?

Believing, stubbornly, that that green land beneath them would blossom once more. Maybe not soon; but again.

If the snipe survived, they would be among the first to see it. Perhaps they believed that the pack of dogs, and Gray Owl's and Ann's advancing torches, had only been one of winter's dreams. Even with the proof—the scribings—of grace's passage before them—the vent-holes still steaming—perhaps they believed it was only one of winter's dreams.

It would be curious to tally how many times any or all of us reject, or fail to observe, moments of grace. Another way in which I think Susan and I differ from most of the anarchists and militia members up here is that we believe there is still green fire in the hearts of our citizens, beneath this long snowy winter—beneath the chitin of the insipid. That there is still something beneath the surface: that our souls and spirits are still of more worth, more value, than the glassine, latticed ice-structures visible only now at the surface of things. We still believe there's something down there beneath us, as a country. Not that we're better than other countries, by any means, but that we're luckier. That ribbons of grace are still passing through and around us—even now, and for whatever reasons, certainly unbeknownst to us, and certainly undeserved, unearned.

Gray Owl, Ann, and the dogs headed south for half a day until they reached the snow-scoured road on which they'd parked. The road looked different, Ann said, buried beneath snowdrifts, and they didn't know whether to turn east or west. The dogs chose west, and so Gray Owl and Ann followed them. Two hours later they were back at their truck, and that night they were back at Gray Owl's cabin; by the next night Ann was home again. She says that even now she still sometimes has dreams about being beneath the ice—about living beneath the ice—and that it seems to her as if she was down there for much longer than a day and a night; that instead she might have been gone for years.

It was twenty years ago, when it happened. Gray Owl has since died, and all those dogs are dead now too. She is the only one who still carries—in the flesh, at any rate—the memory of that passage.

Ann would never discuss such a thing, but I suspect that it, that one day and night, helped give her a model for what things were like for her dogs when they were hunting and when they went on point: how the world must have appeared to them when they were in that trance, that blue zone, where the odors of things wrote their images across the dogs' hot brainpans. A zone where sight, and the appearance of things—*surfaces*—disappeared, and where instead their essence—the heat molecules of scent—was revealed, illuminated, circumscribed, possessed.

I suspect that she holds that knowledge—the memory of that one day and night—especially since she is now the sole possessor—as tightly, and securely, as one might clench some bright small gem in one's fist: not a gem given to one by some favored or beloved individual but, even more valuable, some gem found while out on a walk—perhaps by happenstance, or perhaps by some unavoidable rhythm of fate—and hence containing great magic, great strength.

Such is the nature of the kinds of people living, scattered here and there, in this valley.

The House of Mapuhi
by Jack London

Jack London (1876–1916) wrote about nature's power to sustain or destroy us. But the people in his stories have power as well: They can choose to be arrogant and cruel, or brave and sensible.

Despite the heavy clumsiness of her lines, the *Aorai* handled easily in the light breeze, and her captain ran her well in before he hove to just outside the suck of the surf. The atoll of Hikueru lay low on the water, a circle of pounded coral sand a hundred yards wide, twenty miles in circumference, and from three to five feet above high-water mark. On the bottom of the huge and glassy lagoon was much pearl shell, and from the deck of the schooner, across the slender ring of the atoll, the divers could be seen at work. But the lagoon had no entrance for even a trading schooner. With a favoring breeze cutters could win in through the tortuous and shallow channel, but the schooners lay off and on outside and sent in their small boats.

The *Aorai* swung out a boat smartly, into which sprang half a dozen brown-skinned sailors clad only in scarlet loincloths. They took the oars, while in the stern-sheets, at the steering sweep, stood a young man garbed in the tropic white that marks the European. But he was not all European. The golden strain of Polynesia betrayed itself in the sun-gilt of his fair skin and cast up golden sheens and lights through the glimmering blue of his eyes. Raoul he was, Alexandré Raoul, youngest son of Marie Raoul, the wealthy quarter-caste, who owned and managed half a dozen trading schooners similar to the *Aorai*. Across an eddy just outside the entrance, and in and through and over a boiling tide-rip, the boat fought its way to the mirrored calm of the lagoon. Young Raoul leaped out upon the white sand and shook hands with a tall native. The man's chest and shoulders were magnificent, but the stump of a right arm, beyond the flesh of which the age-whitened bone projected several inches, attested the encounter with a shark that had put an end to his diving days and made him a fawner and an intriguer for small favors.

"Have you heard, Alec?" were his first words. "Mapuhi has found a pearl—such a pearl. Never was there one like it ever fished up in Hikueru, nor in all the Paumotus, nor in all the world. Buy it from him. He has it now. And remember that I told you first. He is a fool and you can get it cheap. Have you any tobacco?"

Straight up the beach to a shack under a pandanus-tree Raoul headed. He was his mother's supercargo, and his business was to comb all the Paumotus for the wealth of copra, shell, and pearls that they yielded up.

He was a young supercargo, it was his second voyage in such capacity, and he suffered much secret worry from his lack of experience in pricing pearls. But when Mapuhi exposed the pearl to his sight he managed to suppress the startle it gave him, and to maintain a careless, commercial expression on his face. For the pearl had struck him a blow. It was large as a pigeon egg, a perfect sphere, of a whiteness that reflected opalescent lights from all colors about it. It was alive. Never had he seen anything like it. When Mapuhi dropped it into his hand he was surprised by the weight of it. That showed that it was a good pearl. He examined it closely, through a pocket magnifying-glass. It was without flaw or blemish. The purity of it seemed almost to melt into the atmosphere out of his hand. In the shade it was softly luminous, gleaming like a tender moon. So translucently white was it, that when he dropped it into a glass of water he had difficulty in finding it. So straight and swiftly had it sunk to the bottom that he knew its weight was excellent.

"Well, what do you want for it?" he asked, with a fine assumption of nonchalance.

"I want—" Mapuhi began, and behind him, framing his own dark face, the dark faces of two women and a girl nodded concurrence in what he wanted. Their heads were bent forward, they were animated by a suppressed eagerness, their eyes flashed avariciously.

"I want a house," Mapuhi went on. "It must have a roof of galvanized iron and an octagon-drop-clock. It must be six fathoms long with a porch all around. A big room must be in the centre, with a round table in the middle of it and the octagon-drop-clock on the wall. There must be four bedrooms, two on each side of the big room, and in each bedroom must be an iron bed, two chairs, and a washstand. And back of the house must be a kitchen, a good kitchen, with pots and pans and a stove. And you must build the house on my island, which is Fakarava."

"Is that all?" Raoul asked incredulously.

"There must be a sewing machine," spoke up Tefara, Mapuhi's wife.

"Not forgetting the octagon-drop-clock," added Nauri, Mapuhi's mother.

"Yes, that is all," said Mapuhi.

Young Raoul laughed. He laughed long and heartily. But while he laughed he secretly performed problems in mental arithmetic. He had never built a house in his life, and his notions concerning house building were hazy. While he laughed, he calculated the cost of the voyage to Tahiti for materials, of the materials themselves, of the voyage back again to Fakarava, and the cost of landing the materials and of building the house. It would come to four thousand French dollars, allowing a margin for safety—four thousand French dollars were equivalent to twenty thousand francs. It was impossible. How was he to know the value of such a pearl? Twenty thousand francs was a lot of money—and of his mother's money at that.

"Mapuhi," he said, "you are a big fool. Set a money price."

But Mapuhi shook his head, and the three heads behind him shook with his.

"I want the house," he said. "It must be six fathoms long with a porch all around—"

"Yes, yes," Raoul interrupted. "I know all about your house, but it won't do. I'll give you a thousand Chili dollars."

The four heads chorused a silent negative.

"And a hundred Chili dollars in trade."

"I want the house," Mapuhi began.

"What good will the house do you?" Raoul demanded. "The first hurricane that comes along will wash it away. You ought to know. Captain Raffy says it looks like a hurricane right now."

"Not on Fakarava," said Mapuhi. "The land is much higher there. On this island, yes. Any hurricane can sweep Hikueru. I will have the house on Fakarava. It must be six fathoms long with a porch all around—"

And Raoul listened again to the tale of the house. Several hours he spent in the endeavor to hammer the house-obsession out of Mapuhi's mind; but Mapuhi's mother and wife, and Ngakura, Mapuhi's daughter, bolstered him in his resolve for the house. Through the open doorway, while he listened for the twentieth time to the detailed description of the house that was wanted, Raoul saw his schooner's second boat draw up on the beach. The sailors rested on the oars, advertising haste to be gone. The first mate of the *Aorai* sprang ashore, exchanged a word with the one-armed native, then hurried toward Raoul. The day grew suddenly dark, as a squall obscured the face of the sun. Across the lagoon Raoul could see approaching the ominous line of the puff of wind.

"Captain Raffy says you've got to get to hell outa here," was the mate's greeting. "If there's any shell, we've got to run the risk of picking it up later on—so he says. The barometer's dropped to twenty-nine-seventy."

The gust of wind struck the pandanus-tree overhead and tore through the palms beyond, flinging half a dozen ripe cocoanuts with heavy thuds to the ground. Then came the rain out of the distance, advancing with the roar of a gale of wind and causing the water of the lagoon to smoke in driven windrows. The sharp rattle of the first drops was on the leaves when Raoul sprang to his feet.

"A thousand Chili dollars, cash down, Mapuhi," he said. "And two hundred Chili dollars in trade."

"I want a house—" the other began.

"Mapuhi!" Raoul yelled, in order to make himself heard. "You are a fool!"

He flung out of the house, and, side by side with the mate, fought his way down the beach toward the boat. They could not see the boat. The tropic rain sheeted about them so that they could see only the beach under their feet and the spiteful little waves from the lagoon that snapped and bit at the sand. A figure appeared through the deluge. It was Huru-Huru, the man with the one arm.

"Did you get the pearl?" he yelled in Raoul's ear.

"Mapuhi is a fool!" was the answering yell, and the next moment they were lost to each other in the descending water.

Half an hour later, Huru-Huru, watching from the seaward side of the atoll, saw the two boats hoisted in and the *Aorai* pointing her nose out to sea. And near her, just come in from the sea on the wings of the squall, he saw another schooner hove to and dropping a boat into the water. He knew her. It was the *Orohena*, owned by Toriki, the half-caste trader, who served as his own supercargo and who doubtlessly was even then in the stern-sheets of the boat. Huru-Huru chuckled. He knew that Mapuhi owed Toriki for trade goods advanced the year before.

The squall had passed. The hot sun was blazing down, and the lagoon was once more a mirror. But the air was sticky like mucilage, and the weight of it seemed to burden the lungs and make breathing difficult.

"Have you heard the news, Toriki?" Huru-Huru asked. "Mapuhi has found a pearl. Never was there a pearl like it ever fished up in Hikueru, nor anywhere in the Paumotus, nor anywhere in all the world. Mapuhi is a fool. Besides, he owes you money. Remember that I told you first. Have you any tobacco?"

And to the grass shack of Mapuhi went Toriki. He was a masterful man, withal a fairly stupid one. Carelessly he glanced at the wonderful pearl—glanced for a moment only; and carelessly he dropped it into his pocket.

"You are lucky," he said. "It is a nice pearl. I will give you credit on the books."

"I want a house," Mapuhi began, in consternation. "It must be six fathoms—"

"Six fathoms your grandmother!" was the trader's retort. "You want to pay up your debts, that's what you want. You owed me twelve hundred dollars Chili. Very well; you owe them no longer. The amount is squared. Besides, I will give you credit for two hundred Chili. If, when I get to Tahiti, the pearl sells well, I will give you credit for another hundred—that will make three hundred. But mind, only if the pearl sells well. I may even lose money on it."

Mapuhi folded his arms in sorrow and sat with bowed head. He had been robbed of his pearl. In place of the house, he had paid a debt. There was nothing to show for the pearl.

"You are a fool," said Tefara.

"You are a fool," said Nauri, his mother. "Why did you let the pearl into his hand?"

"What was I to do?" Mapuhi protested. "I owed him the money. He knew I had the pearl. You heard him yourself ask to see it. I had not told him. He knew. Somebody else told him. And I owed him the money."

"Mapuhi is a fool," mimicked Ngakura.

She was twelve years old and did not know any better. Mapuhi relieved his feelings by sending her reeling from a box on the ear; while Tefara and Nauri burst into tears and continued to upbraid him after the manner of women.

Huru-Huru, watching on the beach, saw a third schooner that he knew heave to outside the entrance and drop a boat. It was the *Hira*, well named, for she was owned by Levy, the German Jew, the greatest pearl-buyer of them all, and, as was well known, *Hira* was the Tahitian god of fishermen and thieves.

"Have you heard the news?" Huru-Huru asked, as Levy, a fat man with massive asymmetrical features, stepped out upon the beach. "Mapuhi has found a pearl. There was never a pearl like it in Hikueru, in all the Paumotus, in all the world. Mapuhi is a fool. He has sold it to Toriki for fourteen hundred Chili—I listened outside and heard. Toriki is likewise a fool. You can buy it from him cheap. Remember that I told you first. Have you any tobacco?"

"Where is Toriki?"

"In the house of Captain Lynch, drinking absinthe. He has been there an hour."

And while Levy and Toriki drank absinthe and chaffered over the pearl, Huru-Huru listened and heard the stupendous price of twenty-five thousand francs agreed upon.

It was at this time that both the *Orohena* and the *Hira*, running in close to the shore, began firing guns and signalling frantically. The three men stepped outside in time to see the two schooners go hastily about and head off shore, dropping mainsails and flying-jibs on the run in the teeth of the squall that heeled them far over on the whitened water. Then the rain blotted them out.

"They'll be back after it's over," said Toriki. "We'd better be getting out of here."

"I reckon the glass has fallen some more," said Captain Lynch.

He was a white-bearded sea-captain, too old for service, who had learned that the only way to live on comfortable terms with his asthma was on Hikueru. He went inside to look at the barometer.

"Great God!" they heard him exclaim, and rushed in to join him at staring at a dial, which marked twenty-nine-twenty.

Again they came out, this time anxiously to consult sea and sky. The squall had cleared away, but the sky remained overcast. The two schooners, under all sail and joined by a third, could be seen making back. A veer in the wind induced them to slack off sheets, and five minutes afterward a sudden veer from the opposite quarter caught all three schooners aback, and those on shore could see the boom-tackles being slacked away or cast off on the jump. The sound of the surf was loud, hollow, and menacing, and a heavy swell was setting in. A terrible sheet of lightning burst before their eyes, illuminating the dark day, and the thunder rolled wildly about them.

Toriki and Levy broke into a run for their boats, the latter ambling along like a panic-stricken hippopotamus. As their two boats swept out the entrance, they passed the boat of the *Aorai* coming in. In the stern-sheets, encouraging the rowers, was Raoul. Unable to shake the vision of the pearl from his mind, he was returning to accept Mapuhi's price of a house.

He landed on the beach in the midst of a driving thunder squall that was so dense that he collided with Huru-Huru before he saw him.

"Too late," yelled Huru-Huru. "Mapuhi sold it to Toriki for fourteen hundred Chili, and Toriki sold it to Levy for twenty-five thousand francs. And Levy will sell it in France for a hundred thousand francs. Have you any tobacco?"

Raoul felt relieved. His troubles about the pearl were over. He need not worry any more, even if he had not got the pearl. But he did not believe Huru-Huru. Mapuhi might well have sold it for fourteen hundred Chili, but that Levy, who knew pearls, should have paid twenty-five thousand francs was too wide a stretch. Raoul decided to interview Captain Lynch on the subject, but when he arrived at that ancient mariner's house, he found him looking wide-eyed at the barometer.

"What do you read it?" Captain Lynch asked anxiously, rubbing his spectacles and staring again at the instrument.

"Twenty-nine-ten," said Raoul. "I have never seen it so low before."

"I should say not!" snorted the captain. "Fifty years boy and man on all the seas, and I've never seen it go down to that. Listen!"

They stood for a moment, while the surf rumbled and shook the house. Then they went outside. The squall had passed. They could see the *Aorai* lying becalmed a mile away and pitching and tossing madly in the tremendous seas that rolled in stately procession down out of the northeast and flung themselves furiously upon the coral shore. One of the sailors from the boat pointed at the mouth of the passage and shook his head. Raoul looked and saw a white anarchy of foam and surge.

"I guess I'll stay with you to-night, Captain," he said; then turned to the sailor and told him to haul the boat out and to find shelter for himself and fellows.

"Twenty-nine flat," Captain Lynch reported, coming out from another look at the barometer, a chair in his hand.

He sat down and stared at the spectacle of the sea. The sun came out, increasing the sultriness of the day, while the dead calm still held. The seas continued to increase in magnitude.

"What makes that sea is what gets me," Raoul muttered petulantly. "There is no wind, yet look at it, look at that fellow there!"

Miles in length, carrying tens of thousands of tons in weight, its impact shook the frail atoll like an earthquake. Captain Lynch was startled.

"Gracious!" he exclaimed, half-rising from his chair, then sinking back.

"But there is no wind," Raoul persisted. "I could understand it if there was wind along with it."

"You'll get the wind soon enough without worryin' for it," was the grim reply.

The two men sat on in silence. The sweat stood out on their skin in myriads of tiny drops that ran together, forming blotches of moisture, which, in turn, coalesced into rivulets that dripped to the ground. They panted for breath, the old man's efforts being especially painful. A sea swept up the beach, licking around the trunks of the cocoanuts and subsiding almost at their feet.

"'Way past high water mark," Captain Lynch remarked; "and I've been here eleven years." He looked at his watch. "It is three o'clock."

A man and woman, at their heels a motley following of brats and curs, trailed disconsolately by. They came to a halt beyond the house, and, after much irresolution, sat down in the sand. A few minutes later another family trailed in from the opposite direction, the men and women carrying a heterogeneous assortment of possessions. And soon several hundred persons of all ages and sexes were congregated about the captain's dwelling. He called to one new arrival, a woman with a nursing babe in her arms, and in answer received the information that her house had just been swept into the lagoon.

This was the highest spot of land in miles, and already, in many places on either hand, the great seas were making a clean breach of the slender ring of the atoll and surging into the lagoon. Twenty miles around stretched the ring of the atoll, and in no place was it more than fifty fathoms wide. It was the height of the diving season, and from all the islands around, even as far as Tahiti, the natives had gathered.

"There are twelve hundred men, women, and children here," said Captain Lynch. "I wonder how many will be here to-morrow morning."

"But why don't it blow?—that's what I want to know," Raoul demanded.

"Don't worry, young man, don't worry; you'll get your troubles fast enough."

Even as Captain Lynch spoke, a great watery mass smote the atoll. The sea-water churned about them three inches deep under the chairs. A low wail of fear went up from the many women. The children, with clasped hands, stared at the immense rollers and cried piteously. Chickens and cats, wading perturbedly in the water, as by common consent, with flight and scramble took refuge on the roof of the captain's house. A Paumotan, with a litter of new-born puppies in a basket, climbed into a cocoanut tree and twenty feet above the ground made the basket fast. The mother floundered about in the water beneath, whining and yelping.

And still the sun shone brightly and the dead calm continued. They sat and watched the seas and the insane pitching of the *Aorai*. Captain Lynch gazed at the huge mountains of water sweeping in until he could gaze no more. He covered his face with his hands to shut out the sight; then went into the house.

"Twenty-eight-sixty," he said quietly when he returned.

In his arm was a coil of small rope. He cut it into two-fathom lengths, giving one to Raoul and, retaining one for himself, distributed the remainder among the women with the advice to pick out a tree and climb.

A light air began to blow out of the northeast, and the fan of it on his cheek seemed to cheer Raoul up. He could see the *Aorai* trimming her sheets and heading off shore, and he regretted that he was not on her. She would get away at any rate, but as for the atoll— A sea breached across, almost sweeping him off his feet, and he selected a tree. Then he remembered the barometer and ran back to the house. He encountered Captain Lynch on the same errand and together they went in.

"Twenty-eight-twenty," said the old mariner. "It's going to be fair hell around here—what was that?"

The air seemed filled with the rush of something. The house quivered and vibrated, and they heard the thrumming of a mighty note of sound. The windows rattled. Two panes crashed; a draught of wind tore in, striking them and making them stagger. The door opposite banged shut, shattering the latch. The white door knob crumbled in fragments to the floor. The room's walls bulged like a gas balloon in the process of sudden inflation. Then came a new sound like the rattle of musketry, as the spray from a sea struck the wall of the house. Captain Lynch looked at his watch. It was four o'clock. He put on a coat of pilot cloth, unhooked the barometer, and stowed it away in a capacious pocket. Again a sea struck the house, with a heavy thud, and the light building tilted, twisted quarter-around on its foundation, and sank down, its floor at an angle of ten degrees.

Raoul went out first. The wind caught him and whirled him away. He noted that it had hauled around to the east. With a great effort he threw himself on the sand, crouching and holding his own. Captain Lynch, driven like a wisp of straw, sprawled over him. Two of the *Aorai*'s sailors, leaving a cocoanut tree to which they had been clinging, came to their aid, leaning against the wind at impossible angles and fighting and clawing every inch of the way.

The old man's joints were stiff and he could not climb, so the sailors, by means of short ends of rope tied together, hoisted him up the trunk, a few feet at a time, till they could make him fast, at the top of the tree, fifty feet from the ground. Raoul passed his length of rope around the base of an adjacent tree and stood looking on. The wind was frightful. He had never dreamed it could blow so hard. A sea breached across the atoll, wetting him to the knees ere it subsided into the lagoon. The sun had disappeared, and a lead-colored twilight settled down. A few drops of rain, driving horizontally, struck him. The impact was like that of leaden pellets. A splash of salt spray struck his face. It was like the slap of a man's hand. His cheeks stung, and involuntary tears of pain were in his smarting eyes. Several hundred natives had taken to the trees, and he could have laughed at the bunches of human fruit clustering in the tops. Then, being Tahitian-born, he doubled his body at the waist, clasped the trunk of his tree with his hands, pressed the soles of his feet against the near surface of the trunk, and began to walk up the tree. At the top he found two women, two children, and a man. One little girl clasped a house-cat in her arms.

From his eyrie he waved his hand to Captain Lynch, and that doughty patriarch waved back. Raoul was appalled at the sky. It had approached much nearer—in fact, it seemed just over his head; and it had turned from lead to black. Many people were still on the ground grouped about the bases of the trees and holding on. Several such clusters were praying, and in one the Mormon missionary was exhorting. A weird sound, rhythmical, faint as the faintest chirp of a far cricket, enduring but for a moment, but in that moment suggesting to him vaguely the thought of heaven and celestial music, came to his ear. He glanced about him and saw, at the base of another tree, a large cluster of people holding on by ropes and by one another. He could see their faces working and their lips moving in unison. No sound came to him, but he knew that they were singing hymns.

Still the wind continued to blow harder. By no conscious process could he measure it, for it had long since passed beyond all his experience of wind; but he knew somehow, nevertheless, that it was blowing harder. Not far away a tree was uprooted, flinging its load of human beings to the ground. A sea washed across the strip of sand, and they were gone. Things were happening quickly. He saw a brown shoulder and a black head silhouetted against the churning white of the lagoon. The next instant that, too, had vanished. Other trees were going, falling and criss-crossing like matches. He was amazed at the power of the wind. His own tree was swaying perilously, one woman was wailing and clutching the little girl, who in turn still hung on to the cat.

The man, holding the other child, touched Raoul's arm and pointed. He looked and saw the Mormon church careering drunkenly a hundred feet away. It had been torn from its foundations, and wind and sea were heaving and shoving it toward the lagoon. A frightful wall of water caught it, tilted it, and flung it against half a dozen cocoanut trees. The bunches of human fruit fell like ripe cocoanuts. The subsiding wave showed them on the ground, some lying motionless, others squirming and writhing. They reminded him strangely of ants. He was not shocked. He had risen above horror. Quite as a matter of course he noted the succeeding wave sweep the sand clean of the human wreckage. A third wave, more colossal than any he had yet seen, hurled the church into the lagoon, where it floated off into the obscurity to leeward, half-submerged, reminding him for all the world of a Noah's ark.

He looked for Captain Lynch's house, and was surprised to find it gone. Things certainly were happening quickly. He noticed that many of the people in the trees that still held had descended to the ground. The wind had yet again increased. His own tree showed that. It no longer swayed or bent over and back. Instead, it remained practically stationary, curved in a rigid angle from the wind and merely vibrating. But the vibration was sickening. It was like that of a tuning-fork or the tongue of a jew's-harp. It was the rapidity of the vibration that made it so bad. Even though its roots held, it could not stand the strain for long. Something would have to break.

Ah, there was one that had gone. He had not seen it go, but there it stood, the remnant, broken off half-way up the trunk. One did not know what happened unless he saw it. The mere crashing of trees and wails of human despair occupied no place in that mighty volume of sound. He chanced to be looking in Captain Lynch's direction when it happened. He saw the trunk of the tree, half-way up, splinter and part without noise. The head of the tree, with three sailors of the *Aorai* and the old captain sailed off over the lagoon. It did not fall to the ground, but drove through the air like a piece of chaff. For a hundred yards he followed its flight, when it struck the water. He strained his eyes, and was sure that he saw Captain Lynch wave farewell.

Raoul did not wait for anything more. He touched the native and made signs to descend to the ground. The man was willing, but his women were paralyzed from terror, and he elected to remain with them. Raoul passed his rope around the tree and slid down. A rush of salt water went over his head. He held his breath and clung desperately to the rope. The water subsided, and in the shelter of the trunk he breathed once more. He fastened the rope more securely, and then was put under by another sea. One of the women slid down and joined him, the native remaining by the other woman, the two children, and the cat.

The supercargo had noticed how the groups clinging at the bases of the other trees continually diminished. Now he saw the process work out alongside him. It required all his strength to hold on, and the woman who had joined him was growing weaker. Each time he emerged from a sea he was surprised to find himself still there, and next, surprised to find the woman still there. At last he emerged to find himself alone. He looked up. The top of the tree had gone as well. At half its original height, a splintered end vibrated. He was safe. The roots still held, while the tree had been shorn of its windage. He began to climb up. He was so weak that he went slowly, and sea after sea caught him before he was above them. Then he tied himself to the trunk and stiffened his soul to face the night and he knew not what.

He felt very lonely in the darkness. At times it seemed to him that it was the end of the world and that he was the last one left alive. Still the wind increased. Hour after hour it increased. By what he calculated was eleven o'clock, the wind had become unbelievable. It was a horrible, monstrous thing, a screaming fury, a wall that smote and passed on but that continued to smite and pass on—a wall without end. It seemed to him that he had become light and ethereal; that it was he that was in motion; that he was being driven with inconceivable velocity through unending solidness. The wind was no longer air in motion. It had become substantial as water or quicksilver. He had a feeling that he could reach into it and tear it out in chunks as one might do with the meat in the carcass of a steer; that he could seize hold of the wind and hang on to it as a man might hang on to the face of a cliff.

The wind strangled him. He could not face it and breathe, for it rushed in through his mouth and nostrils, distending his lungs like bladders. At such moments it seemed to him that his body was being packed and swollen with solid earth. Only by pressing his lips to the trunk of the tree could he breathe. Also, the ceaseless impact of the wind exhausted him. Body and brain became wearied. He no longer observed, no longer thought, and was but semiconscious. One idea constituted his consciousness: *So this was a hurricane*. That one idea persisted irregularly. It was like a feeble flame that flickered occasionally. From a state of stupor he would return to it—*So this was a hurricane*. Then he would go off into another stupor.

The height of the hurricane endured from eleven at night till three in the morning, and it was at eleven that the tree in which clung Mapuhi and his women snapped off. Mapuhi rose to the surface of the lagoon, still clutching his daughter Ngakura. Only a South Sea islander could have lived in such a driving smother. The pandanus-tree, to which he attached himself, turned over and over in the froth and churn; and it was only by holding on at times and waiting, and at other times shifting his grips rapidly, that he was able to get his head and Ngakura's to the surface at intervals sufficiently near together to keep the breath in them. But the air was mostly water, what with flying spray and sheeted rain that poured along at right angles to the perpendicular.

It was ten miles across the lagoon to the farther ring of sand. Here, tossing tree-trunks, timbers, wrecks of cutters, and wreckage of houses, killed nine out of ten of the miserable beings who survived the passage of the lagoon. Half-drowned, exhausted, they were hurled into this mad mortar of the elements and battered into formless flesh. But Mapuhi was fortunate. His chance was the one in ten; it fell to him by the freakage of fate. He emerged upon the sand, bleeding from a score of wounds. Ngakura's left arm was broken; the fingers of her right hand were crushed; and cheek and forehead were laid open to the bone. He clutched a tree that yet stood, and clung on, holding the girl and sobbing for air, while the waters of the lagoon washed by knee-high and at times waist-high.

At three in the morning the backbone of the hurricane broke. By five no more than a stiff breeze was blowing. And by six it was dead calm and the sun was shining. The sea had gone down. On the yet restless edge of the lagoon, Mapuhi saw the broken bodies of those that had failed in the landing. Undoubtedly Tefara and Nauri were among them. He went along the beach examining them, and came upon his wife, lying half in and half out of the water. He sat down and wept, making harsh animal-noises after the manner of primitive grief. Then she stirred uneasily, and groaned. He looked more closely. Not only was she alive, but she was uninjured. She was merely sleeping. Hers also had been the one chance in ten.

Of the twelve hundred alive the night before but three hundred remained. The Mormon missionary and a gendarme made the census. The lagoon was cluttered with corpses. Not a house nor a hut was standing. In the whole atoll not two stones remained one upon another. One in fifty of the cocoanut palms still stood, and they were wrecks, while on not one of them remained a single nut. There was no fresh water. The shallow wells that caught the surface seepage of the rain were filled with salt. Out of the lagoon a few soaked bags of flour were recovered. The survivors cut the hearts out of the fallen cocoanut trees and ate them. Here and there they crawled into tiny hutches, made by hollowing out the sand and covering over with fragments of metal roofing. The missionary made a crude still, but he could not distill water for three hundred persons. By the end of the second day, Raoul, taking a bath in the lagoon, discovered that his thirst was somewhat relieved. He cried out the news, and thereupon three hundred men, women, and children could have been seen, standing up to their necks in the lagoon and trying to drink water in through their skins. Their dead floated about them, or were stepped upon where they still lay upon the bottom. On the third day the people buried their dead and sat down to wait for the rescue steamers.

In the meantime, Nauri, torn from her family by the hurricane, had been swept away on an adventure of her own. Clinging to a rough plank that wounded and bruised her and that filled her body with splinters, she was thrown clear over the atoll and carried away to sea. Here, under the amazing buffets of mountains of water, she lost her plank. She was an old woman nearly sixty; but she was Paumotan-born, and she had never been out of sight of the sea in her life. Swimming in the darkness, strangling, suffocating, fighting for air, she was struck a heavy blow on the shoulder by a cocoanut. On the instant her plan was formed, and she seized the nut. In the next hour she captured seven more. Tied together, they formed a life-buoy that preserved her life while at the same time it threatened to pound her to a jelly. She was a fat woman, and she bruised easily; but she had had experience of hurricanes, and while she prayed to her shark god for protection from sharks, she waited for the wind to break. But at three o'clock she was in such a stupor that she did not know. Nor did she know at six o'clock when the dead calm settled down. She was shocked into consciousness when she was thrown upon the sand. She dug in with raw and bleeding hands and feet and clawed against the backwash until she was beyond the reach of the waves.

She knew where she was. This land could be no other than the tiny islet of Takokota. It had no lagoon. No one lived upon it. Hikueru was fifteen miles away. She could not see Hikueru, but she knew that it lay to the south. The days went by, and she lived on the cocoanuts that had kept her afloat. They supplied her with drinking water and with food. But she did not drink all she wanted, nor eat all she wanted. Rescue was problematical. She saw the smoke of the rescue steamers on the horizon, but what steamer could be expected to come to lonely, uninhabited Takokota?

From the first she was tormented by corpses. The sea persisted in flinging them upon her bit of sand, and she persisted, until her strength failed, in thrusting them back into the sea where the sharks tore at them and devoured them. When her strength failed, the bodies festooned her beach with ghastly horror, and she withdrew from them as far as she could, which was not far.

By the tenth day her last cocoanut was gone, and she was shrivelling from thirst. She dragged herself along the sand, looking for cocoanuts. It was strange that so many bodies floated up, and no nuts. Surely, there were more cocoanuts afloat than dead men! She gave up at last, and lay exhausted. The end had come. Nothing remained but to wait for death.

Coming out of a stupor, she became slowly aware that she was gazing at a patch of sandy-red hair on the head of a corpse. The sea flung the body toward her, then drew it back. It turned over, and she saw that it had no face. Yet there was something familiar about that patch of sandy-red hair. An hour passed. She did not exert herself to make the identification. She was waiting to die, and it mattered little to her what man that thing of horror once might have been. But at the end of the hour she sat up slowly and stared at the corpse. An unusually large wave had thrown it beyond the reach of the lesser waves. Yes, she was right; that patch of red hair could belong to but one man in the Paumotus. It was Levy, the German Jew, the man who had bought the pearl and carried it away on the *Hira*. Well, one thing was evident: The *Hira* had been lost. The pearl-buyer's god of fishermen and thieves had gone back on him.

She crawled down to the dead man. His shirt had been torn away, and she could see the leather money-belt about his waist. She held her breath and tugged at the buckles. They gave easier than she had expected, and she crawled hurriedly away across the sand, dragging the belt after her. Pocket after pocket she unbuckled in the belt and found empty. Where could he have put it? In the last pocket of all she found it, the first and only pearl he had bought on the voyage. She crawled a few feet farther, to escape the pestilence of the belt, and examined the pearl. It was the one Mapuhi had found and been robbed of by Toriki.

She weighed it in her hand and rolled it back and forth caressingly. But in it she saw no intrinsic beauty. What she did see was the house Mapuhi and Tefara and she had builded so carefully in their minds. Each time she looked at the pearl she saw the house in all its details, including the octagon-drop-clock on the wall. That was something to live for.

She tore a strip from her *ahu* and tied the pearl securely about her neck. Then she went on along the beach, panting and groaning, but resolutely seeking for cocoanuts. Quickly she found one, and, as she glanced around, a second. She broke one, drinking its water, which was mildewy, and eating the last particle of the meat. A little later she found a shattered dugout. Its outrigger was gone, but she was hopeful, and, before the day was out, she found the outrigger. Every find was an augury. The pearl was a talisman. Late in the afternoon she saw a wooden box floating low in the water. When she dragged it out on the beach its contents rattled, and inside she found ten tins of salmon. She opened one by hammering it on the canoe. When a leak was started, she drained the tin. After that she spent several hours in extracting the salmon, hammering and squeezing it out a morsel at a time.

Eight days longer she waited for rescue. In the meantime she fastened the outrigger back on the canoe, using for lashings all the cocoanut-fibre she could find, and also what remained of her *ahu*. The canoe was badly cracked, and she could not make it water-tight; but a calabash made from a cocoanut she stored on board for a bailer. She was hard put for a paddle. With a piece of tin she sawed off all her hair close to the scalp. Out of the hair she braided a cord; and by means of the cord she lashed a three-foot piece of broom-handle to a board from the salmon case. She gnawed wedges with her teeth and with them wedged the lashing.

On the eighteenth day, at midnight, she launched the canoe through the surf and started back for Hikueru. She was an old woman. Hardship had stripped her fat from her till scarcely more than bones and skin and a few stringy muscles remained. The canoe was large and should have been paddled by three strong men. But she did it alone, with a make-shift paddle. Also, the canoe leaked badly, and one-third of her time was devoted to bailing. By clear daylight she looked vainly for Hikueru. Astern, Takokota had sunk beneath the sea rim. The sun blazed down on her nakedness, compelling her body to surrender its moisture. Two tins of salmon were left, and in the course of the day she battered holes in them and drained the liquid. She had no time to waste in extracting the meat. A current was setting to the westward, she made westing whether she made southing or not.

In the early afternoon, standing upright in the canoe, she sighted Hikueru. Its wealth of cocoanut palms was gone. Only here and there, at wide intervals, could she see the ragged remnants of trees. The sight cheered her. She was nearer than she had thought. The current was setting her to the westward. She bore up against it and paddled on. The wedges in the paddle-lashing worked loose, and she lost much time, at frequent intervals, in driving them tight. Then there was the bailing. One hour in three she had to cease paddling in order to bail. And all the time she drifted to the westward.

By sunset Hikueru bore southeast from her, three miles away. There was a full moon, and by eight o'clock the land was due east and two miles away. She struggled on for another hour, but the land was as far away as ever. She was in the main grip of the current; the canoe was too large; the paddle was too inadequate; and too much of her time and strength was wasted in bailing. Besides, she was very weak and growing weaker. Despite her efforts, the canoe was drifting off to the westward.

She breathed a prayer to her shark god, slipped over the side, and began to swim. She was actually refreshed by the water, and quickly left the canoe astern. At the end of an hour the land was perceptibly nearer. Then came her fright. Right before her eyes, not twenty feet away, a large fin cut the water. She swam steadily toward it, and slowly it glided away, curving off toward the right and circling around her. She kept her eyes on the fin and swam on. When the fin disappeared, she lay face downward in the water and watched. When the fin reappeared she resumed her swimming. The monster was lazy—she could see that. Without doubt he had been well fed since the hurricane. Had he been very hungry, she knew he would not have hesitated from making a dash for her. He was fifteen feet long, and one bite, she knew, could cut her in half.

But she did not have any time to waste on him. Whether she swam or not, the current drew away from the land just the same. A half hour went by, and the shark began to grow bolder. Seeing no harm in her he drew closer, in narrowing circles, cocking his eyes at her impudently as he slid past. Sooner or later, she knew well enough, he would get up sufficient courage to dash at her. She resolved to play first. It was a desperate act she meditated. She was an old woman, alone in the sea and weak from starvation and hardship; and yet she, in the face of this sea tiger, must anticipate his dash by herself dashing at him. She swam on, waiting her chance. At last he passed languidly by, barely eight feet away. She rushed at him suddenly, feigning that she was attacking him. He gave a wild flirt of his tail as he fled away, and his sandpaper hide, striking her, took off her skin from elbow to shoulder. He swam rapidly, in a widening circle, and at last disappeared.

In the hole in the sand, covered over by fragments of metal roofing, Mapuhi and Tefara lay disputing.

"If you had done as I said," charged Tefara, for the thousandth time, "and hidden the pearl and told no one, you would have it now."

"But Huru-Huru was with me when I opened the shell—have I not told you so times and times and times without end?"

"And now we shall have no house. Raoul told me to-day that if you had not sold the pearl to Toriki—"

"I did not sell it. Toriki robbed me."

"—that if you had not sold the pearl, he would give you five thousand French dollars, which is ten thousand Chili."

"He has been talking to his mother," Mapuhi explained. "She has an eye for a pearl."

"And now the pearl is lost," Tefara complained.

"It paid my debt with Toriki. That is twelve hundred I have made, anyway."

"Toriki is dead," she cried. "They have heard no word of his schooner. She was lost along with the *Aorai* and the *Hira*. Will Toriki pay you the three hundred credit he promised? No, because Toriki is dead. And had you found no pearl, would you to-day owe Toriki the twelve hundred? No, because Toriki is dead, and you cannot pay dead men."

"But Levy did not pay Toriki," Mapuhi said. "He gave him a piece of paper that was good for the money in Papeete; and now Levy is dead and cannot pay; and Toriki is dead and the paper lost with him, and the pearl is lost with Levy. You are right, Tefara. I have lost the pearl, and got nothing for it. Now let us sleep."

He held up his hand suddenly and listened. From without came a noise, as of one who breathed heavily and with pain. A hand fumbled against the mat that served for a door.

"Who is there?" Mapuhi cried.

"Nauri," came the answer. "Can you tell me where is my son, Mapuhi?"

Tefara screamed and gripped her husband's arm.

"A ghost!" she chattered. "A ghost!"

Mapuhi's face was a ghastly yellow. He clung weakly to his wife.

"Good woman," he said in faltering tones, striving to disguise his voice, "I know your son well. He is living on the east side of the lagoon."

From without came the sound of a sigh. Mapuhi began to feel elated. He had fooled the ghost.

"But where do you come from, old woman?" he asked.

"From the sea," was the dejected answer.

"I knew it! I knew it!" screamed Tefara, rocking to and fro.

"Since when has Tefara bedded in a strange house?" came Nauri's voice through the matting.

Mapuhi looked fear and reproach at his wife. It was her voice that had betrayed them.

"And since when has Mapuhi, my son, denied his old mother?" the voice went on.

"No, no, I have not—Mapuhi has not denied you," he cried. "I am not Mapuhi. He is on the east end of the lagoon, I tell you."

Ngakura sat up in bed and began to cry. The matting started to shake.

"What are you doing?" Mapuhi demanded.

"I am coming in," said the voice of Nauri.

One end of the matting lifted. Tefara tried to dive under the blankets, but Mapuhi held on to her. He had to hold on to something. Together, struggling with each other, with shivering bodies and chattering teeth, they gazed with protruding eyes at the lifting mat. They saw Nauri, dripping with sea water, without her *ahu*, creep in. They rolled over backward from her and fought for Ngakura's blanket with which to cover their heads.

"You might give your old mother a drink of water," the ghost said plaintively.

"Give her a drink of water," Tefara commanded in a shaking voice.

"Give her a drink of water," Mapuhi passed on the command to Ngakura.

And together they kicked out Ngakura from under the blanket. A minute later, peeping, Mapuhi saw the ghost drinking. When it reached out a shaking hand and laid it on his, he felt the weight of it and was convinced that it was no ghost. Then he emerged, dragging Tefara after him, and in a few minutes all were listening to Nauri's tale. And when she told of Levy, and dropped the pearl into Tefara's hand, even she was reconciled to the reality of her mother-in-law.

"In the morning," said Tefara, "you will sell the pearl to Raoul for five thousand French."

"The house?" objected Nauri.

"He will build the house," Tefara answered. "He says it will cost four thousand French. Also will he give one thousand French in credit, which is two thousand Chili."

"And it will be six fathoms long?" Nauri queried.

"Ay," answered Mapuhi, "six fathoms."

"And in the middle room will be the octagon-drop-clock?"

"Ay, and the round table as well."

"Then give me something to eat, for I am hungry," said Nauri, complacently. "And after that we will sleep, for I am weary. And to-morrow we will have more talk about the house before we sell the pearl. It will be better if we take the thousand French in cash. Money is ever better than credit in buying goods from the traders."

In the Storm

by James LeMoyne

The news accounts that follow a destructive storm often lean on statistics to describe its effects on people and their property. James Le Moyne's (born 1951) account of Hurricane Andrew and its aftermath in south Florida draws upon his personal sense of loss to convey a notion of the ruin that the 1992 storm inflicted upon his community.

Hurricane Andrew came to south Florida on a sweet, cloud-fleeced day. Just beyond the balcony of my family's twentieth-floor apartment, near downtown Miami, Biscayne Bay was blue and quiet. Herons, ibises, and frigate birds floated on the freshening breeze, over canopies of tropical gumbo-limbo, mahogany, casuarina, ficus, poinciana, and palm.

As daylight faded, we were stuffing books and terra-cotta platters into plastic bags and boxes. An announcer on television told us again to evacuate. I shoved the last of our furniture into an interior hall and hammered boards across the doorway, driving three-inch nails into the bedroom wall. My wife packed baby formula and a few essential documents in her shoulder bag. Then we shared a silent moment in the glass-enclosed home we did not expect to see whole again. I lifted our year-old daughter into my arms, and we fled.

We drove to a friend's concrete-block house about five miles inland, on Romano Avenue, in Coral Gables. The four of us—Emily and I, our daughter, Clara, and Emily's sister Alice—huddled under blankets and sleeping bags on the floor of a small corner room. At three-thirty in the morning a metal storm shutter began to clang above my head. Clara woke, whimpering. Gusts now pounded the walls and windows. Feeling the house tremble, I realized did not know where I had put the flashlight, my shoes, the radio. The wind blew harder. I was afraid a window would shatter. I stood up in the dark and pulled everything off the table so nothing could fly through the air and kill us.

The reassuring hum of the air conditioner stopped as an electrical transformer exploded somewhere. The room was chokingly close. The shutter banged a steady staccato over sudden booms and cracks of things breaking in the street. The hurricane was pawing at the house, trying to get in. Shaken by a new gibberish of howls and whistles outside, I bent my body over Clara to shelter her. What seemed like the whole weight of the sky was slamming the house. If a window or the roof was going to blow, it would happen now. We lay still, held hands, and prayed.

In the gray light, uprooted trees, snapped trees trunks, buckled concrete sidewalks, and ripped power lines covered Romano Avenue. A mango tree had blown into a sailboat trailered behind the house. It was seven in the morning, August 24th. The fleeing sky above Miami was pale and emptied.

Early reports on the radio said central Miami and Miami Beach were largely intact. The worst of the storm had struck between ten and twenty-five miles farther south: in the neighboring towns of Homestead and Florida City, the communities of Goulds and Naranja Lakes, and the densely populated tract-housing suburbs of Perrine, Old Cutler Road, Country Walk, Cutler Ridge, and Kendall. Of this natural and man-made world, some three hundred square miles was severely damaged. About a hundred square miles was blasted or simply gone.

Like more than a million others, we had lost water and power. But the phone worked, and we found another friend, in Sweetwater, fifteen miles northwest, who still had electricity and a trickle of water. I resettled my family there, and then drove home.

The wind had shorn so many street signs, trees, and storefronts that familiar vistas were foreign, almost lunar in their emotional emptiness. There were no working stoplights—at most intersections, no stoplights. Downtown Brickell Avenue, a sparkling, tree-lined boulevard the day before, was an impassable maze of power lines and cleaved trees. Stripped of foliage, Miami was bare and ugly. Beyond the seawall, Biscayne Bay was purple-black with wind-churned mud and torn sea grass.

Our apartment was partly flooded, and the parking garage was under four feet of seawater and a foot of mud. The roof had blown off my office, and files and furniture were flooded. At any other time, this would not have seemed like minor damage.

In Coconut Grove, the sea had surged so far across the bayfront that a hundred yards from the ocean a twenty-two-foot sailboat leaned daintily against a light post, a new piece of Miami's zany public art. A big blue sailing yacht was docked on the four-lane Rickenbacker Causeway, to Key Biscayne. Out on the island, ten-foot seas had washed over the Sandbar, my favorite saloon. Boston John, the bartender, waved toward the remains: "We got waxed."

Fifteen people were killed by the storm that night, most of them crushed or drowned. The wreckage looked so bad it gave rise to rumors that the number fifteen was a lie. Miles Lawrence, a hurricane specialist at the National Hurricane Center, in Miami, said the sustained winds averaged a hundred and forty-five miles per hour, with individual gusts up to a hundred and seventy-five miles per hour. The most powerful may have hit Naranja Lakes; eighty-foot-long steel-reinforced beams weighing several tons were ripped from a housing complex there and tossed more than a block away. Three of the seven people killed inside standing structures died in Naranja Lakes. Other people survived because the wind blew the roof away instead of dropping it on them.

Wooden trusses, tie beams, steel "hurricane straps," bolts, wood sheeting, nails, tarpaper, glue, and shingles or tiles are needed to build a roof sturdy enough for south Florida. The building code in Dade County, where Andrew hit, mandates that most residential construction be able to survive winds of a hundred and nine to a hundred and twenty miles per hour. But it permitted builders to use water-vulnerable particleboard as covering and to substitute staples for nails. Many roofs built that way disintegrated. I had been thinking of buying a house, but now I'm afraid of roofs, unscrupulous builders, and lazy inspectors.

Bob Lamm, who has lived in south Florida for most of his life, spent five years constructing his own house to withstand a major hurricane, with thirty-two-foot-long, seven-and-a-half-inch-wide cedar logs, in the Redland, a farming district near Homestead. Bob says it took Andrew about two hours to tear it apart.

"We lost power at 3 a.m., but I could see with my flashlight that the walls were shaking—I mean solid wood-beam walls were breathing in and out like a lung, moving six and eight inches," Bob told me. "The windows blew, and the whole house began to shake. Oh, Christ! I crawled down into the basement at 4:45 a.m. and didn't come out until five hours later.

"I began to pick up a roof shingle in the living room. Then I looked—there was no reason to be picking up litter." The wind had torn the cedar beams out of the walls and thrown them fifty and eighty feet away. The entire second floor had been lifted and tilted, snapping steel straps. The barn, set in concrete with steel rods, was tossed into an avocado grove. Across the way, a one-by-four-inch wood beam had been driven straight through the concrete-block wall of his next-door neighbor's house.

Bob recalled carefully boarding his windows with three-quarter-inch sheets of plywood. "It didn't do nothing."

My friend Chip Cassidy lived near Country Walk. Chip says he watched in disbelief as the wind lifted a twenty-foot cathedral window from its frame and hurled it across his living room. As his home blew apart around him, Chip pushed his wife and daughter into the Ford Mustang in the garage. Then he stood bracing the garage door while pieces of ceiling fell on him.

"It was like a locomotive roaring right outside the house," he says. "For me, it was the same as Vietnam—absolutely terrifying." Chip won two Silver Stars, a Bronze Star, and a Purple Heart after a battle that nearly wiped out his unit. Bob Lamm, also a Vietnam combat veteran, talked about Hurricane Andrew the same way. Like other survivors of Andrew, they felt the wind as a sentient thing that sought them out. "I could hear it out there," said Bob. "Then it got in the house."

"Hurricane" comes from a Taino Indian word for wind. Severe hurricanes like Andrew are giant tornadoes with a cutting blade of thunderstorms spinning around a calm "eye." Some meteorologists theorize that hurricanes are related to moisture levels over North Africa. During the past two decades of intermittent drought in Africa, hurricane activity has declined, lulling American coast-dwellers into a false sense of security. Some of my friends in central Miami still sound cheeky about hurricanes. But we were only cuffed by Andrew. The hurricane specialist Miles Lawrence says a worse catastrophe in a major coastal city is "just a matter of time."

We were supposedly hurricane-ready, but relief efforts were chaotic and took two weeks to shape up. Meanwhile, tens of thousands of homeless people went without running water, electricity, shelter, and food. The weather, at the height of the Florida rainy season, turned especially wet and hot. I could tell who was living in a damaged house: people whose ankles were covered with mosquito bites were camping in ruins. Nearly three weeks after Andrew, over sixty thousand people still did not have electricity.

The Pentagon appears to be the single public institution able to deal with such a disaster. Soldiers are directing traffic, offering food and shelter, guarding abandoned stores, and clearing streets and homes. In the port of Miami, gray Navy ships off-load crates to Chinooks and other supply helicopters, which chop past the mirrored skyscrapers downtown.

• • •

I have made three visits to the most affected neighborhoods, and in the past month the scene has changed little. Burning rubbish and roofing tar sour the air and stain Miami's skyline a grimy yellow. You can trace the force of the hurricane to its center by the number of jutting rafters and gaping roofs.

Since most street signs are gone, thousands of homes are spray-painted with the owner's name and address, and usually the name of an insurance company and the policy number. One wall just outside Homestead says "Help Your Neighbor," with a squiggly heart and peace sign; another says "Please Help Me. No Insurance. Need Roof. Please!"

Below Southwest 160th Street, Dade County is a militarized zone. "Headquarters First COSCOM Logistics, Support You Can Count On," says a sign in front of what used to be a shopping area. For the next ten miles, shops, homes, and warehouses are ripped out of the ground or hammered into heaps of rubbish. Entire blocks are not identifiable. Steel-and-concrete lampposts are doubled like straws. Hundred-yard-long steel warehouses are reduced to a few metal ribs and pieces of vertebrae.

On the corner of 220th Street, in the poor, black area of Goulds, the Believers in Christ Outreach Ministry was distributing food three weeks after Andrew. A block away, hookers and teenage drug dealers worked the street while families waited out the rain in their broken wooden bungalows roofed with strips of plastic.

In Homestead, people still seem haggard and hurting. The signs are not pleading or welcoming: "Enter and Die," "We Have Guns," "Looters Will Be Shot."

Everywhere, the flimsiness and ugliness of modern building materials is inescapable. Plastic, particleboard, plywood, and drywall skid in loose piles or twist from split walls and ceilings.

"It's like a death," says Joan Lamm, who has lived in South Florida all her life. "It's just all gone—baby books, pictures, clothes, our church, the school, our town."

Florida City, two miles south, fared no better. The Goldcoaster

Mobile Home Park looks like a scrap-metal yard, though the sign out front says "Models on Display." Along the highway heading west to the Everglades, each telephone pole for seven miles was snapped.

Homestead and Florida City were slightly seedy, ornery places, peopled by fishermen, farmers, migrant workers, some retirees, and a growing number of commuters to Miami. Homestead was named for grub farmers tough enough to clear a tangle of flat scrub, brambles, rattlesnakes, and mosquitoes, and to plant the rich soil below. I used to drive down sometimes to drink a beer, eat a taco at the El Toro, and escape the din of Miami. Now, lined up for food stamps, clothes, and medical attention at the Army's tent cities are men and women who have long considered government handouts a sin and have voted Republican ever since they could legally drink beer.

The people I know in the area had just enough money to build or buy their homes; one is underinsured, and others worry about whether to rebuild or to leave.

With several volunteers, my wife and I spent the Sunday of Labor Day weekend in Homestead, clearing fallen trees and debris on Mowry Drive. All the houses had significant damage, but their owners said they would stay and rebuild. As we cleared Mr. Goodspeed's yard, I tried to imagine the lush garden it must have been. Shrivelled orchids lay under a crushed greenhouse. A sprinkler system built to spray water at a height of about five feet, to nurture tropical trees, hanging plants, and vines, was chewed up like most of the foliage it had once made moist and cool. We tossed all of it on garbage heaps.

Across the street my wife and another woman helped Lou Campbell sort out her waterlogged home and clear her yard. Mrs. Campbell, eighty-two years old, is the daughter of one of the founding homesteaders of Homestead. Born and raised here, Lou Campbell has seen hurricanes before, including the killer blow of 1926. She says Andrew was worse. She told my wife she is touched that so many people have reached out to help her. She believes that God sent a tempest to "bring us together."

As I cut and dragged trees and brush in Homestead, I saw almost no cover left for wildlife. I plucked two endangered tree snails, with swirling three-inch shells banded in yellow and gold, from a limb about to be tossed on a burn pile. It took me ten minutes to find a single green place to put them. I saw no birds in a place once filled with birds. Later, Pat Tolle, the information officer at Everglades National Park, told me early surveys show that most birds survived: "They just sort of hunkered down."

The tip of Florida is a brittle strip of limestone and dried seashell between the Atlantic Ocean and the swampland and hardwood hammocks of the Everglades. It is the most fragile and rare subtropical ecosystem in the United States, and for more than a century—since the defeat of the Seminole Indians—man has chopped it into lots and sold it to the highest bidder. In the competition for space and water, the green and moving things that live here and can't live anywhere else have been the losers.

On the one naked remaining trunk of what had been a thicket of trees in Homestead, I saw a twelve-inch iridescent-green Knight anole, a Caribbean lizard that had found a niche in south Florida. In time a predator, the sun, or lack of food would kill it. I shook the three-inch trunk until the anole clambered down. It flashed deep emerald from its flanks and near-blood-red from its distinctive throat sac, pulsing it in fear and anger at my intrusion. Then it bit me hard on my thumb. But I had gloves on, and regretfully let the anole go—on a leafless tree that at least had some protecting branches.

Bill Baggs state park, on Key Biscayne, was my favorite place to take a walk; of its thousands of trees, Andrew left perhaps a dozen. Twenty-five miles of protected mangroves were shredded. The sixty-five-foot-high aviary at Miami Metrozoo collapsed, killing twenty-one rare tropical birds.

Miami is now a sombre and edgy place. We survivors feel small, vulnerable, and hurricane-obsessed. I used to love the blackening rush of the thunderstorms and squalls of high summer. Now I cringe when the wind gusts. Casual conversation here isn't casual. Buying fresh pita at Daily Bread, my local Middle Eastern shop, I asked the salesman, Monem Mazzawi, how he'd weathered Andrew. "I did fine," he said, "but my father and my brother lost their homes." His father, Norman, is seventy-four years old. A Palestinian Christian, he left Nazareth in 1968. "Twenty-three years of hard work gone, just like this," he said, throwing up his hands.

One afternoon, sorting wet office files, unpacking boxes, and otherwise undoing the work of Andrew in my life, I picked up my daughter Clara and escaped with her for a ride in the car, along streets whose leafy corridors once calmed me. On Old Cutler Road, I turned in at the entrance of Fairchild Tropical Garden. A group of botanists were cataloguing the sawed-up trunks of broken tropical hardwoods and palms that had been collected over five decades from around the world. The director told me that an estimated seventy percent of the collection was destroyed or badly damaged—thirteen thousand trees, shrubs, and vines representing five thousand species of rare tropical plants, some from habitats that no longer exist.

The glass-roofed conservatory, which had held orchids and a miniature rain forest, lay in shards. Everywhere, dwarfs and giants of the green world were browning with decay, or held in a traction of wires and wood braces and splints, trying to heal.

Couroupita guianensis, a thick-barreled, silver-barked tree from South America, stood amputated of its upper trunk. The sign at its base said it is known as the cannonball tree, for cannonball-size fruits that "rarely form." I counted eight hefty cannonballs, dark and smooth, carefully taped to surviving limbs, and I wished *Couroupita guianensis* had fired its full volley into Andrew's eye.

Storm Over the Amazon
by Edward O. Wilson

Edward Osborne Wilson (born 1929) is among the preeminent biologists of his generation. His books have twice won the Pulitzer Prize, and the New York Public Library named his The Diversity of Life *one of the outstanding books of the century. Wilson's writing reminds us that great science and great literature flow from the same sources: awareness and imagination.*

The Amazonian forest of Brazil whipsaws the imagination. After two or three days there I grow familiar with the earthy smell and vegetation as though in a Massachusetts woodlot, so that what was recently new and wonderful starts to fade from my senses. Then some small event occurs to shift my conceptual framework, and the mystery comes back in its original force. One night I walked into the forest north of Manaus with a headlamp to study the ground surface and everywhere I saw—diamonds! At regular intervals of several yards, intense pinpoints of white light flashed on and off with each turning of the lamp. They were reflections from the eyes of wolf spiders on the prowl. When the spiders were spotlighted they froze into stillness, allowing me to peer at them from inches away. I could distinguish a wide variety of species by size, color, and hairiness. Where did they all come from? What was their prey, and how could so many kinds exist there in these numbers? By morning they would retreat into the leaf litter and soil, yielding the microterrain to a new set of predators. Because I had come for other purposes, I abandoned their study to the arachnologists who would surely follow.

Each evening after dinner I carried a folding chair to a clearing to escape the noise and stink of the camp I shared with Brazilian field hands. The forest around us was in the process of being clearcut northward along an east-west line, mostly to create short-lived pastures. Even so, what remained was and is one of the few great wildernesses of the world, stretching almost unbroken from where I sat across five hundred miles to the Venezuelan savannas.

Just knowing I was on the edge of that immensity deepened the sense of my own purpose. I stared straight into the dark for hours at a time, thinking in spurts about the ecological research that had attracted me there, dreaming pleasantly about the forest as a reservoir of the unknown, so complicated that its measure will not be taken in my lifetime. I was a would-be conquistador of sorts, searching not for Amazonian gold but for great discoveries to be made in the interior. I fantasized about new phenomena and unborn insights. I confess this without embarrassment, because science is built on fantasies that can be proved true. For me the rain forest is the greatest of fantasy lands, a place of hope still unchained by exact knowledge.

And I strained to catch any trace of sound or light. The rain forest at night is an experience in sensory deprivation, black and silent as a tomb. Life is moving out there all right, but the organisms communicate chiefly by faint chemical trails laid over the surface, puffs of odor released into the air, and body scents detected downwind. Most animals are geniuses in this chemical channel where we are idiots. On the other hand, we are masters of the audiovisual channel, matched in that category only by a few odd groups like birds and lizards. At the risk of oversimplification, I can say that this is why we wait for the dawn while they wait for the fall of darkness.

So I welcomed every meteorite's streak and distant mating flash from luminescent beetles. Even the passage of a jetliner five miles up was exciting, having been transformed from the familiar urban irritant to a rare sign of the continuance of my own species.

Then one August night in the dry season, with the moon down and starlight etching the tops of the trees, everything changed with wrenching suddenness. A great storm came up from the west and moved quickly toward where I sat. It began as a flickering of light on the horizon and a faint roll of thunder. In the course of an hour the lightning grew like a menacing organism into flashes that spread across the sky and illuminated the thunderhead section by section. The sound expanded into focused claps to my left, front, and right. Now the rain came walking through the forest with a hiss made oddly soothing by its evenness of pitch. At this moment the clouds rose straight up and even seemed to tilt a little toward me, like a gigantic cliff about to topple over. The brilliance of the flashes was intimidating. Here, I knew, was the greatest havoc that inanimate nature can inflict in a short span of time: 10,000 volts dropping down an ionizing path at 500 miles an hour and a countersurge in excess of 30,000 amperes back up the path at ten times that speed, then additional back-and-forth surges faster than the eye can follow, all perceived as a single flash and crack of sound.

In the midst of the clamor something distracted my attention off to the side. The lightning bolts were acting like photoflashes to illuminate the wall of the rain forest. In glimpses I studied its superb triple-tiered structure: top canopy a hundred feet off the ground, middle tree layer below that, and a scattering of lowest trees and shrubs. At least 800 kinds of trees had been found along a short transect eastward from the camp, more than occur natively in all of North America. A hundred thousand or more species of insects and other small animals were thought to live in the same area, many of which lack scientific names and are otherwise wholly unstudied. The symmetry was complete: the Amazonian rain forest is the most that life has been able to accomplish within the constraints of this stormy planet.

Large splashing drops turned into sheets of water driven by gusts of wind. I retreated into the camp and waited with my *mateiros* friends under the dripping canvas roof. In a short time leptodactylid frogs began to honk their territorial calls in the forest nearby. To me they seemed to be saying rejoice! rejoice! The powers of nature are within our compass.

For that is the way it is in the nonhuman world. The greatest powers of the physical environment slam into the resilient forces of life and nothing much happens. The next morning the forest is still there, and although a few old trees have fallen to create clearings and the way to new plant growth, the profile stays the same. For a very long time, approximately 150 million years, the species of the rain forest evolved to absorb precisely this form and magnitude of violence. They even coded its frequent occurrence into their genes. Organisms use heavy rain and floods to time their mating and other episodes of the life cycle.

Awe is what I am talking about here. It is the most peculiar human response, an overwhelming feeling of reverence or fear produced by that which is sublime or extremely powerful, sometimes changing perception in a basic way. I had experienced it by seeing a living system in a dramatic and newly symbolic fashion. Far larger storms occur on Venus and Jupiter, but they disclose no life underneath. Nothing like the forest wall exists anywhere else we will ever visit. To drop onto another planet would be a journey into death.

A few days later the grinding of gears announced the approach of the truck sent to return me and two workers to Manaus. We watched it coming across the pastureland, a terrain strewn with fire-blackened stumps and logs, the battlefield the rain forest finally lost. On the ride back I tried not to look at it. No awe there, only defeat and decay. I think that the ultimate irony of organic evolution is that in the instant of achieving self-understanding through the mind of man, it doomed its most beautiful creations.

from Alone

by Richard E. Byrd

Richard E. Byrd (1888–1957) already was a famous explorer when he decided to spend a winter alone in Antarctica. His friends tried and failed to discourage him from the attempt on the grounds that it was too dangerous—that things might go wrong. Things did. Here Byrd recounts perhaps the most frightening moments of his stay.

May was a round boulder sinking before a tide. Time sloughed off the last implication of urgency, and the days moved imperceptibly one into the other. The few world news items which Dyer read to me from time to time seemed almost as meaningless and blurred as they might to a Martian. My world was insulated against the shocks running through distant economies. Advance Base was geared to different laws. On getting up in the morning, it was enough for me to say to myself: Today is the day to change the barograph sheet, or, Today is the day to fill the stove tank. The night was settling down in earnest. By May 17th, one month after the sun had sunk below the horizon, the noon twilight was dwindling to a mere chink in the darkness, lit by a cold reddish glow. Days when the wind brooded in the north or east, the Barrier became a vast stagnant shadow surmounted by swollen masses of clouds, one layer of darkness piled on top of the other. This was the polar night, the morbid countenance of the Ice Age. Nothing moved; nothing was visible. This was the soul of inertness. One could almost hear a distant creaking as if a great weight were settling.

Out of the deepening darkness came the cold. On May 19th, when I took the usual walk, the temperature was 65° below zero. For the first time the canvas boots failed to protect my feet. One heel was nipped, and I was forced to return to the hut and change to reindeer mukluks. That day I felt miserable; my body was racked by shooting pains— exactly as if I had been gassed. Very likely I was; in inspecting the ventilator pipes next morning I discovered that the intake pipe was completely clogged with rime and that the outlet pipe was two-thirds full. Next day—Sunday the 20th—was the coldest yet. The minimum thermometer dropped to 72° below zero; the inside thermograph, which always read a bit lower than the instruments in the shelter, stood at -74°; and the thermograph in the shelter was stopped dead—the ink, though well laced with glycerine, and the lubricant were both frozen. So violently did the air in the fuel tank expand after the stove was lit that oil went shooting all over the place; to insulate the tank against similar temperature spreads I wrapped around it the rubber air cushion which by some lucky error had been included among my gear. In the glow of a flashlight the vapor rising from the stovepipe and the outlet ventilator looked like the discharge from two steam engines. My fingers agonized over the thermograph, and I was hours putting it to rights. The fuel wouldn't flow from the drums; I had to take one inside and heat it near the stove. All day long I kept two primus stoves burning in the tunnel.

Sunday the 20th also brought a radio schedule; I had the devil's own time trying to meet it. The engine balked for an hour; my fingers were so brittle and frostbitten from tinkering with the carburetor that, when I actually made contact with Little America, I could scarcely work the key. "Ask Haines come on," was my first request. While Hutcheson searched the tunnels of Little America for the Senior Meteorologist, I chatted briefly with Charlie Murphy. Little America claimed only -60°. "But we're moving the brass monkeys below," Charlie advised. "Seventy-one below here now," I said. "You can have it," was the closing comment from the north.

Then Bill Haines's merry voice sounded in the earphones. I explained the difficulty with the thermograph. "Same trouble we've had," Bill said. "It's probably due to frozen oil. I'd suggest you bring the instrument inside, and try soaking it in gasoline, to cut whatever oil traces remain. Then rinse it in ether. As for the ink's freezing, you might try adding more glycerine." Bill was in a jovial mood. "Look at me, Admiral," he boomed. "I never have any trouble with the instruments. The trick is in having an ambitious and docile assistant." I really chuckled over that because I knew, from the first expedition, what Grimminger, the Junior Meteorologist, was going through: Bill, with his back to the fire and blandishment on his tongue, persuading the recruit that duty and the opportunity for self-improvement required him to go up into the blizzard to fix a balky trace; Bill humming to himself in the warmth of a shack while the assistant in an open pit kept a theodolite trained on the sounding balloon soaring into the night, and stuttered into a telephone the different vernier readings from which Bill was calculating the velocities and directions of the upper air currents. That day I rather wished that I, too, had an assistant. He would have taken his turn on the anemometer pole, no mistake. The frost in the iron cleats went through the fur soles of the mukluks, and froze the balls of my feet. My breath made little explosive sounds on the wind; my lungs, already sore, seemed to shrivel when I breathed.

Seldom had the aurora flamed more brilliantly. For hours the night danced to its frenetic excitement. And at times the sound of Barrier quakes was like that of heavy guns. My tongue was swollen and sore from drinking scalding hot tea, and the tip of my nose ached from frostbite. A big wind, I guessed, would come out of this still cold; it behooved me to look to my roof. I carried gallons of water topside, and poured it around the edges of the shack. It froze almost as soon as it hit. The ice was an armor plating over the packed drift.

At midnight, when I clambered topside for an auroral "ob," a wild sense of suffocation came over me the instant I pushed my shoulders through the trapdoor. My lungs gasped, but no air reached them. Bewildered and perhaps a little frightened, I slid down the ladder and lunged into the shack. In the warm air the feeling passed as quickly as it had come. Curious but cautious, I again made my way up the ladder. And again the same thing happened; I lost my breath, but I perceived why. A light air was moving down from eastward; and its bitter touch, when I faced into it, was constricting the breathing passages. So I turned my face away from it, breathing into my glove; and in that attitude finished the "ob." Before going below, I made an interesting experiment. I put a thermometer on the snow, let it lie there awhile, and discovered that the temperature at the surface was actually 5° colder than at the level of the instrument shelter, four feet higher. Reading in the sleeping bag afterwards, I froze one finger, although I shifted the book steadily from one hand to the other, slipping the unoccupied hand into the warmth of the bag.

Out of the cold and out of the east came the wind. It came on gradually, as if the sheer weight of the cold were almost too much to be moved. On the night of the 21st the barometer started down. The night was black as a thunderhead when I made my first trip topside; and a tension in the wind, a bulking of shadows in the night indicated that a new storm center was forming. Next morning, glad of an excuse to stay underground, I worked a long time on the Escape Tunnel by the light of a red candle standing in a snow recess. That day I pushed the emergency exit to a distance of twenty-two feet, the farthest it was ever to go. My stint done, I sat down on a box, thinking how beautiful was the red of the candle, how white the rough-hewn snow. Soon I became aware of an increasing clatter of the anemometer cups. Realizing that the wind was picking up, I went topside to make sure that everything was secured. It is a queer experience to watch a blizzard rise. First there is the wind, rising out of nowhere. Then the Barrier unwrenches itself from quietude; and the surface, which just before had seemed as hard and polished as metal, begins to run like a making sea. Sometimes, if the wind strikes hard, the drift comes across the Barrier like a hurrying white cloud, tossed hundreds of feet in the air. Other times the growth is gradual. You become conscious of a general slithering movement on all sides. The air fills with tiny scraping and sliding and rustling sounds as the first loose crystals stir. In a little while they are moving as solidly as an incoming tide, which creams over the ankles, then surges to the waist, and finally is at the throat. I have walked in drift so thick as not to be able to see a foot ahead of me; yet, when I glanced up, I could see the stars shining through the thin layer just overhead.

Smoking tendrils were creeping up the anemometer pole when I finished my inspection. I hurriedly made the trapdoor fast, as a sailor might batten down a hatch; and knowing that my ship was well secured, I retired to the cabin to ride out the storm. It could not reach me, hidden deep in the Barrier crust; nevertheless the sounds came down. The gale sobbed in the ventilators, shook the stovepipe until I thought it would be jerked out by the roots, pounded the roof with sledge-hammer blows. I could actually feel the suction effect through the pervious snow. A breeze flickered in the room and the tunnels. The candles wavered and went out. My only light was the feeble storm lantern.

Even so, I didn't have any idea how really bad it was until I went aloft for an observation. As I pushed back the trapdoor, the drift met me like a moving wall. It was only a few steps from the ladder to the instrument shelter, but it seemed more like a mile. The air came at me in snowy rushes; I breasted it as I might a heavy surf. No night had ever seemed so dark. The beam from the flashlight was choked in its throat; I could not see my hand before my face.

My windproofs were caked with drift by the time I got below. I had a vague feeling that something had changed while I was gone, but what, I couldn't tell. Presently I noticed that the shack was appreciably colder. Raising the stove lid, I was surprised to find that the fire was out, though the tank was half full. I decided that I must have turned off the valve unconsciously before going aloft; but, when I put a match to the burner, the draught down the pipe blew out the flame. The wind, then, must have killed the fire. I got it going again, and watched it carefully.

The blizzard vaulted to gale force. Above the roar the deep, taut thrumming note of the radio antenna and the anemometer guy wires reminded me of wind in a ship's rigging. The wind direction trace turned scratchy on the sheet; no doubt drift had short-circuited the electric contacts, I decided. Realizing that it was hopeless to attempt to try to keep them clear, I let the instrument be. There were other ways of getting the wind direction. I tied a handkerchief to a bamboo pole and ran it through the outlet ventilator; with a flashlight I could tell which way the cloth was whipped. I did this at hourly intervals, noting any change of direction on the sheet. But by 2 o'clock in the morning I had had enough of this periscope sighting. If I expected to sleep and at the same time maintain the continuity of the records, I had no choice but to clean the contact points.

The wind was blowing hard then. The Barrier shook from the concussions overhead; and the noise was as if the entire physical world were tearing itself to pieces. I could scarcely heave the trapdoor open. The instant it came clear I was plunged into a blinding smother. I came out crawling, clinging to the handle of the door until I made sure of my bearings. Then I let the door fall shut, not wanting the tunnel filled with drift. To see was impossible. Millions of tiny pellets exploded in my eyes, stinging like BB shot. It was even hard to breathe, because snow instantly clogged the mouth and nostrils. I made my way toward the anemometer pole on hands and knees, scared that I might be bowled off my feet if I stood erect; one false step and I should be lost forever.

I found the pole all right; but not until my head collided with a cleat. I managed to climb it, too, though ten million ghosts were tearing at me, ramming their thumbs into my eyes. But the errand was useless. Drift as thick as this would mess up the contact points as quickly as they were cleared; besides, the wind cups were spinning so fast that I stood a good chance of losing a couple of fingers in the process. Coming down the pole, I had a sense of being whirled violently through the air, with no control over my movements. The trapdoor was completely buried when I found it again, after scraping around for some time with my mittens. I pulled at the handle, first with one hand, then with both. It did not give. It's a tight fit, anyway, I mumbled to myself. The drift has probably wedged the corners. Standing astride the hatch, I braced myself and heaved with all my strength. I might just as well have tried hoisting the Barrier.

Panic took me then, I must confess. Reason fled. I clawed at the three-foot square of timber like a madman. I beat on it with my fists, trying to shake the snow loose; and, when that did no good, I lay flat on my belly and pulled until my hands went weak from cold and weariness. Then I crooked my elbow, put my face down, and said over and over again, You damn fool, you damn fool. Here for weeks I had been defending myself against the danger of being penned inside the shack; instead, I was now locked out; and nothing could be worse, especially since I had only a wool parka and pants under my wind-proofs. Just two feet below was sanctuary—warmth, food, tools, all the means of survival. All these things were an arm's length away, but I was powerless to reach them.

There is something extravagantly insensate about an Antarctic blizzard at night. Its vindictiveness cannot be measured on an anemometer sheet. It is more than just wind: it is a solid wall of snow moving at gale force, pounding like surf. The whole malevolent rush is concentrated upon you as upon a personal enemy. In the senseless explosion of sound you are reduced to a crawling thing on the margin of a disintegrating world; you can't see, you can't hear, you can hardly move. The lungs gasp after the air sucked out of them, and the brain is shaken. Nothing in the world will so quickly isolate a man.

Half-frozen, I stabbed toward one of the ventilators, a few feet away. My mittens touched something round and cold. Cupping it in my hands, I pulled myself up. This was the outlet ventilator. Just why, I don't know—but instinct made me kneel and press my face against the opening. Nothing in the room was visible, but a dim patch of light illuminated the floor, and warmth rose up to my face. That steadied me.

Still kneeling, I turned my back to the blizzard and considered what might be done. I thought of breaking in the windows in the roof, but they lay two feet down in hard crust, and were reinforced with wire besides. If I only had something to dig with, I could break the crust and stamp the windows in with my feet. The pipe cupped between my hands supplied the first inspiration; maybe I could use that to dig with. It, too, was wedged tight; I pulled until my arms ached, without budging it; I had lost all track of time, and the despairing thought came to me that I was lost in a task without an end. Then I remembered the shovel. A week before, after leveling drift from the last light blow, I had stabbed a shovel handle up in the crust somewhere to leeward. That shovel would save me. But how to find it in the avalanche of the blizzard?

I lay down and stretched out full length. Still holding the pipe, I thrashed around with my feet, but pummeled only empty air. Then I worked back to the hatch. The hard edges at the opening provided another grip, and again I stretched out and kicked. Again no luck. I dared not let go until I had something else familiar to cling to. My foot came up against the other ventilator pipe. I edged back to that, and from the new anchorage repeated the maneuver. This time my ankle struck something hard. When I felt it and recognized the handle, I wanted to caress it.

Embracing this thrice-blessed tool, I inched back to the trapdoor. The handle of the shovel was just small enough to pass under the little wooden bridge which served as a grip. I got both hands on the shovel and tried to wrench the door up; my strength was not enough, however. So I lay down flat on my belly and worked my shoulders under the shovel. Then I heaved, the door sprang open, and I rolled down the shaft. When I tumbled into the light and warmth of the room, I kept thinking, How wonderful, how perfectly wonderful.

from Song of the Sirens
by Ernest K. Gann

Ernest K. Gann (1910–1991) wrote 23 adventure novels, but his two memoirs have outlived them all. Fate is the Hunter *recounts his career as a commercial pilot.* Song of the Sirens *describes his life as a sailor, ship owner and commercial fisherman. Piloting a newly-acquired fishing boat (which tended to roll more than most) from Seattle to San Francisco, Gann and his shipmates encountered weather that proved too much for one of them.*

His name was Kimball and he had joined us for the passage down to San Francisco because he thought it would be an adventure. Alas.

He was a very big and agreeable man renowned for his athletic prowess, concerning which he was pleasingly deprecatory. There was about him some bluster but no more than is natural to big and hearty men suddenly released from their city desks and allowed to prance around in the fresh air. While we were still in the smooth waters of Puget Sound with the *Mike* gliding along like a respectable matron on her way to church, Kimball would look up at the surrounding snow-capped mountains, be compelled to breathe deeply, then hammer his chest with his fists, and then breathe deeply again. And between thumpings and inhalations he would exclaim, "Magnificent! . . . Magnificent!" And I thought how true and tragic that a man of *his* magnificent dimensions was not in some way daily concerned with those mountains rather than employing his muscles to shuffle papers.

As the hours passed I found Kimball's enthusiasm touching, for everything that he saw and sensed excited him to new parades of jubilant adjectives. Even the wretched stew which I cooked and stirred with the handle of a crescent wrench because I was simultaneously engaged in repairing the stove, Kimball pronounced as absolutely *cordon bleu!* He was everywhere about the *Mike,* trying to find spoons and plates so we could eat my indigestible goulash, cleaning the port debris off deck, exclaiming over the chart as if it would momentarily reveal some pirate treasure, and climbing up and down the ladder leading to the flying bridge like an amiable gorilla. We were pleased that our guest was so enjoying himself.

Before the gale had more than announced its coming Kimball began to crumble. We were preoccupied with the *Mike*'s astonishing style of rolling, and the wind was nearly full upon us before I realized that Kimball, who apparently thought all boats rolled like the *Mike,* had been following me around like a worried puppy. We were still so freshly out of port that there were many things to be attended and wherever I went—to the engine room to secure tools and oil against the rolling, or on my hands and knees checking the bilges and the stern bearing, or in the pilothouse greasing the automatic-pilot chain, or fussing with the oil control to the stove, which leaked and stank more than it should—there was Kimball panting at my heels. I wanted to tell him to go away and read some of the magazines he had brought, but then I saw his eyes and they were not at all the same eyes I had observed before.

We were in the deckhouse, which was compact but comfortable enough during those few seconds of each minute when it assumed an angle of less than 30 degrees. The galley occupied the after part of the deckhouse, my bunk and the sink took up the port side, and a bench and table—which served as a catchall for tools, tobacco, personal possessions of every description—and dining area took what space was left. There was not much room between anything, which was good since the distance a man could be catapulted before coming up against something solid was all the less. Beyond the forward bulkhead was the wheelhouse, which was entered via a narrow swinging door. A heavy sliding door next to the odiferous diesel stove led aft to the open deck. It was closed now against the considerable commotion outside.

With the wind had come an abrupt lowering of the overcast and then even lower scud which raced across the water at masthead height. There was little left of the afternoon light, yet I could see that Kimball's eyes had become dilated and there was a look of wildness and dismay behind them that concerned me even more than the *Mike*'s ridiculous gymnastics. Hoping to revive his exuberant spirits, I tried a few lame jollities about the carefree life of a sailor, to which he failed to respond.

Soon LaFrenier called to me from the wheelhouse, where he had been on watch, and said he had a fine radio bearing on Astoria. During the few minutes it required to pull out the chart and plot it I forgot about Kimball and the increasing wind. To counter our disappointment in the *Mike*'s motion there was now revealed an attribute which we could not have discovered in port. The separate engine room below confined the noise of the Mack engine, so that in the deckhouse only a rather pleasant and throaty humming was audible, and its extraordinarily heavy construction quite isolated the occupants from the outside weather. Now, with sea and wind making up a symphony of nasty noise, the *Mike* plowed onward like a liner. Only her rolling marked the turmoil outside; it was so quiet in the deckhouse I could distinctly hear the rattle of two dishes motivated by the slight engine vibration. When I turned to the dish locker with a bit of rag to silence them, there was Kimball again.

He was standing between the stove and the locker with his back to the sink and I saw that he was shivering. I refused to believe my eyes, which insisted that somehow he had shrunk two feet, but there was no question about his attempt to communicate. His mouth opened and closed several times without a sound and his arms were linked across his mighty chest as if to squeeze air for his voice. I asked him, foolishly, if he was feeling all right.

He tried to reply but failed, and churlishly I left him to stand in his muteness while I went forward to LaFrenier. If possible I wanted him to obtain another radio bearing to cross with the one from Astoria and thus fix our position nicely before other events intruded, as in such weather they were bound to do. When I returned to the deckhouse after a few minutes I was rather surprised to see Kimball still there—in my preoccupation I had actually forgotten he was aboard. He had not loosed the embrace of himself with his powerful arms, and his eyes had become dead agates. He had found his voice.

"Did you know it was snowing outside?" he asked in a monotone.

"Sure. It's just a little squall."

"Is it going to be worse?"

"Probably."

LaFrenier called back a new bearing—this time from the lightship, at Cape Flattery. I bent over the chart immediately, as much to avoid Kimball's fish eyes as in my desire to plot the bearing.

"There are thousands of hailstones on deck," Kimball said. "You can't stand up. Can't you call the Coast Guard?"

"For what?"

"To come help us?"

Crossing the new bearing didn't agree with my dead-reckoning position very well and I was annoyed at my apparent error. But before I could find it and justify the accuracy of the lightship bearing I had to be rid of Kimball and his beseechings. My impatience festered as I explained we were perfectly all right and had no need of any assistance and the *Mike* could ride out this little blow with the greatest of ease, and the very best thing he could do now was climb in his nice warm bunk with some magazines and forget where he was. I glanced suggestively at the hatch hole, which was in the deck at the forward end of the deckhouse. Descent through it was made via a straight steel ladder to the engine room and also the fo'c'sle, where there were six bunks.

Kimball shook his head. "I couldn't go down there," he said slowly. In a way I couldn't blame him. It was much noisier below because the bulkhead between the fo'c'sle and engine room was only plywood and the seas meeting the *Mike*'s steady progress did not divide without protest. And there was the psychological block of going *down* into extremely unstable confinement—the primitive sense of being trapped.

Kimball's eyes had returned from the dead and I suddenly became aware of what I should have recognized long before. He was utterly terrified.

I foresaw little prospect of using my own bunk this night, so I suggested Kimball might like to try it for size even though its height above the waterline in comparison with his own greatly multiplied the force generated by the *Mike*'s rolling. He moved slowly toward it, grabbing at everything he could reach for balance. He seemed to be in a trance and again I had the distinct impression that he had diminished remarkably in stature.

I put the bunk's fiddle board in place for him so he wouldn't roll out and drop the 5 feet to the deck and gave him a heist when the *Mike* rolled in the bunk's favor. When he was in and secure at last, I found I was panting with the exertion of fighting the roll of the *Mike* against the eccentric tumbling of his lumplike mass. I smiled at him while I caught my breath and said, "Now, rockaby, baby . . . when the wind blows—" then I stopped. For there were his eyes searching me out, and I tried to pity him, yet ashamedly found myself hating him. His behavior was all the more distressing because he had been such a noble physical specimen and now I could only think that he was letting us down; he was letting the entire human race down, exposing by his miserable exhibition how vulnerable to fear we all are. His abject eyes spoke plainly enough to me and they said, You are a fraud with your careless air. There is nothing genuine about the way you pretend to dismiss this gale, there is nothing honest about the phrases you employ to convince either yourself or me that all is well, or anything true in your heart. Because you are also afraid and simply lack the courage to admit it.

I did not like what his eyes seemed to say. I wanted to throw him overboard.

Now that he was lying down he reminded me of a battle painting in the Louvre which included a fallen warrior whose eyes were so rendered that they followed every movement of the viewer and seemed to censure his survival. Now it seemed to me that here between us totally different men there was on his part a frightening advantage, because having abandoned all pride he no longer had need to pose and could at his own pleasure mock all who would pretend they were strong.

As had its predecessor of two years before, the gale continued all through that night and the next day. LaFrenier and I had relieved each other so that one or the other of us could slip down into the fo'c'sle for a few hours' rest, such as it was. By the third exchange of watch neither of us heard the cacophony of noises below; hence we were fatigued yet still far from exhausted. Even so a taut anxiety seemed to possess me and in time I knew it was not due to the storm. It was Kimball's eyes and body, both of which seemed inescapable. He lay flat on his back with a peculiar corpselike rigidity and his big hands were clasped firmly across his chest as in death. His face appeared to be carved in wax and at first I wondered if men, like birds and certain animals, could die of fright.

If Kimball was dead his eyes were certainly not. From time to time it was necessary to pass through the deckhouse on one duty or another, which meant passing him reposed in my bunk. And always it would be the same—there were Kimball's eyes following me though his head remained absolutely motionless. Now, however, his eyes had ceased their beseeching and become openly contemptuous, saying without any apparent assistance whatever from Kimball himself, Ahoy, faker! When will your stiff back bend and your intestines ravel. When will you scream silently for mercy and grovel in your own indignities, since it must come to all men.

I could not tell Kimball how I was a veteran of his catechism, so during one unavoidable encounter with his eyes I paused long enough to ask, "Why the hell don't you close your eyes and go to sleep?"

To my surprise the dead Kimball answered me: "How can I?"

"How can't you?" I said, bitter with envy because my own body yearned for sleep. "You've got the best bunk in the ship."

At least his eyes protested my cruelty, which was much better than if he had simply accepted it. I thought of asking LaFrenier to come back and perhaps convince Kimball I was not deliberately punishing him with the whips of wind and sea and that his torment would soon end. Then I remembered LaFrenier's bedside manner, which was that of a priest administering Extreme Unction, and decided against it.

Just as I started away from Kimball, the *Mike* twisted over a larger than average wave and took such a violent roll I was thrown against the lockers below the bunk. When I rose, rubbing at my bruised rib cage, I heard Kimball say as if he were asking the time, "Aren't you ever afraid?"

"No," I lied. Fear in confined areas is like typhus, for it can infect the population so fast that mere worry can become panic in minutes. I knew I must not speak to Kimball again or remain in his vicinity, so I fled to the wheelhouse and slammed the door after me.

The indomitable LaFrenier was perched on the small seat which folded up from the bulkhead. His eyes were half closed and he was crooning softly. When I entered he paused, then went on to finish his rendition before he said, "I think it will be dawn soon."

"It better be. Our friend is giving me the willies."

LaFrenier nodded his head. "*Sí.*"

We watched the angry light arrive like the first day of Creation, and either awe or fatigue forced LaFrenier into silence, so there were only the moaning of the autopilot in labor, the metallic hiss of spray when it struck the pilothouse windows, and the subdued rumble of the wind.

"Let's swear all over again we will never go to sea in March."

"*Sí.*"

LaFrenier's predilection for Spanish had only increased since our albacore trips in Mexican waters, and now I found it irritating. Why in God's name couldn't he stick to his native language? I was about to ask him caustically for an explanation of his fancy when I realized that if I was angry with such a staunch shipmate, then indeed I must be on the verge of breaking, and the true cause was not to be found in him but in my own waning endurance and a childish envy of the man-shell who had usurped my bunk.

"And in the future let's not invite strangers to share our lot."

"*Sí.*"

Having said my piece and conveniently forgotten that I had invited Kimball to use my bunk, my pique had scattered as quickly as it had joined, and we were content and relatively comfortable until the edge of dawn revealed the sharp-gouged summits of the seas and rising beyond them a sky of prison-gray. In the heavier squalls it was still snowing, but the cozy little wheelhouse had become a soothing oasis, not only from the elements but from the defeat which lurked in the gloom behind us.

As the *Mike*'s pugnacious bow became more clearly outlined and we saw how easily she tackled each sea, we developed a new and almost maudlin affection for her. Roll she might, but here in the wheelhouse there was a sense of doughty power and even a feeling of inherent stability.

By nine o'clock the wind had diminished until it was only blowing a fresh force-6. It was providential, because in contrast to the sea room we had had in the *Fred Holmes* two years before, we were now less than 10 miles offshore.

There were times when, rising on a great swell, we thought we could see the land stretching darkly along the eastern horizon. At other times, particularly in the squalls, there was not more than a few yards' visibility. Our "patient," as we now called Kimball, seemed to have achieved a state of mental and physical suspension so that he had managed to deny even the basic needs. He had not relieved himself for at least a day and a half. Perhaps we should have let him rest in peace if our own longing for land had not been so powerful.

We used Kimball as our principal excuse and persuaded ourselves that a port known as Umpqua River was close at hand and offered quick shelter. We were very tired or we would never have made such a foolish decision, for during a blow the safest place for any seaworthy boat *is* at sea—not messing about with the dangers of shallow water. If we had ever attempted entrance to the Umpqua River before, we would most certainly have remained as far offshore as possible.

It was actually no more than a wound in the beach and we approached it just before noon with good visibility. We could see a dark line of pine trees marking the shore and from the wildly careening flying bridge we could make out a pair of stone breakwaters extending seaward perhaps five hundred yards. Outside the breakwaters the seas were jagged with gray beards foaming along their tops. When they charged the breakwaters, they exploded mightily, yet there were moments in between when a smartly handled boat might pass.

We held off for almost an hour, easing up and down, our engine deliberately slowed so that its drive matched the wind and we would hold position. We studied the sequence of the larger waves and judged the intervals between their crashing on the bar which served as a dangerous threshold to the breakwaters. And we decided it could be done—if we were to approach boldly and not equivocate. Demurring, even for a moment, would find us overtaken just as we were in the narrow entrance; caught wrong by a pursuing wave and we must be cast against the stones no matter how we or the *Mike* labored to escape.

Unless we were extraordinarily lucky. It was very obvious that once we were committed to the entrance of the Umpqua River on such a morning there could be no turning back.

The *Mike*'s helm was very stiff and her rudder not as large as it should be, hence steering was plain work, even in relatively smooth water. There were two wheels, one in the wheelhouse at deck level, and one on the flying bridge. Watching the seas scamper between the break-waters, I realized steering was going to be a wrestling match and so sent LaFrenier down to follow me through on the lower wheel. Working together, I hoped we could spin the helm faster.

We stood just off the entrance, still waiting for what I knew not except a possible recharge of daring. From my elevated position I had a clear view of the slot between the breakwaters and the action of the seas around them. The legend of the "seventh wave" is almost true. For some mysterious reason *about* every seventh wave is larger than all those before and after, and frequently when the seventh wave has passed there is a relatively flat area during which the seas appear to subside and gather themselves for the next major assault. This area is known as a "smooth." You wait for such a time if you are going to come about in a sailing ship or bear around on the opposite tack. You look for a smooth when you must maneuver a powerboat in difficult ocean conditions. The time duration of a smooth is rarely more than a minute or so, although fortunately the greater the major seas, the longer the interval of relative peace.

Now I waited, the wheel firm in my hands, my rubber boots placed wide apart to counter the *Mike*'s wild rolling, and I wondered if Kimball had called upon his personal devils to set this stage for my ordeal.

The wind had eased again and scud no longer flew off the waves. I could not see or talk to LaFrenier, but I could feel his extra strength flowing through the helm whenever I turned the rudder. Also just behind me was the exhaust stack, and in it I could hear the reassuring grumbling of the Mack diesel.

I warned myself that I must be patient. Now, now? No. Not now. Wait!

I saw a granddaddy wave approaching, which is a fisherman's way of saying a wave is enormous. The *Mike*'s flying bridge was approximately 15 feet above the water, yet I could not see over this wave. It was a pigmy compared to those we had seen in the *Fred Holmes*, but locally it was everything.

The *Mike* rose swiftly upward with its approach, lifting like a toy. The crest slipped beneath and I gasped at the realization of its speed. At the summit of the wave I could see for miles: the curved inlet beyond the breakwaters, and the rumpled sea slicing across the distant horizon to the west. And nowhere could I observe any sea to compare with this granddaddy.

As we skidded down its black backside I glanced once again to seaward and saw that the smooth matched its creator. Now!

Even as I jammed on full throttle and spun the wheel I heard the thunder of the granddaddy colliding with the breakwater. For an instant everything was lost in spray and foam; then the two ends of the breakwater came squirting upward like surfacing submarines. We were plowing full speed for the narrow separation between them.

I was pleased with my timing. For a few minutes we rode perfectly steady in the huge smooth valley. Steering was easy.

But it soon became apparent that my estimate of our distance to the breakwater had not been so shrewd; I had thought it would take us two minutes, perhaps three, to reach the entrance at full speed. Now it looked as if it would be closer to five minutes.

And a new granddaddy was making up to seaward.

We could not turn away and try again. We would be caught broadside to both seas and wind in shallow water. We had to hold course for the entrance.

We almost made it. Thirty seconds in an airplane can be an eternity. It can also become a very long time in a boat if it makes the difference between entering a harbor under control or being hurled into it.

I glanced over my shoulder, saw it coming, and whispered the name of Jesus. I slammed at the throttle lever to make sure it was full on, which it had been anyway, and the futile gesture made me feel all the more helpless. Our maximum speed was 9 knots. How could we hope to escape a wave that was coming on at 18 or better?

I felt the initial lift just before the *Mike*'s bow was even with the breakwaters' heads. We rose rapidly and the breakwaters seemed to sink.

The *Mike* paused as if to gather her maximum strength. The engine maintained its heaving snoring, yet we made no apparent progress. Instinctively I hunched my shoulders.

We rose still farther until I thought the very bottom of our keel must actually be several feet above the breakwaters. Then the crest hit our stern with a great sickening thump and we were propelled forward so fast I could feel our self-created wind against my face. The *Mike* slewed to port and drove straight for the northern breakwater. I spun the helm hard over, pushed hopelessly at the throttle again and tried to tell myself there was still space enough for the *Mike* to respond and turn away from the pile of great stones.

I jammed down on the wheel with all my strength. It made no difference. The wheel was already hard against the stops.

The change came very suddenly. The wave passed on down the

channel, leaving us again at a standstill in the following trough. In spite of the queasy sensation of being trapped, I now thought we stood a chance. We wallowed helplessly for a moment; then our propeller regained authority and with the helm hard over we charged toward the opposite breakwater.

The wrestling match I had anticipated had begun. It lasted for perhaps three minutes. We fought and hung on. Once the *Mike* rolled over so far I seemed to be looking straight down at the water, and though I stood high on the flying bridge, I had the crazy notion that I could reach out and plunge my hand in the sea.

Gradually, like a spawning salmon fighting upstream, we made our way far enough into the channel so that there was some protection from the breakwaters. We made a final controlled surf down a rapidly expiring granddaddy, and with the engine still growling full out, slid into smooth water.

I sighed, and the *Mike* seemed to join me.

Our decision to enter at all had been bad seamanship. Given a trifling less luck and we would certainly have been tossed upon one breakwater or the other.

Kimball appeared on deck soon after we entered Umpqua River. He had found his voice, and after some overpolite inquiries as to our whereabouts announced that he had made a mistake in his original estimate of his free time. He must return to his job at once. We understood and we were grateful for his consistency, for it would have been deeply disturbing if he had suddenly found courage to say he was leaving because he was afraid of being afraid.

He swung his impressive bulk up to the dock with the grace of a true athlete, and his smile and hand wave were hearty, as befitted a sailor home from the sea. Not until he turned his broad shoulders and strode jauntily toward the bus station did we find our relief turning to pity. What was it like to live in a perpetual masquerade? What tales he must contrive when friends inquire of his great adventure.

from Arctic Dreams
by Barry Lopez

Barry Lopez (born 1945) often writes about landscapes and animals. His work generally comes around to themes like tolerance, dignity and compassion. An encounter with the elements during his Arctic travels nearly killed Lopez. He characteristically seized the opportunity to imagine more fully the life and longings of early Arctic explorers.

We left our camp on Pingok Island one morning knowing a storm was moving in from the southwest, but we were not worried. We were planning to work in open water between the beach and the edge of the pack ice, only a few miles out, making bottom trawls from an open 20-foot boat. The four of us were dressed, as usual, in heavy clothes and foul-weather gear.

You accept the possibility of death in such situations, prepare for it, and then forget about it. We carried emergency and survival equipment in addition to all our scientific gear—signal flares, survival suits, a tent, and each of us had a pack with extra clothing, a sleeping bag, and a week's worth of food. Each morning we completed a checklist of the boat and radioed a distant base camp with our day plan. When we departed, we left a handwritten note on the table in our cabin, saying what time we left, the compass bearing we were taking, and when we expected to return.

My companions, all scientists, were serious about this, but not solemn or tedious. They forestalled trouble by preparing for it, and were guided, not deterred, by the danger inherent in their work. It is a pleasure to travel with such people. As in other walks of life, the person who feels compelled to dramatize the risks or is either smugly complacent or eager to demonstrate his survival skills is someone you hope not to meet.

Our camaraderie came from our enthusiasm for the work and from exhilaration with the landscape, the daily contact with seabirds, seals, and fish. We rarely voiced these things to each other; they surfaced in a word of encouragement or understanding around rough work done in unending dampness and cold. Our mutual regard was founded in the accomplishment of our tasks and was as important to our survival as the emergency gear stowed in a blue box forward of the steering console.

We worked through the morning, sorting the contents of bottom trawls and vertical plankton tows. Around noon we shut the engines off and drifted under overcast skies, eating our lunch. The seas were beginning to slap at the hull, but we had another couple of hours before they built up to three or four feet—our match, comfortably. We decided, then, to search for seals in the ice front before heading in. An hour later, by a movement of the ice so imperceptible it was finished before we realized it, we were cut off from the sea. The wind, compacting the ice, was closing off the channels of calm water where we had been cruising. We were suddenly 200 yards from open water, and a large floe, turning off the wind and folding in from the west, threatened to close us off even deeper in the pack. Already we had lost steerageway—the boat was pinned at that moment on all four sides.

In those first hours we worked wordlessly and diligently. We all knew what we faced. Even if someone heard our distress call over the radio, we could not tell him precisely where we were, and we were in pack ice moving east. A three-day storm was coming on. The floes might crush the boat and drive it under, or they could force it out of the water where we would have it for shelter.

We took advantage of any momentary opening in the ice to move toward open water, widening the channels with ice chisels, pushing with the twin 90-horsepower engines, the four of us heaving at the stern and gunnels. We were angling for a small patch of water within the pack. From there, it seemed, after a quick reconnoiter ahead on foot, we might be able to get out to the open sea. Thirty feet shy of our patch of water, we doubted the wisdom of taking ice chisels to one particular chunk of weathered pressure ice that blocked our path. Fractured the wrong way, its center of gravity would shift and the roll could take the boat under. The only way around it was to pull the boat, which weighed 3,000 pounds, completely out of the water. With an improvised system of ice anchors, lines, and block and tackle, and out of the terrific desire to get free, we set to. We got the boat up on the floe, across it, and back into the water.

Had that been open water, we would have cheered. As it was, we exchanged quick glances of justifiable but not foolish hope. While we had been winching the boat over the ice toward it, this patch of water had been closing up. And another large floe still separated us from the ocean. Where the surf broke against it, it fell a sheer four feet to the sea. Even if we got the boat over that ice, we could never launch it from such a precipice.

Two stayed in the boat. I and one other went in opposite directions along the floe. Several hundred yards to the east I found a channel. I looked it over quickly and then signaled with the upraised shaft of my ice chisel for the others. It was barely negotiable to begin with, and in the few minutes it took to get the boat there, the channel closed. We put the prow of the boat against the seaward floe and brought both engines up to full power, trying to hold it against the wind. The ice beside it continued to move east. The channel started to open. With the engines roaring, the gap opened to six feet. With a silent, implicit understanding each of us acted decisively. The man at the helm reversed the engines, heeled the boat around, and burst up the channel. We made 20 quick feet, careened the boat over on its port gunnel, and pivoted through a 120° turn. One ran ahead, chopping swift and hard at the closing ice with a chisel. Two of us heaved, jumping in and out of the boat, stabbing at chunks of ice closing on the props. One man remained at the throttles. Suddenly he lunged away, yanking the starboard engine clear of fouling ice. The man ahead threw his ice chisel into the boat and jumped across to help lift at the port gunnel. We could *feel* how close. The starboard side of the boat slid off the ice, into the water. The bow lifted on the open sea. There was nothing more for our legs to strain against. We pulled ourselves over the gunnel and fell into the boat, limp as feed sacks. Exhausted. We were out.

We were out, and the seas were running six feet. And we were miles now from a shore that we could not see. In the hours we had been in the ice, the storm had built considerably, and we had been carried we did not know how far east. The seas were as much as the boat could handle, and too big to quarter—we had to take them nearly bow on. The brief views from wave crests showed us nothing. We could not see far enough through the driving sleet and spray, and the arctic coast here lies too low, anyway. We could only hope we were east of Pingok, the westernmost of the barrier islands, and not to the west, headed down into Harrison Bay, where the wind has a greater fetch and the shore is much farther on.

We took water over the bow and shouted strategy to each other over the wind and the sound of engines screaming as the props came out of the water. We erected a canvas shelter forward to break the force of the sea and shed water. We got all the weight we could out of the bow. A resolute steadiness came over us. We were making headway. We were secure. If we did not broach and if we were far enough to the east, we would be able to run up on a leeward shore somewhere and wait out the storm.

We plowed ahead. Three of us stood hunched backward to the weather.

I began to recognize in the enduring steadiness another kind of calmness, or relief. The distance between my body and my thoughts slowly became elongated, and mulled like a dark, carpeted corridor. I realized I was cold, that I was shivering. I sensed the dry pits of warmth under my clothes and, against this, an opening and closing over my chest, like cold breath. I realized with dreamlike stillness that the whole upper right side of my body was soaked. The shoulder seams of my foul-weather gear were torn open.

I knew I had to get to dry clothes, to get them on. But desire could not move my legs or arms. They were too far away. I was staring at someone, then moving; the soaked clothes were coming off. I could not make a word in my mouth. I felt suspended in a shaft in the earth, and then imagined I was sitting on a bare earthen floor somewhere within myself. The knowledge that I was being slammed around like a wooden box in the bottom of the boat was like something I had walked away from.

In dry wool and protected by a tarp from the seas, I understood that I was safe; but I could not understand the duration of time. I could not locate any visual image outside myself. I concentrated on trying to gain a sense of the boat; and then on a rhythmic tensing and loosening of my muscles. I kept at it and at it; then I knew time was passing. There was a flow of time again. I heard a shout. I tried to shout myself, and when I heard an answer I knew that I was at the edge of time again, and could just step into it. I realized I was sitting up, that I was bracing myself against heavy seas.

The shouts were for the coast. We had found Pingok.

We anchored the boat under the lee shore and went into the cabin and changed clothes and fixed dinner. Our sense of relief came out in a patter of jokes at each other's expense. We ate quietly and went to bed and slept like bears in winter.

The storm blew for two days. We nearly lost the boat when an anchor line parted, and got wet and cold again trying to secure it; but that seemed no more than what we had chosen by coming here. I went for a long walk on the afternoon of the second day, after the storm had become only fretful gusts and sunlight threatened to break through the low clouds.

I still felt a twinge of embarrassment at having been reduced from a

state of strength to such an impassive weight, to a state of disassocia-
tion, so quickly. But I did not dwell on it long. And we would go out
again, when the seas dropped. We would go into the ice again. We
would watch more closely; but nothing, really, had changed.

With the experience so fresh in my mind, I began thinking of frail
and exposed craft as I walked down the beach, of the Irish carraughs
and Norse knarrs that brought people across the Atlantic, bucking pack
ice streaming southward on the East Greenland Current. My God, what
had driven them? All we know is what we have deduced from the
records of early historians. And the deference those men showed to
their classical predecessors, to Ptolemy, Solinus, and Isidore, their own
nationalism and religious convictions, their vanity, and the shape of
the ideas of their age—all this affected what they expressed. And when
it was translated, or when they themselves translated from others,
interpolations, adaptation, and plain error colored the historical
record further. So the early record of arctic exploration is open to inter-
pretation. And this refined history is less real, less harrowing than what
had happened to us in the boat. It is events mulled and adjudicated.

I wanted to walk the length of the seaside beach on Pingok,
knowing the storm was dying away. I brooded over the fates of those
early immigrants, people whose names no one knows, who sailed in
ships of which there are neither descriptions nor drawings, through ice
and storms like this one—but so much farther from a shore, with
intentions and dreams I could only imagine.

The earliest arctic voyages are recorded in the Icelandic sagas and
Irish imramha. But they were written down hundreds of years after the
fact by people who did not make the journeys, who only heard about
them. The Norse Eddas and Icelandic sagas, wrote the arctic explorer
and historian Fridtjof Nansen, are "narratives somewhat in the light of
historical romances, founded upon legend and more or less uncertain
traditions." The same can be said of the imramha and the records of
Saint Brendan's voyage, though in tone and incident these latter are different from the sagas.

In the following pages, beginning in a time before the sagas, the notion of a road to Cathay, a Northwest Passage, emerges. The quest for such a corridor, a path to wealth that had to be followed through a perilous landscape, gathers the dreams of several ages. Rooted in this search is one of the oldest of all human yearnings—finding the material fortune that lies beyond human struggle, and the peace that lies on the other side of hope.

I should emphasize two points. Few original documents point up the unadorned character, the undisguised sensibilities, of the participants in these dramas. And the most common simile of comparison for these journeys—the exploits of astronauts—falls short. The astronaut is suitably dressed for his work, professionally trained, assiduously looked after en route, and nationally regarded. He possesses superb tools of navigation and observation. The people who first came into the Arctic had no photograph of the far shore before they left. They sailed in crude ships with cruder tools of navigation, and with maps that had no foundation or geographic authority. They shipwrecked so often that it is difficult to find records of their deaths, because shipwreck and death were unremarkable at the time. They received, for the most part, no support—popular or financial. They suffered brutally and fatally from the weather and from scurvy, starvation, Eskimo hostility, and thirst. Their courage and determination in some instances were so extreme as to seem eerie and peculiar rather than heroic. Visions of achievement drove them on. In the worst moments they were held together by regard for each other, by invincible bearing, or by stern naval discipline. Whether one finds such resourceful courage among a group of young monks on a spiritual voyage in a carraugh, or among worldly sailors with John Davis in the sixteenth century, or in William Parry's snug winter quarters on Melville Island in 1819–20, it is a sterling human quality.

In the journals and histories I read of these journeys I was drawn on by a sharp leaning in the human spirit: pure desire—the complexities of human passion and cupidity. Someone, for example, had to pay for these trips; and whoever paid was looking for a way to be paid back. Rarely was the goal anything as selfless as an increase in mankind's geographical knowledge. An arctic voyage in quest of unknown riches, or of a new passage to known riches, could mean tangible wealth for investors, and it could mean fame and social position for a captain or pilot. For a common seaman the reward might only mean some slip of the exotic, or a chance at the riches himself—at the very least a good story, probably something astounding. Enough, certainly, to sign on.

As I read, I tried to imagine the singular hunger for such things, how desire alone might convey a group of people into those fearsome seas. The achievement of one's desires may reveal what one considers moral; but it also reveals the aspiration and tack of an individual life, and the tenor of an age. In this light, one can better understand failures of nerve in the Arctic, such as Bering's in the Chukchi Sea in 1728—he simply did not have Peter the Great's burning desire to define eastern Russia. And one can better understand figures in arctic exploration so obsessed with their own achievement that they found it irksome to acknowledge the Eskimos, unnamed companions, and indefatigable dogs who helped them.

Arctic history became for me, then, a legacy of desire—the desire of individual men to achieve their goals. But it was also the legacy of a kind of desire that transcends heroics and which was privately known to many—the desire for a safe and honorable passage through the world.

As I walked the beach I stopped now and then to pick over something on the storm-hardened shore—bits of whale vertebrae, waterlogged feathers, the odd but ubiquitous piece of plastic, a strict reminder against romance.

The narratives I carried in my head that afternoon fascinated me, but not for what they recorded of geographic accomplishment or for how they might be used in support of one side or another of a controversy, such as whether Frederick Cook or Robert Peary got to the Pole first. They held the mind because of what they said about human endeavor. Behind the polite and abstemious journal entries of British naval officers, behind the self-conscious prose of dashing explorers, were the lives of courageous, bewildered, and dreaming people. Some reports suggest that heroic passage took place for many just offstage. They make clear that others struggled mightily to find some meaning in what they were doing in those regions, for the very act of exploration seemed to them at times completely mad. They wanted to feel that what they were doing was necessary, if not for themselves then for the nation, for mankind.

The literature of the arctic exploration is frequently offered as a record of resolute will before the menacing fortifications of the landscape. It is more profitable I think to disregard this notion—that the land is an adversary bent on human defeat, that the people who came and went were heroes or failures in this. It is better to contemplate the record of human longing to achieve something significant, to be free of some of the grim weight of life. That weight was ignorance, poverty of spirit, indolence, and the threat of anonymity and destitution. This harsh landscape became the focus of a desire to separate oneself from those things and to overcome them. In these arctic narratives, then, are the threads of dreams that serve us all.

from Genesis

by Wallace Stegner

Wallace Stegner (1909–1993) wrote novels, stories and essays, most of them about the American West. "Genesis," set among cowboys in Canada's Saskatchewan province, is about a young Englishman (Rusty) on his first cattle drive. Stegner's stories often are parables of sorts, but he was no mere moralist. He knew how to make—out of smells, sounds, behavior and small occurrences—a world that matters.

Sometime before the gray afternoon howled itself out, Ray Henry shouldered into his sheepskin and went outside. The rest lay in their blankets, which they had inhabited too long for their blankets' good or their own, in their postures that were like the postures of men fallen in war. Panguingue sprawled with his drawn-up knees wide, his whiskered face glimmering a vacant grin straight upward. Little Horn and Buck were unexpected angles of arms and legs, Slip lay curled as if around a mortal body wound. Spurlock had locked his hands under the back of his head and crossed his knees under the covers. They listened to the undiminished wind. After what may have been ten minutes Jesse rose and said he guessed he'd take a look at the Clydes. He followed his jet of white breath outside, and they lay on.

Their cloth house shook, and gave way, and shuddered stiff and tight again. They heard the whistle and scream go flying through and away, and in a lull Buck said, "This one's the worst one yet." They lay considering this for quite a long time. At last Rusty heard the sound of feet, and with a relief that astonished him he cried, "Here they are!"

But no one entered. The wind pounded through and over and past. It had a curving sound; it dipped to the ear like telegraph wires to the eye. Everyone in the tent was listening for the steps Rusty had announced. At last Spurlock grumbled, "Just fawncy." Panguingue blurted a laugh.

"Christ A'mighty!" Slip said abruptly, and snapped nimble as a monkey out of his bed. He was stepping in his slippers across Ray Henry's tarp when the flap opened and Ray and Jesse stooped in on a flurry of snow. Slippers sat quietly down again on his blankets. His leathery, deeply lined, big-nosed face said nothing. Neither did any of the other smudged and whiskered faces around the tent. But they were all sitting up or half propped on their elbows; the concern that had moved Slip had been a fear in all of them. In silence they watched Ray throw down beside the cold stove three or four round cake-like chunks of ice. Rusty reached across and picked up a frozen cowchip.

"Are we burning ice now?"

With a wipe of a bare hand around on his wet, beef-red face, the foreman said, "We may be lucky to have that to burn, it's drifting pretty deep all over."

"Still from the northwest?" Buck asked.

"Oh, dear," said Little Horn. "All those poor little calves and their mamas. They'll be clear the hell and gone down to Wood Mountain."

"Or else they'll be piled up in some draw," Ray said.

"You think it's pretty bad, then," Rusty said—a small, inconsequent, intrusive voice of ignorance and greenness that he himself heard with shame and dismay.

"Yes, kid," Ray said. "I think it's pretty bad."

They ebbed away into silence. With only a few sticks of wood left Jesse gave them no more for supper than warm gravy poured over frozen biscuits; not even coffee. Part of the stove, while the gravy was warming, held two of the cowchips that Ray had kicked up from under the snow, and the smell of wetted and baking manure flavored their supper. But at least the cakes dried out enough so that Jesse could use them for the breakfast fire.

The single candle gave a blotted light. When they were all still Rusty saw the humps of bedrolls fuming like a geyser basin with their eight breaths, until Little Horn said, "Well, nighty-night, kids," and blew out the candle. The wind seemed to come down on their sudden darkness with such violence that in the cold tent they lay tensely, afraid something would give. Both Slip and Little Horn had pulled their goatskin chap over their beds for extra cover. Rusty's icy hands were folded into his armpits; he wore all his clothes except sheepskin and boots. He blew his breath into the air, moved his sore shoulder experimentally, smelled his own stale nest, thinking Holy Mother, if my people could see me now! There was a brief, vivid picture of rescuers in the spring reverently uncovering eight huddled figures, identifying each one, folding the tarp back over the frozen face. His head was full of vague heroisms related to Commodore Peary and the North Pole.

Once the thought popped whole and astonishing into his head: I might, except for one or two decisions made in excitement and stuck to through tears and argument, be sleeping in my old room right now, and if I opened my eyes I would see the model of the *Kraken* hanging from the ceiling like a ship of thanksgiving in a Danish church. Except for the excitement that his father thought wild whimsy and his mother thought heartlessness, he might be getting his exercise these days pushing a punt up and down the Cher, disturbing the swans (Swans! From here they sounded fabulous as gryphons), or drinking too much port with sporty undergraduates from his college, or sitting on some cricket pitch, or (assuming he *hadn't* chosen Oxford and the family's program) he might be guiding the tiller of the yawl with his backside while he shouted questions, jeers, comments, or other conversation at sailors leaning over the stern rails of old rustpots anchored in the stream off Spithead.

The fact that he was here in a tent on the freezing Saskatchewan plains, that one decision rashly made and stubbornly stuck to had taken him not only out of the university, out of home, out of England, but out of a whole life and culture that had been assumed for him, left him dazed. A good job he didn't have much chance to think, or he might funk it yet, and run straight home with his tail tucked. He was appalled at the effectiveness of his own will.

A numbness like freezing to death stole through him gradually, Panguingue restored him to wakefulness with a kick in the head, and he cursed Panguingue with a freedom he would not have adopted toward anyone else in the outfit. Sometime during or just after the flurry of profane protest he fell asleep.

Solitary flutes, songs from the Vienna woods, chirpings and twitterings so that he opened his eyes thinking *Birds?* and heard the awakening sounds of the outfit, and old Jesse whistling with loose lips while he stood over the stove. He lifted a can and tipped it in a quick gesture; the tent filled with the smell of kerosene. Jesse hobbled about in his boots like an old crone. His right knee crooked upward, there was a swoop and a snap, and a match popped into flame across his tight seat. The stove *whoofed* out a puff of smoke. The lids clanged on. Fire gleamed through the cracks in the ash door and Jesse shoved the coffee pot against the stovepipe. Looking, Rusty saw that Ray, Slip, and Buck were missing.

He sat up. "I say! The wind's died!"

"You say, hey?" Jesse said.

Rusty hustled to the door and looked out. Deep tracks went through the drift that curved all around them; the sky was palest blue, absolutely clear. Ray was trotting the Clydes up and down a fifty-foot trampled space, getting them warm. Their breasts and rumps and legs were completely coated in ice. Buck and Slip already had saddles on the night ponies. Whatever had been brown in the landscape had disappeared. There were no scraggly patches of bare grass in the snow waves, but packed, rippled white ran off into the southeast where the sun was just rising. He could almost see the plain move as if a current ran strongly toward where the sun squatted on the rim and sent its dazzle skipping across the million little wave crests into his eyes. Spurlock, looking over his shoulder, swore foully. "Here goes for some more God damn snow-blindness." He stepped past Rusty and blew his nose with his fingers, first one nostril, then the other.

Rusty shouted over to Ray, "Working weather!"

"Yeah." He laughed his dry laugh through his nose. "Come here and curry some of the ice out of these studs."

"Uh-huh!" Spurlock said behind Rusty, with I-told-you-so emphasis. The boy stared at him. "Working weather!" Spurlock said. "Jesus Christ! I guess."

His guess was right. Within minutes of the time Rusty woke he was working; they paused only long enough to bolt a steak and gulp scalding coffee and warm their hands over the fire; their last wood and all the cowchips had gone into it. Before they had more than spread their palms to the beautiful heat, Slip and Buck came in with the horse herd.

"Jesse," Ray said, "you better tear down here and get loaded and beat it on a beeline for Horse Camp. If we ain't there when you get there, which we won't be, you can improve your time and warm your blood gettin' in wood, and there ain't any such thing as too much. The rest of you is goin' to round up every cow within fifteen miles downwind, and we're going to put them all in the corrals at Horse Camp before we sleep any more. So pick you a pony with some bottom."

They looked at the shaggy, scrawny, long-maned and long-tailed herd picking at the wisps of a few forkfuls of hay that the boys had thrown out. There was not a pony among them whose ribs did not show plainly under the rough winter hair. Here and there one stood spraddled, head hanging, done in, ready to fall.

"Boneracks," Little Horn said. "Some of them ponies ain't goin' to make it, Boss."

"Then we got to leave them," Ray said. "They can maybe make out, poor as they are, but unless we get a chinook this is starvin' time for cattle."

They saddled and rode out, Ray, Slip, Panguingue, and Rusty to the southeast, straight into the sun, Spurlock and Buck and Little Horn to the northeast. They would pinch everything in to the middle and then swing and bring them back. The tent was already coming down as they rode off.

They rode a long way before they raised any cattle. When they did, down in a draw, they were humped in the deep snow, making no effort to get out. They stood and bellowed; they moved as if their blood had frozen thick, and they had among them range steers, including a few longhorns, which the boys did not want at all but had no time to cut out. They threw them all into a bunch, and attended by an intensely black and unlikely looking crow, rode on into the diamond glitter, gradually swinging eastward so that they could get some relief by ducking their heads and pulling their hats clear down on the sun side. Ray kept them pushing hard through the difficult going, knee high sometimes, hock high the next moment, crusted just enough to hold the horse's weight for a split second before he broke down through. It was hard enough in the saddle; it must have been a good deal worse under it.

"Got to hustle," Ray said. "For some reason I'm gettin' so I don't trust the damn weather." They fanned out, riding wide. Far north, across a spread of flats and one or two shallow coulees whose depressions could hardly be seen in the even glare, the black dots that were Spurlock and Little Horn and Buck were strung out across a mile or so of snow. They headed in toward the center of their loop every sad whiteface whose red hide showed. The cattle bellowed, blinking white eyelashes, and they moved reluctantly, but they moved. The crow flapped over, following companionably, flying off on some investigation of his own and returning after a few minutes to coast over and cock his wise eye down and caw with laughter to hear them talk.

About noon, far to the south and east of where they had camped, they came to the river, angling down from the northwest in its shallow valley. The willows along the banks looked thin as a Chinaman's whiskers, hardly more than weeds, but they held a surprising number of cattle, which the outfit flushed out by the dozens and scores and hazed, plunging and ducking and blindly swinging back until a horse blocked them or a rope cut across their noses, up onto the flats. They had everything in that herd: whiteface, shorthorn, longhorn, all sorts of crosses; steers, cows, bulls, calves; T-Down, Circle Diamond, Turkey Track. Ray pointed some out to Rusty when they rested their ponies for a minute on the flat and let Slip chase a half-dozen whiteface yearlings back into the bottoms. "The Seventy-Six," he said. "Their range is way up by Gull Lake, on the CPR. They've drifted twenty-five miles."

Whatever they were, whoever they belonged to, if they could not be easily cut out the riders swept them in and drove them westward, pushing them without a pause toward Horse Camp. The afternoon changed from blue-white to lavender. The crow had left them— disgusted, Rusty thought, that they never stopped to eat and threw away no scraps. The trampled waste of snow bloomed for a minute or two a pure untroubled rose, and the sun was gone as if it had stepped in a hole. Gray-blue dusk, grateful to their seared eyes, lay in every slightest hollow; the snowplain was broken with unexpected irregularities. The "drag" of cows and calves slowed, poked along, stopped, and had to be cursed and flogged into starting. Their ponies, poor boneracks, plodded gamely, and if a cow tried to break away or swing back they had to gather themselves like a tired swimmer taking one last stroke. Their breath was frozen all over them, stirrups and overshoes were enameled in ice; Rusty could hear his pony wheezing in his pipes, and his skinny ewe neck was down. He stumbled in the trodden snow.

It grew dark, and they went on, following Jesse's track, or whatever track it was that Ray kept, or no track at all, but only his wild animal's sense of direction. The faint eruption of color in the west was gone; and then as the sky darkened, the stars were there, big and frosty and glittering, bright as lamps, and Rusty found the Dipper and Cassiopeia and the Pole Star, his total astronomy. He moved in his saddle, lame and numb, his face stiff, his shoulder aching clear down across his collarbone into his chest. Ahead of him, a moving blur on the snow, the herd stumbled and clicked and mooed, the joints of their random longhorns cracked, the traveling steam went up. Off to his right he heard Buck trying to sing—a sound so strange, revelatory, and forlorn that he had to laugh, and startled himself with the voiceless croak he produced.

How much farther? Up above, the sky was pure; the Northern Lights were beginning to flare and stretch. He heard his old friend the wolf hunting down the river valleys and coulees of his ordained home and speaking his wolfish mind to the indifferent stars. Lord God, how much longer? They had been in the saddle since six, had eaten nothing since then. Neither horse nor rider could take much more of this. But nobody said, We can stop now. Nobody said, We'll camp here. They couldn't, obviously. Jesse had taken their bubble of shelter God knew how many more empty miles to Horse Camp. He thought to himself, with a qualm of panic, My God, this is *desperate*. What if we don't find him? What if a horse should give clear out?

He gave his pony clumsy mittened pats; he enlisted its loyalty with words; it plodded and stumbled on.

Eventually there was a soft orange bloom of lights, and shouts cut through the luminous murk, and as he stopped, confused, Ray Henry came riding from his left and they crowded the cattle into a tighter mass. Over their moving backs and the sounds of their distress and irritation he heard poles rattle; someone ki-yi-ed. Ray pushed his horse against the rear cattle and in his almost-gone whisper drove and urged them on. They moved, they broke aside, they were turned back; the mass crawled ahead, tedious, interminable, a toss and seethe of heads and horns, until suddenly it had shrunk and dwindled and was gone, and Panguingue was down in the snow, ramming gate poles home. The whole world smelled of cow.

They sat there all together, stupid with cold and fatigue; they dismounted like skeletons tied together with wire. Ray croaked, "Let's see if Jesse ain't got a spare oat or two for these ponies," and they walked toward the wagon and the bloom of the tent. The air, which had been bright at sunset and in the first hour of dark, was blurred as if a fog were rising from the snow; beyond the tent the faint shadow of the coulee fell away, but the other side was misted out. Rusty's eyes were so longingly on Jesse's shadow as he hopped around the stove, obviously cooking, that he fell over the pile of willows stacked by the wagon: Jesse had not wasted his time; there was cooking wood for a week.

"Dad," Ray called, "you got any oats? These ponies are about done." The white head appeared in the flap, a hand with a fork in it held the canvas back, the soft old voice said, "I got a couple-three bushel left, I guess. That has to hold the Clydes and the night horses till we get back to the ranch."

"They'll have to get along," Ray said. "I'm afraid we're going to lose some ponies anyway. They just don't have the flesh for this kind of a job."

Rusty stood with the reins in his hand, letting Jesse and Ray heave the oat bag out of the wagon. The tent with its bloom of light and its smell of frying was a paradise he yearned for as he had never yearned for anything, but he had to stand there and care for the horse first, and he hated the poor beast for its dependence. It was no tireder than he was. Nevertheless Ray's was an inescapable example. He unsaddled and threw the saddle into the wagon; he tramped a little hollow in the snow and poured out a quart or two of oats and pulled his pony's bridle and let him drop his head to them. One after the other the outfit did the same. After what seemed an hour Rusty found the tent flap and crept in. The little stove was red hot; the air was full of smoke. Jesse had unrolled their beds for them. Rusty stepped over Buck and fell full length and shut his eyes. What little strength he had left flowed out of him and was soaked up; his bones and veins and skin held nothing but tiredness and pain.

Jesse hopped around, juggling pans, going on cheerfully. He had thought by God they were never going to get in. Chopped wood till he like to bust his back. (Yeah, said somebody, *you* did a day's work!) Horse herd come all the way with him, right along behind the pilot. Those few scraps of hay the other day made tame ponies of the whole bunch. Looks like you guys got a pretty good herd of calves, considering. Anybody like a cup of coffee now?

"By God," he said after a short silence, you fellers look *beat*."

And after another little silence in which nobody spoke, but somebody groaned or grunted, Jesse said, "Here, I don't reckon coffee has got enough nourishment for the occasion."

Beside Rusty, Buck rolled over. Rusty opened his eyes. Slip and Little Horn had rolled over too. Ray was sitting on his bed, holding a quart of whiskey, shaking his head. "Jesse," he said, "by God, remind me to raise your wages."

Their common emotion while Ray worked on the cork was reverence. They sat or lay around in a ring, as bleary a crew as ever ate with its fingers or blew its nose with the same all-purpose tool, and they watched each motion of his thick wrist and big dirty hand. None of them had shaved for more than two weeks; they had all, except possibly Buck, lost any right to browbeat Panguingue about his filthiness. They felt—or at least Rusty did—that they had endured much and labored incredibly. He wondered, as the greenest hand there, how well he had done, and hoped he had done at least passably, and knew with unaccustomed humility that he could not have done more. Considering everything, the three hundred-odd cattle they had finally brought to the Horse Camp corrals were an achievement. The work still to be done, the separating and weaning, and the driving of calves and bulls to the home ranch, could only be trifling after what they had been through.

The stove's heat beat on their bearded red faces, the candles gleamed in their bloodshot eyes. They watched Ray Henry's thick hands, and when the cork slipped out of the neck with a soft *pok* some of them smiled involuntarily, and Panguingue giggled, a high, falsetto sound that set off another round of smiles and made Jesse say, "Listen at old Pan, he sounds like a jack after a mare."

Ray held the bottle to the light and looked through it; he shook it and watched the bead rise. He was like a priest before an altar. He would not hurry this. "Well," he said at last, "here's looking at you, boys," and tipped the bottle to his blackened mouth. They watched the contents gurgle around the spark of candle that lived inside the amber bottle. He let the bottle down. "Whah!" he said. "Kee-rist!" and wiped the neck politely with the heel of his palm and passed it to Slip, whose bed lay beside his next to the wall. The smell of whiskey cut through the smoke of the tent; they sat like Indians in the medicine lodge and passed the ceremonial vessel around, and each, as he finished, wiped the neck carefully with his palm. Slip to Jesse, Jesse to Little Horn, Little Horn to Spurlock, Spurlock to Panguingue. Panguingue drank and shook his head and wiped the neck once and started to pass the bottle and then, as if not satisfied, wiped it again. Rusty loved him for it, he loved them all; he felt that he had never known so mannerly a group of men. Buck took the bottle from Panguingue, and from Buck it came to the greenhorn, its neck flavored with all their seven mouths and hands. He raised it to his mouth and let its fire wash down his throat and felt it sting in his cracked lips. His eyes watered. He lowered the bottle and choked down a cough, and as he passed the bottle back to Ray and talk broke out all at once, he took advantage of the noise and cleared his throat and so was not shamed.

"Well, Jesse," Ray said, "what do you think? Want to save that little-bitty dab?"

"Why, I can't see it'd be much good from now on," Jesse said.

They passed it around again, and their tongues were loosened. They told each other how cold it had been and how hard they had worked. Jesse had made up a raisin-and-rice pudding, practically a pailful. It was pure ambrosia; they ate it all and scraped the kettle, and for a few minutes after supper Rusty even roused up enough strength to get out the harmonica. There was not the slightest remnant left of the irritability they had felt with one another in the snowed-in time; the boy could feel how they had been welded and riveted into a society of friends and brothers. Little Horn sang some filthy verses of "The Old Chisholm Trail." Spurlock supplied some even filthier ones from "Johnny McGraw." The whole bunch joined in a couple of songs.

Then all at once they were done in again. The talk dropped away, Rusty put the harmonica in his pocket. They went outside and walked a few steps from the tent and stood in a row and made water, lifting their faces into the night air that was mistier than ever, and warmer than any night since they had left the ranch.

"I don't know," Ray said, sniffing for wind. "I don't quite like the looks of the sky."

"Oh but hell," they said. "Feel how warm it is."

He gave in doubtfully to their optimism. The mild air might mean snow, but it also might mean a chinook coming in, and that was the best luck they could hope for. There was not enough grass bare, even out on the flats, to give the cattle a chance to feed. Rusty had never seen or felt a chinook, but he was so positive this was the birth of one that he offered to bet Little Horn and Panguingue a dollar each that it was a chinook coming. They refused, saying they did not want to hoodoo the weather. Ray remarked that such weather as they had had couldn't be hoodooed any worse. They kicked the snow around, smelling the night air soft in their faces; it smelled like a thaw, though the snow underfoot was still as dry and granular as salt. Every minute or so a hungry calf bawled over in the corral.

"Well," Ray said, "maybe this is our break."

Rusty hardly heard him. His eyes were knotted, the nerves and veins snarled together, the lids heavy with sleep. Back inside the tent there was a brief flurry of movement as they crawled in. Somebody cursed somebody else feebly for throwing his chaps across him. He heard the fire settle in the stove; after a minute or two he was not sure whether it was the stove or the first whiffling of some sleeper. Then he was asleep too, one of the first.

But not even his dead tiredness could lift from him the habits of the last ten days. In his dreams he struggled against winds, he felt the bite of cold, he heard the clamor of men and animals and he knew that he had a duty to perform, he had somehow to shout "Here!" as one did at a roll call, but he was far down under something, struggling in the dark to come up and to break his voice free. His own nightmared sounds told him he was dreaming, and moaning in his sleep, and still he could not break free into wakefulness and shove the dream aside. Things were falling on him from above; he sheltered his head with his arms, rolled, and with a wrench broke loose from tormented sleep and sat up.

Panguingue was kicking him in the head through the blankets. He was freezing cold, with all his blankets wound around his neck and shoulders like shawls. By the light of a candle stuck on the cold stove he saw the rest all in the same state of confused, unbelieving awakening. There was a wild sound of wind; while he sat leaning away from Panguingue's feet, stupidly groping for his wits, a screeching blast hit the tent so hard that old Jesse, standing by the flap, grabbed the pole and held it until the shuddering strain gave way a little and the screech died to a howl.

Rusty saw the look of disbelief and outrage on every face; Panguingue's grin was a wolfish baring of teeth, his ordinary dull-witted good nature shocked clear out of him. "What is it?" Rusty asked idiotically. "Is it a chinook?"

"Chinook!" Buck said furiously.

He yanked his stiff chaps on over his pants and groped chattering for his boots. They were all dressing as fast as their dazed minds and numbed fingers would let them. Jesse let go the tent pole to break some willow twigs in his hands and shove them into the stove. At that moment the wind swooped on them again and the tent came down.

Half dressed, minus mittens, boots, mackinaws, hats, they struggled under the obliterating canvas. Somebody was swearing in an uninterrupted stream. Rusty stumbled over the fallen stovepipe and his nostrils were filled with soot. Then the smothering canvas lifted a couple of feet and somebody struck a match to expose them like bugs under a kicked log, dismayed and scuttling, glaring around for whatever article they needed. He saw Jesse and Ray bracing the front pole, and as the match died he jumped to the rear one; it was like holding a fishing rod with a thousand pound fish on: the whole sail-like mass of canvas flapped and caved and wanted to fly. One or two ropes on the windward side had broken loose and the wall plastered itself against his legs, and wind and snow poured like ice water across his stockinged feet. "Somebody get outside and tie us down," Ray's grating whisper said. Little Horn scrambled past, then Spurlock. Panguingue crawled toward the front flap on hands and knees, Slip and Buck followed him. Braced against the pole, old Jesse was laughing; he lit a match on his pants and got a candle going and stuck it in its own drip an the stove. The stovepipe lay in sooty sections across the beds.

Ropes outside jerked; the wall came away from Rusty's legs, the tent rose to nearly its proper position, the strain on the pole eased. Eventually it reached a wobbly equilibrium so that he could let go and locate his boots in the mess of his bed. The five outsiders came in gasping, beating their numbed hands. In the gray light of storm and morning, they at looked like old men; the blizzard had sown white age in their beards.

"*God* A'mighty!" Slip said, and wiped away an icicle from under his nose.

"Cold, uh?" Ray whispered.

"Must be thirty below."

"Will the tent hold?"

"I dunno," Slip said. "Corner ropes is onto the wheels, but one of the middle ones is pulled plumb out."

They stood a second or two, estimating the strain on the ropes, and as if to oblige their curiosity the wind lit on them and heeled them halfway over again. The whole middle of the windward wall bellied inward; the wind got under the side and for an instant they were a balloon; Rusty thought for certain they would go up in the air. He shut his eyes and hung on, and when he looked again three of the boys had grappled the uplifting skirt of the cloth and pinned it down.

"We got to get in off these flats," Jesse said.

"I guess," Ray said. "The question is how. It's three-four miles to the river."

"We could keep the wind on our left and drift a little with it. That'd bring us in somewhere below Bates Camp."

"Well," Ray said, and looked at the rest of them, holding the tent down, "we haven't got much choice. Slip, you reckon we could find any horses in this?

"I reckon we could try."

"No," Ray said. "It'd be too risky. We couldn't drive them against this wind if we found them."

"What about the cattle?" Buck said

"Yeah," said Link Horn. "What about them?"

"D'you suppose," Ray whispered, and a spasm like silent mirth moved his iron face, "after we get things ready to go, you boys could pull about three poles out of the corral gate?"

"You mean turn 'em loose?"

"I mean turn 'em loose."

Ed Spurlock said, "So after all this, we wind up without a single God damn calf?" and Ray said, "You rather have a corral full of dead ones?"

Rusty leaned against the swaying pole while the furious wind whined and howled down out of the Arctic, and he listened to them with a bitterness that was personal and aggrieved. It seemed to him atrocious, a wrong against every principle and every expectation, that the devoted and herculean labors of eight good men should be thwarted by a blind force of nature, a meteorological freak, a mere condition of wind and cold.

Now on with the boots over feet bruised and numb from walking stocking-footed on the frozen ground, and on with the overshoes, and stamp to get life going. Now button the sheepskin collar close and pull the fur cap down, earlaps and forehead piece, leaving exposed only the eyes, the chattering jaw, the agonized spuming of the breath *huh-huh-huh, huh-huh-huh-huh*. Clumsy with clothing, beat mittened hands in armpits, stoop with the others to get the stovepipe together, the grub box packed, the beds rolled. "Keep out a blanket apiece," Ray Henry says.

The tent tugs and strains, wanting to be off. In the gray light, snow sifts dry as sand down through the open stovepipe thimble and onto the stove—a stove so useless that if anyone touched it with a bare hand he would freeze fast.

As in a nightmare where everything is full of shock and terror and nothing is ever explained, Rusty looks around their numb huddle and sees only a glare of living eyes, and among them Panguingue eyes that roll whitely toward the tent roof to ask a question.

"We'll leave it up till we get set," Ray says. "It ain't a hell of a lot, but it's something."

They duck outside, and shielding faces behind shoulders and collars, drive into the wind. The paralyzing wind hammers drift against eyelids, nose, and lips, and their breath comes in gasps and sobs as they throw things into the wagon. Jesse and Ray are harnessing the Clydes over their yellow blankets, Slip pounds ice off the blanket of the night pony getting ready to throw the saddle on. From their feet plumes of drift streak away southward. Beyond the figures in the squirming dusk the whole visible world moves—no sky, no horizon, no earth, no air, only this gray-white streaming, with a sound like a rush of water, across and through it other sounds like howling and shouting far off, high for a moment and lost again in the whistle and rush.

The cheek Rusty has exposed feels scorched as if by flame. Back in the icy, half-cleared tent, the hollow of quiet amid the wind seems a most extravagant sanctuary, and he heaves a great breath as if he has been running. He does not need to be told that what moves them now is not caution, not good judgment, not anything over which they have any control, but desperation. The tent will not stand much more, and no tent means no fire. With no horses left but the Clydes and one night pony, they will have to walk, and to reach either of the possible shelters, either Stonepile or Bates Camp, they will have to go north and west, bucking the wind that just now, in the space of a dozen breaths, has seared his face like a blowtorch. He has a feeling outraged and self-pitying and yet remotely contemplating a deserved punishment, a predicted retribution, the sort of feeling that he used to have in childhood when something tempted him beyond all caution and all warnings and he brought himself to a caning in the iodine- and carbolic-smelling office where his father, the doctor, used to look him down into shame before laying the yardstick around his legs. They have got what they deserved for daring Authority; the country has warned them three separate times. Now the punishment.

Into the wagon, jumbled any old way, goes everything the tent holds—grub box, saddles, stove, stovepipe, kerosene can—and again they gather in the still, icy hollow, strangely empty without the stove. Ray Henry has two lariats in his hands, Buck an axe, and Jesse a lighted lantern. The foreman wipes his nose on the back of his mitt and squints at old Jesse. "Dad, you sure you want to drive? It'll be colder up there than walkin'."

The old-timer shakes the lantern, and his eyes gleam and his square teeth gleam. "Lantern between m'feet, buffler robe over the top," he says, "I don't care how cold I get upstairs if I'm warm from the tail down."

"Long as you don't set yourself afire,"' Ray says. "How about somebody ridin' up there with you?"

"Dee-lighted!" Jesse says, flashing his teeth like Teddy Roosevelt, and they laugh as if they were all short of wind. The foreman's gray thinking eyes go over them. When his look pauses on Rusty Cullen, the boy's breath is held for a moment in sneaking hope, for he has never been so miserable or so cold; the thought of going out there and fighting across six miles of snowflats in the terrible wind has paralyzed his nerve. Also, he tells himself, he is the injured one; his arm still hurts him. The possibility pictures itself seductively before him: to ride, bundled under the buffalo robe and with the lantern's warmth. Like a child pretending sleep when a night emergency arises and the rain beats in an open window or the wind has blown something loose; to sit snug beside old Jesse, relieved of responsibility, while the grownups take care of it . . . He cannot read the foreman's gray eyes; he feels his own wavering down. A crawl of shame moves in his guts, and he thinks, If he picks me it will be because I'm the weakest as well as the greenest.

The thinking eye moves on. "Slip," Ray says. "you ain't got the feet for walkin'. You can spell Dad with the lines. It'll be bad on the hands."

To cover his relief Rusty is beating his hands rhythmically in his armpits and jiggling on nerveless feet. He watches Ray pass the lariats to Little Horn. "If you're tied together, we won't lose nobody."

"Where'll you be?"

"I'll be ridin' pilot."

They are all moving constantly, clumsily. Spurlock has wrapped a woolen muffler around his mouth so that only his restless eyes show. Buck and Panguingue already have hung blankets over their heads and shoulders. Little Horn pulls off a mitt to pat the chimney of

Jesse's lantern with a bare hand. "Well," Ray says, "I guess it's time she came down."

They lurch outside. Rusty, unsure of what to do, astonished at their instant obedience, finds himself standing stupidly while Buck with the butt of the axe knocks out one picket pin, then another, and chops off the ropes that tie the tent to the wheels. Jesse and Panguingue, at the ends, reach inside the flaps and lift and yank at the poles, and down it comes in a puddle of frozen canvas that they fall upon and grapple together and heave into the wagon. They curse and fight the wind, pushing and folding the tent down, throwing the poles and two saddles on it to hold it, hauling and lashing the wagon cover tight. Rusty looks back at where their shelter has been and his insides are pinched by cold panic. Drift is already streaking across the patch of thawed and refrozen grass; the little space their living warmth has thawed there in the midst of the waste looks as passionately and finally abandoned as the fresh earth of a grave.

Little Horn is tying them together, using the rope to snug and hold the blankets they have wrapped around themselves, when out of the tattered edge of storm cattle appear, longhorns that swerve away at a stumbling half-trot. After them and among them, a streaming miserable horde, come the whitefaces and shorthorns, cow's and calves, some steers, a few bulls, with no noise except an occasional desperate blat from a calf, and the clicking of longhorn hooves and joints carried headlong southward by the wind. Well-fleshed and round-bellied no more than a week ago, they stream and flinch past, gaunt ghosts of themselves, and Rusty thinks sullenly, while Little Horn ties the rope tight around him and their four hands tuck the blanket under, that it has been human foolishness that has brought the cattle to this condition. Driven all day by cowboys, and every other night by blizzards, they have eaten hardly anything for days. Left alone, yarding up in the coulees and river bottoms, they could at least have gnawed willows.

He is furious at their violent futile effort, and at Ray Henry for insisting upon it. Inhuman labor, desperate chances, the risk of death itself, for what? For a bunch of cattle who would be better off where their instinct told them to go, drifting with the storm until they found shelter. For owners off in Aberdeen or Toronto or Calgary or Butte who would never come out themselves and risk what they demanded of any cowboy for twenty dollars a month and found.

The tip of his mitt is caught under the rope; he tears it loose, and for a moment Little Horn's barely exposed eyes glint sideways, surprised. Out of the storm behind the last straggling cattle rides Ray Henry, already plastered white. He waves, somebody shouts, the wind tears the sound away and flings it across the prairie, the Clydes jerk sideways, the frozen wheels of the wagon crackle loose and crush through a crested foot-deep drift. The five walkers bunch up to get the protection of the wagon for their faces and upper bodies; the wind under the box and through the spokes tears at their legs as they swing half around and jolt off angling across the storm—northeast, Rusty judges, if the wind is northwest—following the stooped figure of the foreman on the horse. As they pass the corrals, Rusty sees the stained ground humped with carcasses already whitening under the blast of snow and wind.

He huddles his blanket across his chest, clenching and unclenching his numb hands; he crowds close to the others, eager to conform; he plants his feet carefully, clumsily, in the exact footprints of Ed Spurlock, and he tries to keep the rope between them just slack enough so that it does not drag and trip him. His face, unless he carelessly falls behind, is out of the worst lash of the wind; with walking, he has begun to feel his feet again. It seems possible after all—they can walk under these conditions the necessary five or six miles to shelter. He is given confidence by the feel of the rope around his waist, and the occasional tug when Spurlock or someone else up ahead stumbles or lurches, or when he feels Little Horn coming behind. Beside his cheek the wheel pours dry snow, and every turning spoke is a few inches gained toward safety.

Once, as they bounced across the flats, Slippers leaned out and shouted something down to Buck, leading the single-file walkers. An unintelligible word came down the line, the wheels beside them rolled faster, and they were forced into a trot to keep up. Rusty staggered sideways in the broken snow, kept himself from falling under the wheel by a wild shove against the wagon box, lurched and was yanked forward into step so roughly that it kinked his neck. The line of them jogged, grunting in cadence, trotting awkwardly armless, wrapped in their blankets, beside the ponderous wagon. Eventually Buck shouted up at the seat, and they slowed to a walk, but the run had done them good. The blood was out at their edges and extremities again. Rusty felt it sharp and stinging in his cheeks.

Up ahead, revealed and half covered, and revealed and nearly obscured, moving steadily through the lateral whip and crawl of the storm, went the whitened horse, the humped white figure of Ray Henry. Once when Rusty looked he was down, walking and leading the pony. A few minutes later he was up again. The plain stretched on, interminable. Rusty dropped his head turtle-fashion, wiped an edge of the blanket across his leaking and freezing nose, concentrated on putting his feet precisely into the tracks of Ed Spurlock. Dreamlike and hypnotic, body moved, brain moved, but both sluggishly, barely awake. Life was no more than movement, than dull rhythm. Eyes were aware only of the drooping rope, the alternating feet ahead, and once in a while the glimpse of Ray Henry moving through the blizzard out at the edge of visibility. Walking or riding, he went with the inevitability of a cloud driving across the sky; to look up and find him not there would have been a shock and a dismay. And yet he went ambiguously too, something recognized or remembered from an old charade or pantomime or tableau. Leader or Betrayer, urgent, compulsive, vaguely ominous, so that one hurried to keep him in sight and cursed him for the way he led on, and on.

In the thudding hollows of the skull, deep under the layered blanket, the breath-skimmed sheepskin, inside the stinging whiskered face and the bony globe that rode jolting on the end of the spine, deep in there as secret as the organs at the heart of a flower or a nut inside shell and husk, the brain plodded remotely at a heart's pace or a walking pace, saying words that had been found salutary for men or cattle on a brittle and lonesome night, words that not so much expressed as engendered what the mind felt: sullenness, fear, doubt.

Up ahead the foreman moved steadily, dusky stranger, silent companion, and if he did not "bend upon the snowshoe with a long and limber stride," he had a look as tireless and unstoppable as if he had in fact been that Spirit Hunter, that Walker of the Snow, one of the shapes with which the country deluded frightened men.

The wind had changed, and instead of driving at their legs under the box between the spokes was coming much more from behind them. Rusty felt Little Horn's hand on his back, but when he turned to see what was wanted, Little Horn shook his head at him from under the blanket hood: only a stumble, or the wind hustling him along too fast. The pour of dry snow from the wheel blew on forward instead of sideward into their faces. Except for his hands and his impossible leaky nose, he was not cold. They must have come more than half of the three miles that would bring them to the river, where there would be protection among the willows and under the cutbanks, and where they might even choose to make some sort of shelter of the wagon and the tent—build a big wood fire and thaw out and wait for the storm to blow by. He hoped they would; he did not relish the thought of turning into the wind, even in the more sheltered river valley.

He saw the Walker coming back, bent double, his face turned aside. When he reached them his pony turned tail to wind and Jesse cramped the Clydes around and they stood for a brief conference. It seemed that the wind had not changed. The horses simply wouldn't head across it, and kept swinging. That meant they would hit the river lower down, and have a longer upwind pull to Bates.

Only Ray's eyes showed through the mask-like slot of a felt cap that came clear down around his throat. To Jesse and Slip he whisper-shouted something that Rusty could not hear, and mounted and rode off again. The wagon crunched after him, the segmented ten-footed worm beside it took up its lockstep. Deafened by fur and wool, anesthetized by cold and the monotony of walking, the next-to-last segment, joined to the segments before and behind by a waist of half-inch hard-twist rope, plodded on, thinking its own dim thoughts, which were concerned with cosmic injustice and the ways of God to man.

Why couldn't there be, just at this moment, the lucky loom of an unknown or unexpected cowcamp, the whiff of lignite smoke on the wind? Why, just once, could not rescue come from Heaven, instead of having to be earned foot by foot? He dreamed of how warmth would feel in the face, the lovely stink of four or five shut-in cowboys in a hot shack, and he sucked and sniffed at the drooling of his mouth and nose, a hateful, inescapable oozing that turned to ice in his beard and on his lips.

Head down, he plodded on, one step and then another. Once as he put his foot in the print that Spurlock's foot had just left, he caught the heel of Spurlock's overshoe with his toe, and saw Spurlock fling an irritable snarl over the shoulder. Oh, the hell, he thought. Can't you be decent even when we're like this? The rope tugged tight around him, he hopped to get in step again, walking carefully, left, right, left, right, wiping his leaking nose against the blanket's edge and feeling slick ice there.

> *Sancta Maria, speed us!*
> *The sun is falling low;*
> *Before us lies the valley*
> *Of the Walker of the Snow!*

Later—hours or days, for time whipped and snaked past in unceasing movement like the wind and the trails of drift, and all its proportions were lost—Rusty bumped into Spurlock and an instant later felt Little Horn bump into him in turn. The wagon had stopped, and Ray was back, leading his pony by the bridle. His visor of felt was iron-stiff with ice, so that he pulled it down and craned his neck and lifted his chin to shout over it to Jesse, perched on the high seat beside Slip with the buffalo robe folded up around him under the armpits. Rusty, squinting to see what they were looking at, felt the sticky drag of ice on his lashes as if his eyes were fringed with crickets' legs, and saw that ahead of them the land fell away beyond an edge where the grass was blown bare. Ahead or below, the ground-hugging trails of drift were gone, leaving only air murky as dusk, with fitful swirls and streaks of dark at its bottom which he realized were brush. He dragged at his wet nose. The river.

But the brief, gratified expectation he had that this would be an easier stage lasted no more than two minutes. The hills dipping down to the floodplain were gullied and washed, and drifted deep. Even with Ray riding ahead to try the going, the wheels dropped into holes and hollows, rose over knobs; the wagon canted at perilous angles, groaning and jolting its way slanting, with the wind almost dead behind it. Pulling out wide from the rocking wagon, the men were caught in the open wind and blown along. Rusty saw the Clydes braced back in the breeching, their hairy fetlocks coming up out of the snow rattling with balls of ice, and their muscular haunches bunching under the blankets, and then here came Slip digging out from under the buffalo robe to throw his weight on the brake. Ice against ice, shoe slid on tire and held nothing; the wagon rolled heavily down upon the Clydes, who braced lower, slipping. The walkers jumped aside and then, as the wagon lumbered past them, jumped to the endgate to try to hold it back. Its ponderous weight yanked them along, their dug heels plowed up snow. They could feel it under their hands getting away, they knew it without Jesse's yell that snapped off on the wind above their heads. Jesse rose half to his feet, braced between seat and box. The wagon jackknifed sharply as he swung the Clydes along the sidehill to slow them. The left side dropped down, the right heaved up, and with a neat final motion like the end of a crack-the-whip the wagon tipped over and cast off Slip in a spidery leap down the hillside. Jesse, hanging to the tilted seat to the end, slid off it to land on his feet with the reins in one hand and the lantern in the other. By the time Ray discovered what had happened and rode back, he had unhooked the Clydes and got them quiet. The wagon lay with its load bulging out of the lashed cover, the busy wind already starting to cover it with snow.

• • •

Rusty would not have believed that in that wind and cold it was possible to work up a sweat, but he did. It was a blind and furious attack
they launched on the tipped wagon, unloading almost everything and
carrying it down to more level ground where the abrupt hill aproned
off, stacking it there while they floundered back to dig and pry at the
jackknifed wheels. Ray hitched on with his saddle horse, they heaved
while their held breath burst out of them in grunts and straining
curses, until they righted it, and straightened the wheels, and a spoke
at a time got them turning; three of them carrying the tongue and the
others ready to push or hold back, they angled it down onto leveler
and smoother ground.

There they wasted not a second, but hitched up and loaded as if they
raced against time. When the muffled-up figure of Spurlock started to
heave a saddle up, and slipped and fell flat on its back with the saddle
on its chest, Rusty coughed out one abrupt bark of laughter, but no one
else laughed. Panguingue and Buck picked the saddle off Spurlock's
chest and tossed it aboard and before Spurlock was back on his feet
Little Horn and Buck were starting to tie together the worm of walkers.
Up where Jesse and Slip were fussily folding the buffalo robe around
and under them it looked bitterly cold, but down where Rusty stood it
was better. He could feel his hands all the way, his feet all but the tips
of the toes. Where the fur cap covered it, his forehead was damp, and
under the ponderous layers of clothing and blanket his body itched a
little with warmth. He was winded, and dead tired, and his shoulder
ached as if the fierce haul and heave of the unloading and loading had
pulled it from its socket, but the dismay of the accident was worked off.
They were all right, they would make it yet.

He twisted to help Little Horn tuck the blanket ends under the rope,
and at that moment Spurlock, moving awkwardly in front, put his foot
down crooked, reeled against him, landed on his foot and anchored
him there, and bore him helplessly over in the drift. If it had been
anyone else, Rusty might have laughed, reassured and warmed by work

as he was; but since it was Spurlock he rose to one knee anticipating trouble. He was not wrong; the hand he put on Spurlock's arm was knocked off angrily, and through the layers of the muffler the words were savage: ". . . the Christ you're doing!"

The boy's anger blew up instant and hot, and he bounded to his feet, freeing his elbows from the blanket. They faced each other, tied together by four feet of rope like gladiators coupled to fight to the death, and then the shadow above them made itself felt and Rusty looked up to see Ray Henry sitting hands-on-horn and looking down on them.

"What's trouble?" the foreman said.

The unintelligible growl that came out of Spurlock's muffled mouth could have told him nothing, but Rusty pulled the collar away from his chin and said passionately, "Look, put me somewhere else in this line! I'm not going to stand for . . . "

"What's trouble?" Ray said again.

"He keeps stumbling around and falling down and then blaming me . . . ."

"If he falls down, help him up," Ray croaked, and kneed his frosted pony around and rode off in front. The wheels jerked, the icy axles shrieked, their feet automatically hopped to get in step, and they were walking again. Rusty pulled his chin back inside the collar and went sullenly, furious at the injustice of the rebuke, and alert to make the most of any slightest slip or stumble ahead of him.

Down in the bottoms among the willows the wind was less, and they could bring the horses to turn halfway into it, feeling for the river. But if the wind was less, the snow was deeper; the Clydes floundered belly deep and the wagon box scraped up a great drift that piled up over the doubletree and against the stallions' rumps and finally stopped them dead. They shoveled it away and cleared the Clydes' feet, never quite sure whether or not they would have their brains kicked out. Then they fell into two lines out in front and tramped a way for the horses and the wagon wheels down through smothered rosebushes and between clumps of willow whose bark gleamed red under the hood of snow. Ten feet of it was enough to wind a man; they panted their way ahead, turned to tramp backward and deepen the track, stopped every twenty yards to dig away the snow that the wagon box scooped up. They worked like people fighting a fire, exhausted themselves and stood panting a minute and fell to it again, frenzied for the easy going on the river ice.

The wagon eased over the edge of a bushy bank, the Clydes plunged as Jesse took them over straight on. The front wheels went down, pushing the stallions out onto the ice. Just as Rusty saw them lunging to pull the wagon through, a jerk from behind dragged him over in the drift and the whole line of walkers came down. When they got to their feet there was the wagon on the river.

Getting up watchfully, Rusty thought he felt Spurlock yanking at the rope, and he yanked back harshly. Sunk between the muskrat cap and the muffler, and blindered on both sides by the wings of the mackinaw collar, Spurlock's eyes peered out like the eyes of a fierce animal peering from a crack in the rock, but he turned away without a word, giving Rusty at least the smoldering satisfaction of having yanked last, of having finished something that the other had started.

The cutbank partially shielded them from the wind. Upriver was a straight reach with an irregular streak of clear, blown ice down its center, grading up to shelving drifts against both banks. Drift skated and blew down it like dust down an alley. The last lap of the road to shelter lay before them as smooth as a paved highway.

Ray Henry, leading his pony down the broken bank, stopped by them a moment where they hung panting on the wagon. "Everybody all right?"

They looked at him from among their wrappings.

"Ed?" Ray said.

It seemed to Rusty terribly unjust that particular attention should have been paid to Spurlock rather than to himself. It meant that the foreman still looked upon Spurlock as in the right, himself in the wrong. It meant that he had no concern for the one of his men who was hurt, and might be in trouble. He saw Ray's eyes within the visor that was like the helmet of a hero, and his unhappiness that he had lost prestige and respect drove words to his lips, impulsive and too eager, anything to be recognized and accepted again. He did not care about Spurlock, actually; he was already ashamed of that quarrel. But he wanted Ray Henry to notice him, and so he said, "What do we do now, Ray? Camp here till it's over?"

"Not hardly," Ray said. "The Clydes have had all the fresh air they need."

"How much farther?"

"Three miles, maybe four."

"Do we ride from here?"

The gray, thinking eye examined him from within the helmet of ice-hardened felt. The foreman said, "You reckon you're any more petered than them studs?"

He went stooping and slipping out in front to confer with Jesse and Slip, and Rusty, avoiding Little Horn's eyes and with his back to Spurlock and the others, watched the smothered rosebushes on the bank quiver in a gust. The slow warmth under all his wrappings might have come from the heavy work of getting the wagon through the brush and the drifts, but it might just as well have been shame, and he hated them all for never giving a man a chance, for taking things wrong, for assuming what should not be assumed. He hadn't been wanting to quit, he had asked only for information. Sullenly he waited, resolved to keep his mouth shut and plod it out. Once they got back to the ranch, he could simply leave the job; he was under no obligation to stay at it any longer than he pleased to. Neither Ray nor anyone else could compel a man to stick it through months of this kind of thing, no matter how short-handed the T-Down was. There was sure to be a great change as soon as he announced he was leaving. He could see Ray Henry's face—all their faces. Every man who left, left more for the remaining ones to do. Too late, chaps. Sorry. Ta-ta, gentlemen. Enjoy the winter.

In the river bottom the wind was louder, though he felt it less. The bare willows and the rosebushes, bent like croquet wickets into the drifts, whistled with it, the cutbank boomed it back in hollow eddies, every corner and edge and groove of the valley gave it another tongue.

More than out on the flats, even, it echoed with hallucinatory voices, shouts, screams, whistles, moans, jeers. Rusty concentrated on it. He had only been asking a perfectly reasonable question, considering that they were running for their lives and still had an unknown distance to go. Would it be so terrible to climb up and let those big strong horses pull them for a little while along the level ice? Would it, for that matter, be entirely unheard of to sacrifice the Clydes, if necessary, to save eight lives? He asked himself what about a leader who thought more of his horses than of his men.

The blood in his veins was sluggish with cold, his mind was clogged with sullen hatred. Ray, shouting up to Jesse and Slip, and Spurlock, weaving bearlike from one foot to the other, were both part of a nightmare which he loathed and wanted to escape, but the numbness held him and he stood spraddling, squinting from behind the wagon box, hearing the shouts of those ahead torn from their lips and flung streaming down the ice to become part of the headlong illusory wailing that blew and moaned around the river's bends. His mind, groping among images, was as clumsy as his mittened unfeeling hands would have been, trying to pick up a coin from the snow. He thought of old Jesse's friend down by Sheridan, with his frozen conversation, and of how others had explained, not so humorously, the voices that haunted the wind in this country.

> *For I saw by the sickly moonlight*
> *As I followed, bending low,*
> *That the walking of the stranger*
> *Left no footmarks on the snow.*

The voices of all the lost, all the Indians, *métis*, hunters, Mounted Police, wolfers, cowboys, all the bundled bodies that the spring uncovered and the warming sun released into the stink of final decay; all the starving, freezing, gaunt, and haunted men who had challenged this country and failed; all the ghosts from smallpox-stilled Indian camps, the wandering spirits of warriors killed in their sleep on the borders of the deadly hills, all the skeleton women and children of the starving winters, all the cackling, maddened cannibals, every terrified, lonely, crazed, and pitiful outcry that these plains had ever wrung from human lips, went wailing and moaning over him, mingled with the living shouts of the foreman and the old-timer, and he said, perhaps aloud, remembering the legend of the Crying River, and the voices that rode the wind there as here, *Qu'appelle? Qu'appelle?*

Heartless and inhuman, older than earth and totally alien, as savage and outcast as the windigo, the cannibal spirit, the wind dipped and swept upon them down the river channel, tightening the lightly sweating inner skin with cold and the heart with fear. Rusty watched Ray hump his back and shake off the worst of the blast, saw the arm wave. The wagon rolled again. Ed Spurlock, unready, was pulled sideways a stumbling step or two by the tightening of the rope, and Rusty got one clear look into the brown, puckered eyes. Out of his fear and misery and anger he sneered, "Learn to walk!" But if Spurlock heard he made no sign. In a moment he was only the hooded, blanketed, moving stoop, not human, not anything, that Rusty imitated movement for movement, step for step, plodding up the river after the wagon.

Exhaustion and cold are a kind of idiocy, the mind moves as numbly as the body, the momentary alertness that a breathing spell brings is like the sweat that can be raised under many clothes even in the bitterest weather; when the breathing spell is over and the hard work past, mind and body are all the worse for the brief awakening. The sweaty skin chills, the images that temporary alertness has caught scrape and rasp in the mind like edged ice and cannot be dislodged or thought away or emptied out, but slowly coagulate there.

For Rusty they were the images of fear. No matter how much he tried to tie his mind to the plod-plod-plod of foot after foot, he heard the spirit of that bitter country crying for cold and pain. Under his moving feet the ice passed, now clear, with coin-like bubbles in it, now coated with a pelt of dry smooth snow, now thinly drifted. The world swung slowly, the dry snow under their feet blew straight sideward, then quar-

tered backward; his quickly lifted eyes saw that the right bank had
dropped to a bar and the left curved up in a cutbank. The wind lashed
his face so that he hunched and huddled the blanket closer, leaving
only the slightest hole, and still the wind got in, filled the blanket,
threatened to blow it off his back. His eyes were full of water and he
wiped them free, terrified that they would freeze shut. With his head
bowed clear over, almost to the rope, he stumbled on. Through the slits
of sight remaining to him he saw that the drift now was blowing
straight backward from Spurlock's feet. The river had swung them
directly into the wind. The line of walkers huddled to the left until they
were walking bunched behind the feeble protection of the wagon.

The wagon stopped, the line of walkers bumped raggedly to a halt.
Rusty had forgotten them; he was surprised to find them there, glaring
from the frozen crevices of their clothes. From out in front Ray Henry
came looming, a huge indomitable bulk, leading the pony whose bony
face was covered with a shell of ice, the hairy ears pounded full of
snow, the breast of the blanket sheathed. He unlooped the halter rope
and tied it to the endgate, pulled the bridle and hung it on the saddle
horn. For a minute he rubbed and worked at the pony's face, turned
grunting, and said from inside his visor, "They just can't buck it. We're
gonna have to lead 'em." He helped Little Horn pull open the loose,
frozen knot in the rope and free himself from the others. "Rusty," he
said, "see if you can find a blanket up in the load somewhere."

Rusty found the blanket, the foreman and Little Horn flapped off
with it, the walkers huddled back to the wagon, eyeing the miserable
pony which now took half their shelter. After a minute or two the yell
came back, they turned, they stirred their stiffened legs and moved
their wooden feet. The wind shrieked around the wagon, between the
spokes, along the axles and the snow-clogged reach, and Rusty, colder
now than at any time since he had awakened half frozen in his blankets, heard the blizzardy bottoms wild with voices. *Qu'appelle? . . .
Qu'appelle? . . . Qu'appelle?*

In an hour, or four hours, or ten minutes, the river blessedly bent
rightward, and the wind went screaming and flying above them but

touched them only in swoops and gusts. There was a stretch where the inshore drifts let them go close up under the bank, and for a brief time the air was almost still, the snow settling almost gently as on any winter's day, a day to put roses in the cheeks.

Sancta Maria, speed us!

During that brief, numbed lull Spurlock tangled his feet and fell again, pulling over Panguingue ahead of him. Rusty, hopping awkwardly to keep from getting entangled with the sliding, swiveling figures, saw Buck squat and grab the rope to maintain his balance against the drag of the fallen ones. There went the three of them, helplessly dragged along on back or feet, and here came Rusty, a lead-footed dancer, prancing and shouting in their wake until those up ahead heard and they stopped.

Ray was back again. Panguingue and Buck stood up and cleared the rope, but Spurlock sat on the ice with his head down, pawing at his face and heaving his shoulders under the blanket. Rusty stayed back in scorn and contempt, sure that the blame would somehow be pinned on him. He was the proper scapegoat; everything that happened was caused by his awkwardness.

Ray was stooping, shaking Spurlock's shoulder. His hand worked at the muffler around Spurlock's face. Then he straightened up fierce and ready and with so much power left that Rusty moved a step back, astonished. "The lantern!" Ray shouted, and lunged around the line of walkers to reach and take the lantern from Jesse's hand. Back at Spurlock, stooping to hold the lantern directly against the muffler, he said over his shoulder, "Rusty, unhitch yourself and rustle some wood. We're gonna have to stop and thaw out."

The knot was stiff with ice, his fingers like sticks, but he got loose and stumped around in the deep snow breaking dead stalks out of willow clumps. Slip appeared to help him, and Rusty said, pausing a second in his fumbling, "What's the matter with Spurlock?"

"Smotherin'," Slip said. "God damn muffler froze to his whiskers."

"Are we going to camp here?"

"Why?" said Slip in surprise. "Do you *want* to?"

Rusty floundered down the bank with his handful of twigs, watched Panguingue cone them on the ice and souse them with kerosene. The smell cut his nostrils, and he sniffed back the wetness and spat in the snow. It was that drooling that had got Spurlock in trouble. Drool and freeze fast. Dully curious, he watched Ray moving the lantern glass around on the frozen wool, while Buck pulled on the unfrozen ends. Spurlock's head was pulled out of his collar; he looked like a fish on a hook. Then Panguingue found a match and reached across Buck to scratch it on the dry bottom of the lantern. The little cone of sticks exploded in bright flame.

"More," Panguingue said thickly.

Little Horn, who had led the Clydes around in a half circle was already up over the endgate, unlashing the wagon cover. Stupidly Rusty watched as he loosened it all across the windward side and dropped it in the lee, and then, comprehending, he helped tie it to the spokes to make a windbreak. The fire had burned out its splash of kerosene, and was smoldering in the snow until Panguingue swished it again and it blazed up. "More!" he said. "We need wood."

"In the wagon," Jesse said. "What do you think I chopped all that wood for yesterday?"

He climbed the wheel to burrow into the uncovered load, and his face with its bowed mustaches emerged from under the tangled tent like a walrus at a waterhole and he winked in Rusty's face, handing him out wood two and three sticks at a time. His manner was incredible to the boy. He acted as if they were out on a picnic or a berry picking and were stopping for lunch. Buck and Ray were holding Spurlock's face close to the little fire and working away at the muffler. The wind, here, was only a noise; they squatted in their bivouac with the fire growing and sputtering in the water of its melting, and they gathered close around it, venturing their faces a little out of their coverings.

Spurlock cursed clearly for the first time, the muffler came loose in Buck's hands. Ray set the lantern aside while Spurlock breathed deeply and passed his hands around on his face.

"Stick her right in," Jesse said. "That's the quickest way to thaw her. Set those weeds on fire."

They sat knee to knee, they put their mittens on sticks of wood in the snow and held stiff red hands in the very flames, they opened collars and exposed smarting faces. Life returned as pain; far down his legs Rusty felt a deep, passionate ache beginning in his feet. He knew from the burn of his cheeks and the chilblain feel of his fingers that he would have some frostbite to doctor. But he loved the snug out-of-the-wind shelter, the fire, even the pain that was beginning now and would get worse. For no matter how they came out, or whether they camped here to wait out the storm or went on after a rest to Bates, which couldn't be more than another mile or two, he would go with a knowledge that warmed him like Jesse's lantern under the robe: it hadn't been *he* that cracked. And what a beautiful and righteous and just thing it was that the one who did crack should be Spurlock! In triumph and justification he looked across the fire at the sagging figure, but he couldn't make the restless reddened eyes hold still. Spurlock hadn't said a word since they released him from the smothering scarf.

A half hour later, when Ray said they must go on, Rusty received the words like a knife in his guts. He had been sitting and secretly willing that they should stay. But he glanced again across the fire and this time caught Ed Spurlock's moving eyes, and the eyes ducked like mice. He told himself that if he was unwilling, Spurlock was scared to death. When they lashed the wagon cover back on and tied themselves together again and hooded the Clydes in the red Hudson's Bay blanket and Little Horn and Ray swung them by the bits and the forlorn night pony stretched his neck and came unwillingly, Rusty had a feeling that the moving line literally tore Spurlock from the side of the fire, now sunk into the crust and sizzling out blackly at the edges in steam and smoke.

The river swung, and the wind got at them. It swung wider, and they were plucked and shoved and blinded so that they walked sideward with their backs to the bar and their faces turned to the fantastic pagoda-roof of snow along the cutbank. In fury and anguish they felt how the river turned them. Like things with an identical electrical

charge, their faces bent and flinched away, but in the end there was no
evading it. The wagon stopped and started, stopped and started. The
feet that by the fire had felt renewed life began to go dead again, the
hands were going back to wood, the faces, chafed and chapped and
sore, were pulled deep into the wool and fur. Gasping, smelling wet
sheepskin and the tallowy smell of muskrat fur, feeling the ice at their
very beards and the wind hunting for their throats, they hunched and
struggled on.

Rusty, bent like a bow, with every muscle strained to the mindless
plod, plod, plod of one foot after the other, and his eyes focused
through the blanket's crack on Spurlock's heels, saw the feet turn sideward, the legs go out of sight. Apparently Spurlock had simply sat
down, but the rope, tightening on him, pulled him over. Sliding on the
ice, hauled after the backward-walking, braced, and shouting Panguingue, he was trying to untie the rope around his waist with his mittened hands.

Again their yells were torn away downwind, voices to blend with the
blizzard's crying, or thaw out to haunt hunters or cowboys in some soft
spring. They dragged Spurlock a hundred feet before those up in front
heard. Then Rusty stood furiously over him and cursed him for his
clumsiness and cried for him to get up, but Spurlock, straightening to
sit with his arms hung over his knees, neither looked up nor stood up.
He mumbled something with his head down.

"Lone," he mumbled, "rest minute."

Rusty's leg twitched; he all but kicked the miserable bundle. Slip and
Jesse or both were shouting from the wagon seat, Ray Henry was coming
back—for the how many'th time? They were utterly exposed, the wind
whistled and the drift blinded them. He dropped his mouth again to
Spurlock's ear, shouted again. Panguingue was hauling at Spurlock's
armpits. "Can't sit down," he said. "Got to keep him movin'."

Not until then did the understanding grow into Rusty's mind, a slow
ache of meaning like the remote feeling in his feet. Spurlock was done.
It wasn't just awkwardness, he wasn't just quitting, he was exhausted.
The danger they had been running from, a possibility in which Rusty

had never thoroughly believed, was right among them. This was how a man died.

His hands found an arm under blanket and coat, and he and Panguingue helped Spurlock's feeble scrambling until they had him on his feet. They held him there, dragged down by his reluctant weight, while Ray peered grimly into his face. "He's played out," Panguingue said, and Rusty said, "Couldn't we put him in the wagon? He can't walk any farther."

Ray said, "Put him in the wagon he'd be froze stiff in twenty minutes." His hands went out to Spurlock's shoulders and he shook him roughly. "Ed! You hear? You got to keep movin'. It's only another mile. Just keep comin'."

"'mall right," Spurlock said. "Just rest minute."

"Not a damn minute," Ray said. "You rest a minute and you're dead."

Spurlock hung between Rusty and Panguingue until they were holding almost his whole weight. "You hear, Ed?" Ray said, glaring from his visor like a hairy animal. "You stop to rest, you're dead. Come on now, stand up and walk."

Somehow he bullied strength into the legs and a glitter of life into the eyes. Then he drove back against the wind to take the bridle of the off horse, and the halting, laborious crawl moved on. But now Rusty and Panguingue had hitched their ropes around and walked one on each side of Ed Spurlock, each with a hand under the rope around his waist to haul him along, and to support him if he started to go down. He came wobbling, and he murmured through the blanket they had wrapped over his whole head, but he came.

Rusty's shoulder ached—he ached all over, in fact, whenever he had any feeling at all—and the strain of half supporting Spurlock twisted his body until he had a stabbing stitch in his side. The hand he kept in Spurlock's waist rope was as unfeeling as an iron hook.

A mile more, Ray said. But the river led them a long time around an exposed loop. He had all he could do to force himself into the blast of snow and wind that faded and luffed only to howl in their faces again more bitterly than ever. When Spurlock, stumbling like a sleepwalker, hung back or sagged, trying to sit down, Rusty felt Panguingue's strength and heard Panguingue's stout cursing. His own face was so stiff that he felt he could not have spoken, even to curse, if he tried; he had lost all feeling in his lips and chin. His inhuman hook dragged at Spurlock's waist rope, he threw his shoulder across to meet Panguingue's when the weight surged too far forward, and he put foot after foot, not merely imbecilic now with cold and exhaustion, but nearly mindless, watching not the feet ahead, for there were none now, with three of them abreast and Buck trailing them behind, but the roll of the broad iron tire with the snow spume hissing from it.

He watched it hypnotically, revolving slowly like the white waste of his mind where a spark of awareness as dim as the consciousness of an angleworm glimmered. His body lived only in its pain and weariness. The white waste on which the wheel moved broke into dark angles, was overspread by blackness that somehow rose and grew, strangely fluid and engulfing, and the air was full of voices wild and desolate and terrible as the sound of hunting wolves. The led pony reared and broke its halter rope and vanished somewhere. Then Rusty felt himself yanked sideward, falling into Spurlock and Panguingue in an encumbered tangle, seeing even as he fell, shocked from his stupor, that the endgate was clear down, the hub drowned in black water that spread across the snow. Kicking crabwise, he fled it on his back, helped by someone hauling on the rope behind, until they stood at the edge of the little shallow rapid and saw Jesse and Slip in the tilted wagon ready to jump, and the round wet heads of stones among the broken ice, and the Clydes struggling, one half down and then up again, Little Horn hanging from the bits, hauled clear of the ice as they plunged. There was a crack like a tree coming down, the stallions plunged and steadied, and then Ray was working back along the broken tongue to get at the singletrees and unhook the tugs and free them.

Ray was standing on the broken tongue and calming the stallions with a hand on each back while he yelled downwind. Rusty pulled at his cap, exposed one brittle ear, and heard the foreman shouting, "Get him on up to the cabin . . . two or three hundred yards . . . right after you."

So with hardly a pause longer than the pause of their falling side-ward away from the crunch of ice and the upwelling of water from the broken shell of the rapid, he and Panguingue were walking again, cast free from the rope and supporting Spurlock each with one arm around his shoulders, the other hands locked in front of him. He drooped and wobbled, mumbling and murmuring about rest. He tricked them with sudden lurches to left or right; when he staggered against them his weight was as hard to hold as a falling wall. Twice he toppled them to the ice. Compelled to watch where he walked, Rusty had to let the blanket blow from head and face, and without its protection he flinched and gasped, blinded, and felt the ice forming stickily along his eyelashes, and peered and squinted for the sight of the dugway that would lead them out of the channel and up the cutbank and across a little flat to the final security, so close now and so much more desper-ately hard to reach with every step.

The river bent, they dragged their burden along, they yielded to his murmurings and to their own exhaustion and let him sag a minute onto the ice, and then hauled and dragged him onto his feet and stag-gered on. The right bank was low and brushy; the wind came across it so that they leaned and fought across its whipping edge. Rusty freed his left hand and scoured the wrist of the mitten across his eyes and looked into the blast for the slant of the dugway, and saw nothing but the very throat of the blizzard. It was more than muscle and will could endure; panic was alive in his insides again. Even a hundred yards was too much; they could fall and die before the others could overtake them, right here within a few rods of safety. He gasped and sucked at his drooling lip, lost his hold on Panguingue's hand, felt with anguish how Spurlock slid away and went down.

Somehow they got him up again; somehow they struggled another hundred feet along the ice, and now a cutbank curving into a left-hand bend cut off some of the wind, and Rusty heard Panguingue grunt and felt the veer and stagger as he turned in toward the bank. Rusty still could not see it, but starting up, slipping, he put a hand down to stay himself and felt the dugway. Strengthless, they leaned into the bank; Spurlock tried to lie back; they held him with difficulty, and lifting the blanket to took into his face, Rusty saw his eyes frozen wholly shut with teardrops of ice on the lashes. Above the dark beard the cheek-bones were dead white.

When they tried to move him again, he sagged back against the bank and gave them his limp arms to haul at, and their combined strength was not enough to get him onto his feet, much less to start him up the steep dugway. They tried to drag him and stopped exhausted after six feet. The glare of uncertainty, fear, helplessness, was in Panguingue's glimmer of eyes and teeth. Rusty understood him well enough. Leave him? The others would soon come along. But if they didn't come in a few minutes he would be dead. Again they lifted and hauled at Spurlock, got him halfway, and felt him slip and go comfortably down again. Panguingue let go. "We better try to get up to the cabin. Schulz might be there."

"Suppose he isn't?"

He heard the forlorn, hopeless sound of Panguingue's snuffling. The face looked at him, bearded clear to the eyes.

"You go," Rusty said. "I'll wait here with him."

A snuffle, a momentary look, and Panguingue ducked away, scrambling with hands and feet, to disappear over the dugway edge.

For a while Rusty lay beside Spurlock on the slope, his blanket huddled over to cover both their faces, and simply waited, without mind or thought, no longer afraid, not hopeful, not even aware or sentient, but simply waiting while the gasp of breath and hammer of heart labored toward some slowing point. He could not feel his feet at all; his hands were clubs of wood. Driven inward from its frontiers, his life concentrated itself in his chest where heart and lungs struggled.

A little later there was a stage in which his consciousness hung above him, like the consciousness in a dream where one is both actor and observer, and saw him lying there, numb already nearly to the knees, nearly to the elbows, nose and lips and forehead and the tender sockets of the eyes gone feelingless, ears as impersonal as paper ears pinned to his head. What he saw was essentially a corpse huddling over another corpse. He recognized the fact without surprise or alarm. This was the way it ended, this was the way they would be found.

Under the blanket's hood were a darkness and stillness. He felt how absurd it was, really. Absurd for men to chase around an arctic prairie wearing themselves and their cattle to death. Absurd. Take a rest, now, and . . .

Coming? Who? *Qu'appelle?* Old wolf, old walker of the snow, old windigo, *qu'appelle?* He smiled. It was a joke between them.

He heard now neither the wind nor the dry rustle of his mind. Inside the blanket the air was still, red-dusky, not cold. But as he moved to make his legs more comfortable the hillside toppled, a dull anguish of unwilling sensation spread in his throat, and he struggled back up, straightening the elbow that had given way and let him fall across Spurlock's up-jutting face. A powder flash of terror lighted up his whole head. The imprint of Spurlock's chin, unyielding as stone, ached in his Adam's apple. The face of a corpse—his too? But it was not his own pain so much as the appalling rigidity of Spurlock's jaw that shocked him. The man was dying, if not dead. Something had to be done, he couldn't just wait for help from Panguingue or the others.

His hands clutched and shook the stiffening bundle, the unfeeling hooks tried to close, to lift. "Ed! Ed, come on! We're almost there, man! Get up, you can't lie here. Only a little way farther. Ed! *Ed!* You hear? God damn it, Ed, get up! Come on, move!"

His eyes were full of catastrophic tears; he dashed them away with a fold of the blanket and threw a look up the dugway and gulped a burning throatful of the wind. He heard the voices wail and howl around the eaves of the riverbank, and he bent and slapped and pounded and tugged, screaming at the clownish, bearded, ice-eyed, and white-cheek-boned face that turned and whimpered under his attack.

Gasping, he stopped a moment, threw another look upward. The top of the bank was less than thirty feet above him. Beyond that, within two hundred feet, should be the cabin. Five minutes, no more than ten even on hands and knees. He looked in anguish for the outfit, possibly coming up the river ice, and saw only trails of drift vanishing around the bend. The boys rendering their fantastic duty to the horses could not possibly come in time. And Panguingue must have found the shack deserted or he would have been back by now. Was he stopping to build a fire, or was he too exhausted to come back? Or was he lying in the snow himself, somewhere between the cutbank and the cabin?

"Ed! Wake up! Get up and walk! It's only a little way!"

Hopeless; inert and hopeless. He could not help the tears, though he knew they would be his blindness and his death. "Please, Ed! Please, come on!"

In a clumsy frenzy he hauled and yanked and dragged; his frantic strength skidded Spurlock a yard or two up the dugway, and when Spurlock began mumblingly to resist with arms and legs, Rusty attacked him with three times more fury and by slaps and kicks and blows reinforced his resistance until, miraculously, Spurlock was on his feet. With hooks and shoulder Rusty helped him, braced him, shoved him upward, moved him a step, and another; and crying encouragement, panting, winded and dead-armed and dead-legged, forced the man foot by foot up the dugway path until he felt the ground level off and the wind fling itself full against them.

They toppled and almost fell. Spurlock sagged and started to sit down and Rusty barely managed to hold him. He could not see more than a bleared half-light—no objects at all. His tears were already ice, his lashes stitched together, and he could make no move to clear his sight without letting Spurlock slip away, probably for the last time. Savagely he rasped his face across the snow-slick wool of Spurlock's blanketed shoulder; with what little vision he could gain he glared straight into the wind for the dark wall or icicled eaves that would be the cabin. The wind drove down his throat; his shouting was strangled and obliterated; it was like trying to look and shout up a waterfall. The wilder-

ness howled at him in all its voices. He was brought to a full stop, sight-
less, breathless, deafened, and with no strength to move and barely
enough to stand, not enough—frantically not enough—to hold the
weight of Ed Spurlock that despite every effort he could make slid away
and down.

With a groan Rusty let him go. Both hands rose to rub the
wristlets of his mittens across his scaled eyes. Pain stabbed through his
eyeballs as if he had run across them with sandpaper, but he broke the
threads of ice that stitched him shut, and looked again into the gray and
howling wind, saw a square darkness, a loom of shadow in the murk,
and thought in wonder, My God, we've been right against the shack all
the time, and then the darkness moved and the wind's voice fell from
whine and howl to a doglike barking, and Panguingue was there
shouting in his face.

Relief was such pure bliss to him that he was rendered imbecilic
by it, and stood mouth open and cheeks stretched to force open his
eyes, watching Panguingue try to pull Spurlock erect. He loved Panguingue, the stoutest and decentest and bravest and most depend-
able man alive. Merely his presence brought not only hope but
assurance. It would be no trouble now. And even while he was
bending to help he heard the unmistakable dig and clump of the
Clydes behind him, and turned to see them clear the dugway with
tennis balls of ice rattling in their fetlocks and Jesse hanging to the
lines behind them, and then the others—one, then another, then
another, leading the pony.

What had been impossible was suddenly easy, was nothing. Among
them they hoisted Spurlock to his feet. Rusty felt an arm around him, the
urge of someone else's undiminished strength helping him along
through a thigh-deep drift that gave way abruptly to clear ground. His
head sounded with hollow kickings and poundings and with one last
defeated howl of wind, and he saw icicles under the shack's eaves like
yard-long teeth, and the wind stopped, the noises fell, the light through
his sticky eyelids darkened, his nostrils filled with smells of mice,
kerosene, sheepskins, ham rind, sardines, and a delirious tropical odor

of cinnamon and cloves like his mother's spice cupboard, and someone steered him and turned him and pushed on his shoulders, and Ray Henry's whisper said, "OK, kid, take a load off your feet." He felt safety with his very buttocks as he eased himself down on the rustly hay-stuffed tick of a bunk.

Later he sat with his aching feet in a dishpan of snow and water, and when the pain in his hands swelled until it seemed the fingers would split like sausages, he stooped and numbed the ache into bearability in the same dishpan. His eyes were inflamed and sore; in each cheek a spot throbbed with such violence that he thought the pulse must be visible in the skin like a twitching nerve. His ears were swollen red-hot fungi, his nose that had run and drooled incontinently all the way through the blizzard was now so stuffed and swollen that he gurgled for air. He knew how he looked by looking at Little Horn, who had got wet to the knees when the Clydes went through the rapid, and who sat now on an apple box with first one foot and then the other in a bucket of snow. Little Horn's skin showed like a flaming sun-burn through his reddish beard. He had innocent blue eyes like Jesse's, and the same blunt chin. When he was twenty years older he would look a good deal like Jesse—they were members of the same tribe. Now he lifted one tallowy foot from the deep snowprint in the pail and set it tenderly on the floor and lifted the other into its place, and looked across at Rusty with his mild ironic eye and shook his head in acknowl-edgment of something.

Ray and Jesse were squatting by the bunk against the side wall where Spurlock lay. Each had a blotched foot in his hands, each was mas-saging it and sousing it with snow. At the head of the bunk Buck worked on Spurlock's hands. Spurlock's fiery face looked straight upward; his teeth were set; he said nothing. Back by the door Slip and Panguingue had just finished washing each other's faces with snow. All of them, emerged from their cumbersome wrappings, looked disheveled as corpses dredged from a river. Rusty marveled at their bony hairless feet, their red hands, their vulnerable throats. They were making a good deal of talkative noise, their skins were full of the happiness of rescue, and not yet quite full of pain.

Little Horn looked at Panguingue's wet face. He said to Rusty, "Ain't that the way it goes? Of all the people that might of froze their feet and got a good wash out of it, who is the one God damn boy in the outfit without even a frozen toe but old Pan?"

Jesse said from the end of Spurlock's bunk, "Cold couldn't get through that crust."

"B.S.," Panguingue said. "I'm just tougher than you. And besides, I froze my face damn good."

"Snow washed some of the protective layer off," Little Horn said. "No, more I think of it, more I think you shouldn't make any mistake and wash them feet till spring, Pan. We'll need somebody around to do the chores while we get well."

"Hey, by God," Panguingue said. "How about my face?"

"Just leave it go. A little proud flesh would improve it."

"B.S.," said Slip, in imitation of Panguingue's growl, and he and Panguingue threatened each other with pans of snow. From the other bunk Ray Henry said, "Feelin' 'em yet?"

"You're damn right," Ed Spurlock said through his teeth.

"Better let 'em set in the water for a while," Ray said. "The slower they come back the better." He stood up, looking at Rusty. "Rusty, you needin' that dishpan for a while?"

"No, take it." He moved his feet carefully out onto the dirty board floor, and the foreman shoved the pan under Spurlock's dangling feet. Standing over Rusty, burly, matted-haired, grave-eyed, totally enigmatic to the boy but restored to his position of authority and respect, he said, "How you doin'? Feelin' yours?"

"Enough," Rusty said. He raised his head a little. "What's the cure for frostbite?"

"Whiskey," Jesse said from beside Spurlock.

"Fine," said Little Horn. "Just what we ain't got."

"If we had some rocks we could have some rock and rye," Slip said. "If we had some rye."

"No particular cure," Ray said to Rusty. "Thaw it out slow, keep away from heat, little arnica if you get sores, cut it out if you get gangrene. And wait."

"How long?"

"Depends how bad you are. You and Little Horn, maybe a week, ten days. Ed maybe two-three weeks. It's the hands and feet that lay you up."

"What do we do, stay here till we're well?"

"I expect we'll cobble up that tongue and beat it for the ranch soon as it clears off."

"Vacation with pay," Little Horn said. "Peach pies. Whiskey every hour, while Panguingue does the chores. I tell you, Rusty, there's no life like a cowboy's."

But Rusty was thinking of the two weeks they had just gone through, and of the cattle that had gone streaming miserably downwind from the Horse Camp corrals, the gaunt exhausted horses that had hung around the tent and wagon until the wind literally blew them away. "What about the calves?" he asked. "And what about the horses?"

"Horses we'll have to round up, some of them anyway. They'll winter out all right, but we need work ponies."

"You mean—ride out there and hunt through all that country and drive them on back to the ranch?"

"Uh-huh."

"I tell you," Little Horn said, and lifted his left foot out of the bucket and raised his right tenderly in, "there's no business like the cow business to make a man healthy and active. There's hardly a job you can work at that'll keep you more in the open air."

Rusty smelled the coffee that Jesse had put on the fire as soon as he got it going. He saw the flaw of moisture the spout cast on the stovepipe, and he moved his pain-distended hands cautiously, cradling them in his lap. The shack's growing warmth burned in his cheeks. Over on the other side of the stove Slippers' face, purple in the bare patches, black where the beard grew, brooded with its eyes on the floor. This was the leathery little man who would ride out to bring the ponies back across sixty miles of rough country. And maybe one or two others—maybe himself—with him. The very notion, at that moment, moved the boy to something like awe.

"What about the calves?" he said.

For the first time expression—disgust? anger? ironic resignation?— flickered across Ray's chapped, bearded mouth. "The calves. Well, the ones that ain't dead by the time this one blows out may find some willows to gnaw in a coulee, and if we get a chinook they'll have feed and come through all right. If we don't get a chinook the wolves are gonna be very fat by spring."

"But we aren't going to try rounding them up again."

Ray turned away with the flicker widening momentarily on his mouth. "I wouldn't worry about it," he said.

"Don't be impatient," Little Horn said, and hissed sharply as he moved his foot and bumped the pail. He set the heel on the floor and looked at the swollen toes, looked at his sausage-like fingers, shook his head. On the bunk Spurlock raised one foot from the dishpan. "Wait a minute," Jesse said. "Got enough of that footbath for a while?"

He helped the legs with their rolled-up pants to straighten out in the bunk. In the silence that came down as the pain of returning blood preoccupied them Rusty heard the undiminished wind shriek along the icicled eaves of the shack and swoop away. Smoke puffed out around the rings of the stove lids, lay there for a minute like fat white circular worms, and was sucked in again. Shaggy as cavemen, weatherbeaten and battered, they huddled back against the walls and away from the stove and contemplated each in his own way the discomforts of the outraged flesh. Each retired within his skinful of pain and weariness, and among them Rusty Cullen, as weary as any, as full of pain as any—pain enough to fill him to the chin and make him lock his jaw for fear of whimpering. He made note that none whimpered, not even Spurlock; the worst was an occasional querulous growl when one moved too fast. Jesse, the old-timer, the knowing one, Nestor and patriarch, unfrozen except for a touch on the fingers and ears, moved between them in stockinged feet and flipped the coffeepot lid with the edge of his palm, saving his tender fingertips, and looked in. The mystic smells of brotherhood were strong in the shack. The stove lids puffed out worms of smoke once more, and once more sucked them inward. The wind went over and around them, the ancient implacable wind, and tore away balked and shrill.

The Rusty Cullen who sat among them was a different boy, outside and inside, from the one who had set out with them two weeks before. He thought that he knew enough not to want to distinguish himself by heroic deeds: single-handed walks to the North Pole, incredible journeys, rescues, whatnot. Given his way, he did not think that he would ever want to do anything alone again, not in this country. Even a trip to the privy was something a man might want to take in company.

The notion insinuated itself into his head, not for the first time, that his sticking with Spurlock after Panguingue left was an act of special excellence, that the others must look upon him with a new respect because of it. But the tempting thought did not stand up under the examination he gave it. Special excellence? Why hadn't anyone praised him for it, then? He knew why: because it was what any of them would have done. To have done less would have been cowardice and disgrace. It was probably a step in the making of a cowhand when he learned that what would pass for heroics in a softer world was only chores around here.

Around him he heard the hiss of air drawn between clenched teeth, he saw the careful, excruciating slowness of hands and feet being moved in search of more comfortable positions, he saw and smelled and felt how he was indistinguishable from the other seven. His greenness did not show, was perhaps not quite so green as it had been. And he did not take it ill, but understood it as a muffled acceptance or acknowledgement, when Spurlock sniffed thickly and said to the sagging springs above his nose, "Is that coffee I smell, Jesse, or is it only fawncy?"

The Half-Skinned Steer
by Annie Proulx

Annie Proulx (born 1935) writes some of the sharpest, most surprising prose around. The people in her stories work their ways through difficult lives at the mercy of nature's powerful whims and each other's behavior, whether cruel or kind.

In the long unfurling of his life, from tight-wound kid hustler in a wool suit riding the train out of Cheyenne to geriatric limper in this spooled-out year, Mero had kicked down thoughts of the place where he began, a so-called ranch on strange ground at the south hinge of the Big Horns. He'd got himself out of there in 1936, had gone to a war and come back, married and married again (and again), made money in boilers and air-duct cleaning and smart investments, retired, got into local politics and out again without scandal, never circled back to see the old man and Rollo bankrupt and ruined because he knew they were.

They called it a ranch and it had been, but one day the old man said it was impossible to run cows in such tough country where they fell off cliffs, disappeared into sinkholes, gave up large numbers of calves to marauding lions, where hay couldn't grow but leafy spurge and Canada thistle throve, and the wind packed enough sand to scour windshields opaque. The old man wangled a job delivering

mail, but looked guilty fumbling bills into his neighbors' mail-
boxes.

Mero and Rollo saw the mail route as a defection from the work of
the ranch, work that fell on them. The breeding herd was down to
eighty-two and a cow wasn't worth more than fifteen dollars, but they
kept mending fence, whittling ears and scorching hides, hauling cows
out of mudholes and hunting lions in the hope that sooner or later the
old man would move to Ten Sleep with his woman and his bottle and
they could, as had their grandmother Olive when Jacob Corn disappointed her, pull the place taut. That bird didn't fly and Mero wound
up sixty years later as an octogenarian vegetarian widower pumping an
Exercycle in the living room of a colonial house in Woolfoot,
Massachusetts.

One of those damp mornings the nail-driving telephone voice of a
woman said she was Louise, Tick's wife, and summoned him back to
Wyoming. He didn't know who she was, who Tick was, until she said,
Tick Corn, your brother Rollo's son, and that Rollo had passed on,
killed by a waspy emu though prostate cancer was waiting its chance.
Yes, she said, you bet Rollo still owned the ranch. Half of it anyway. Me
and Tick, she said, we been pretty much running it the last ten years.

An emu? Did he hear right?

Yes, she said. Well, of course you didn't know. You heard of Down
Under Wyoming?

He had not. And thought, what kind of name was Tick? He recalled
the bloated gray insects pulled off the dogs. This tick probably thought
he was going to get the whole damn ranch and bloat up on it. He said,
what the hell was this about an emu? Were they all crazy out there?

That's what the ranch was now, she said, Down Under Wyoming.
Rollo'd sold the place way back when to the Girl Scouts, but one of the
girls was dragged off by a lion and the G.S.A. sold out to the Banner
ranch next door who ran cattle on it for a few years, then unloaded it
on a rich Australian businessman who started Down Under Wyoming
but it was too much long-distance work and he'd had bad luck with
his manager, a feller from Idaho with a pawnshop rodeo buckle, so

he'd looked up Rollo and offered to swap him a half-interest if he'd run the place. That was back in 1978. The place had done real well. Course we're not open now, she said, it's winter and there's no tourists. Poor Rollo was helping Tick move the emus to another building when one of them turned on a dime and come right for him with its big razor claws. Emus is bad for claws.

I know, he said. He watched the nature programs on television.

She shouted as though the telephone lines were down all across the country, Tick got your number off the computer. Rollo always said he was going to get in touch. He wanted you to see how things turned out. He tried to fight it off with his cane but it laid him open from belly to breakfast.

Maybe, he thought, things hadn't finished turning out. Impatient with this game, he said he would be at the funeral. No point talking about flights and meeting him at the airport, he told her, he didn't fly, a bad experience years ago with hail, the plane had looked like a waffle iron when it landed. He intended to drive. Of course he knew how far it was. Had a damn fine car, Cadillac, always drove Cadillacs, Gislaved tires, interstate highways, excellent driver, never had an accident in his life knock on wood, four days, he would be there by Saturday afternoon. He heard the amazement in her voice, knew she was plotting his age, figuring he had to be eighty-three, a year or so older than Rollo, figuring he must be dotting around on a cane too, drooling the tiny days away, she was probably touching her own faded hair. He flexed his muscular arms, bent his knees, thought he could dodge an emu. He would see his brother dropped in a red Wyoming hole. That event could jerk him back; the dazzled rope of lightning against the cloud is not the downward bolt, but the compelled upstroke through the heated ether.

He had pulled away at the sudden point when it seemed the old man's girlfriend—now he couldn't remember her name—had jumped the track, Rollo goggling at her bloody bitten fingers, nails chewed to the quick, neck veins like wires, the outer forearms shaded with hairs, and the cigarette glowing, smoke curling up, making her wink her bulged mustang eyes, a teller of tales of hard deeds and mayhem. The old man's hair was falling out, Mero was twenty-three and Rollo twenty and she played them all like a deck of cards. If you admired horses you'd go for her with her arched neck and horsy buttocks, so high and haunchy you'd want to clap her on the rear. The wind bellowed around the house, driving crystals of snow through the cracks of the warped log door and all of them in the kitchen seemed charged with some intensity of purpose. She'd balanced that broad butt on the edge of the dog food chest, looking at the old man and Rollo, now and then rolling her glossy eyes over at Mero, square teeth nipping a rim of nail, sucking the welling blood, drawing on her cigarette.

The old man drank his Everclear stirred with a peeled willow stick for the bitter taste. The image of him came sharp in Mero's mind as he stood at the hall closet contemplating his hats; should he bring one for the funeral? The old man had had the damnedest curl to his hat brim, a tight roll on the right where his doffing or donning hand gripped it and a wavering downslope on the left like a shed roof. You could recognize him two miles away. He wore it at the table listening to the woman's stories about Tin Head, steadily emptying his glass until he was nine-times-nine drunk, his gangstery face loosening, the crushed rodeo nose and scar-crossed eyebrows, the stub ear dissolving as he drank. Now he must be dead fifty years or more, buried in the mailman sweater.

The girlfriend started a story, yeah, there was this guy named Tin Head down around Dubois when my dad was a kid. Had a little ranch, some horses, cows, kids, a wife. But there was something funny about him. He had a metal plate in his head from falling down some cement steps.

Plenty of guys has them, said Rollo in a challenging way.

She shook her head. Not like his. His was made out of galvy and it eat at his brain.

The old man held up the bottle of Everclear, raised his eyebrows at her: Well, darlin?

She nodded, took the glass from him and knocked it back in one swallow. Oh, that's not gonna slow *me* down, she said.

Mero expected her to neigh.

So what then, said Rollo, picking at the horse shit under his boot heel. What about Tin Head and his galvanized skull-plate?

I heard it this way, she said. She held out her glass for another shot of Everclear and the old man poured it and she went on.

Mero had thrashed all that ancient night, dreamed of horse breeding or hoarse breathing, whether the act of sex or bloody, cutthroat gasps he didn't know. The next morning he woke up drenched in stinking sweat, looked at the ceiling and said aloud, it could go on like this for some time. He meant cows and weather as much as anything, and what might be his chances two or three states over in any direction. In Woolfoot, riding the Exercycle, he thought the truth was somewhat different: he'd wanted a woman of his own without scrounging the old man's leftovers.

What he wanted to know now, tires spanking the tar-filled road cracks and potholes, funeral homburg sliding on the backseat, was if Rollo had got the girlfriend away from the old man, thrown a saddle on her and ridden off into the sunset?

The interstate, crippled by orange pylons, forced traffic into single lanes, broke his expectation of making good time. His Cadillac, boxed between semis with hissing air brakes, snuffled huge rear tires, framed a looming Peterbilt in the back window. His thoughts clogged as if a comb working through his mind had stuck against a snarl. When the traffic eased and he tried to cover some ground the highway patrol pulled him over. The cop, a pimpled, mustached specimen with mismatched eyes, asked his name, where he was going. For the minute he couldn't think what he was doing there. The cop's tongue dapped at the scraggy mustache while he scribbled.

Funeral, he said suddenly. Going to my brother's funeral.

Well you take it easy, Gramps, or they'll be doing one for you.

You're a little polecat, aren't you, he said, staring at the ticket, at the pathetic handwriting, but the mustache was a mile gone, peeling through the traffic as Mero had peeled out of the ranch road that long time ago, squinting through the abraded windshield. He might have made a more graceful exit but urgency had struck him as a blow on the humerus sending a ringing jolt up the arm. He believed it was the horse-haunched woman leaning against the chest and Rollo fixed on her, the old man swilling Everclear and not noticing or, if noticing, not caring, that had worked in him like a key in an ignition. She had long gray-streaked braids, Rollo could use them for reins.

Yah, she said, in her low and convincing liar's voice. I'll tell you, on Tin Head's ranch things went wrong. Chickens changed color overnight, calves was born with three legs, his kids was piebald and his wife always crying for blue dishes. Tin Head never finished nothing he started, quit halfway through a job every time. Even his pants was half-buttoned so his wienie hung out. He was a mess with the galvy plate eating at his brain and his ranch and his family was a mess. But, she said. They had to eat, didn't they, just like anybody else?

I hope they eat pies better than the ones you make, said Rollo, who didn't like the mouthful of pits that came with the chokecherries.

His interest in women began a few days after the old man had said, take this guy up and show him them Indan drawings, jerking his head at the stranger. Mero had been eleven or twelve at the time, no older. They rode along the creek and put up a pair of mallards who flew downstream and then suddenly reappeared, pursued by a goshawk who struck the drake with a sound like a handclap. The duck tumbled through the trees and into deadfall trash and the hawk shot as swiftly away as it had come.

They climbed through the stony landscape, limestone beds eroded by wind into fantastic furniture, stale gnawed breadcrusts, tumbled bones, stacks of dirty folded blankets, bleached crab claws and dog teeth. He tethered the horses in the shade of a stand of limber pine and led the anthropologist up through the stiff-branched mountain mahogany to the overhang. Above them reared corroded cliffs brilliant with orange lichen, pitted with holes and ledges darkened by millennia of raptor feces.

The anthropologist moved back and forth scrutinizing the stone gallery of red and black drawings: bison skulls, a line of mountain sheep, warriors carrying lances, a turkey stepping into a snare, a stick man upside-down dead and falling, red ochre hands, violent figures with rakes on their heads that he said were feather headdresses, a great red bear dancing forward on its hind legs, concentric circles and crosses and latticework. He copied the drawings in his notebook, saying rubba-dubba a few times.

That's the sun, said the anthropologist who resembled an unfinished drawing himself, pointing at an archery target, ramming his pencil into the air as though tapping gnats. That's an atlatl and that's a dragonfly. There we go. You know what this is; and he touched a cloven oval, rubbing the cleft with his dusty fingers. He got down on his hands and knees, pointed out more, a few dozen.

A horseshoe?

A horseshoe! The anthropologist laughed. No boy, it's a vulva. That's what all of these are. You don't know what that is, do you? You go to school on Monday and look it up in the dictionary.

It's a symbol, he said. You know what a symbol is?

Yes, said Mero, who had seen them clapped together in the high school marching band. The anthropologist laughed and told him he had a great future, gave him a dollar for showing him the place. Listen, kid, the Indians did it just like anybody else, he said.

He had looked the word up in the school dictionary, slammed the book closed in embarrassment, but the image was fixed for him (with the brassy background sound of a military march), blunt ochre tracing on stone, and no fleshy examples ever conquered his belief in the subterranean stony structure of female genitalia, the pubic bone a proof, except for the old man's girlfriend whom he imagined down on all fours, entered from behind and whinnying like a mare, a thing not of geology but flesh.

Thursday night, balked by detours and construction, he was on the outskirts of Des Moines and no farther. In the cinderblock motel room he set the alarm but his own stertorous breathing woke him before it rang. He was up at five-fifteen, eyes aflame, peering through the vinyl drapes at his snow-hazed car flashing blue under the motel sign SLEEP SLEEP. In the bathroom he mixed the packet of instant motel coffee and drank it black without ersatz sugar or chemical cream. He wanted the caffeine. The roots of his mind felt withered and punky.

A cold morning, light snow slanting down: he unlocked the Cadillac, started it and curved into the vein of traffic, all semis, double- and triple-trailers. In the headlights' red glare he missed the westbound ramp and got into torn-up muddy streets, swung right and right again, using the motel's SLEEP sign as a landmark, but he was on the wrong side of the interstate and the sign belonged to a different motel.

Another mudholed lane took him into a traffic circle of commuters sucking coffee from insulated cups, pastries sliding on dashboards. Halfway around the hoop he spied the interstate entrance ramp, veered for it, collided with a panel truck emblazoned STOP SMOKING! HYPNOSIS THAT WORKS!, was rammed from behind by a stretch limo, the limo in its turn rear-ended by a yawning hydroblast operator in a company pickup.

He saw little of this, pressed into his seat by the air bag, his mouth full of a rubbery, dusty taste, eyeglasses cutting into his nose. His first thought was to blame Iowa and those who lived in it. There were a few round spots of blood on his shirt cuff.

A star-spangled Band-Aid over his nose, he watched his crumpled car, pouring dark fluids onto the highway, towed away behind a wrecker. A taxi took him, his suitcase, the homburg funeral hat, in the other direction to Posse Motors where lax salesmen drifted like disorbited satellites and where he bought a secondhand Cadillac, black like the wreck, but three years older and the upholstery not cream leather but sun-faded velour. He had the good tires from the wreck brought over and mounted. He could do that if he liked, buy cars like packs of cigarettes and smoke them up. He didn't care for the way it handled out on the highway, throwing itself abruptly aside when he twitched the wheel and he guessed it might have a bent frame. Damn, he'd buy another for the return trip. He could do what he wanted.

He was half an hour past Kearney, Nebraska, when the full moon rose, an absurd visage balanced in his rearview mirror, above it a curled wig of a cloud, filamented edges like platinum hairs. He felt his swollen nose, palped his chin, tender from the stun of the air bag. Before he slept that night he swallowed a glass of hot tap water enlivened with whiskey, crawled into the damp bed. He had eaten nothing all day yet his stomach coiled at the thought of road food.

He dreamed that he was in the ranch house but all the furniture had been removed from the rooms and in the yard troops in dirty white uniforms fought. The concussive reports of huge guns were breaking the window glass and forcing the floorboards apart so that he had to walk on the joists and below the disintegrating floors he saw galvanized tubs filled with dark, coagulated fluid.

On Saturday morning, with four hundred miles in front of him, he swallowed a few bites of scorched eggs, potatoes painted with canned *salsa verde*, a cup of yellow coffee, left no tip, got on the road. The food was not what he wanted. His breakfast habit was two glasses of mineral water, six cloves of garlic, a pear. The sky to the west hulked sullen, behind him smears of tinselly orange shot through with blinding streaks. The thick rim of sun bulged against the horizon.

He crossed the state line, hit Cheyenne for the second time in sixty years. There was neon, traffic and concrete, but he knew the place, a railroad town that had been up and down. That other time he had been painfully hungry, had gone into the restaurant in the Union Pacific station although he was not used to restaurants and ordered a steak, but when the woman brought it and he cut into the meat the blood spread across the white plate and he couldn't help it, he saw the beast, mouth agape in mute bawling, saw the comic aspects of his revulsion as well, a cattleman gone wrong.

Now he parked in front of a phone booth, locked the car although he stood only seven feet away, and telephoned the number Tick's wife had given him. The ruined car had had a phone. Her voice roared out of the earpiece.

We didn't hear so we wondered if you changed your mind.

No, he said, I'll be there late this afternoon. I'm in Cheyenne now.

The wind's blowing pretty hard. They're saying it could maybe snow. In the mountains. Her voice sounded doubtful.

I'll keep an eye on it, he said.

He was out of town and running north in a few minutes.

The country poured open on each side, reduced the Cadillac to a finger-snap. Nothing had changed, not a goddamn thing, the empty pale place and its roaring wind, the distant antelope as tiny as mice, landforms shaped true to the past. He felt himself slip back, the calm of eighty-three years sheeted off him like water, replaced by a young man's scalding anger at a fool world and the fools in it. What a damn hard time it had been to hit the road. You don't know what it was like, he told his ex-wives until they said they did know, he'd pounded it into their ears two hundred times, the poor youth on the street holding up a sign asking for work, and the job with the furnace man, *yatata yatata ya*. Thirty miles out of Cheyenne he saw the first billboard, DOWN UNDER WYOMING, *Western Fun the Western Way*, over a blown-up photograph of kangaroos hopping through the sagebrush and a blond child grinning in a manic imitation of pleasure. A diagonal banner warned, *Open May 31*.

So what, Rollo had said to the old man's girlfriend, what about that Mr. Tin Head? Looking at her, not just her face, but up and down, eyes moving over her like an iron over a shirt and the old man in his mailman's sweater and lopsided hat tasting his Everclear and not noticing or not caring, getting up every now and then to lurch onto the porch and water the weeds. When he left the room the tension ebbed and they were only ordinary people to whom nothing happened. Rollo looked away from the woman, leaned down to scratch the dog's ears, saying, Snarleyow Snapper, and the woman brought a dish to the sink and ran water on it, yawning. When the old man came back to his chair, the Everclear like sweet oil in his glass, glances resharpened and inflections of voice again carried complex messages.

Well well, she said, tossing her braids back, every year Tin Head butchers one of his steers, and that's what they'd eat all winter long, boiled, fried, smoked, fricasseed, burned and raw. So one time he's out there by the barn and he hits the steer a good one with the axe and it drops stun down. He ties up the back legs, hoists it up and sticks it, shoves the tub under to catch the blood. When it's bled out pretty good he lets it down and starts skinning it, starts with the head, cuts back of the poll down past the eye to the nose, peels the hide back. He don't cut the head off but keeps on skinning, dewclaws to hock up the inside of the thigh and then to the cod and down the middle of the belly to brisket to tail. Now he's ready to start siding, working that tough old skin off. But siding is hard work—(the old man nodded)—and he gets the hide off about halfway and starts thinking about dinner. So he leaves the steer half-skinned there on the ground and he goes into the kitchen, but first he cuts out the tongue which is his favorite dish all cooked up and eat cold with Mrs. Tin Head's mustard in a forget-me-not teacup. Sets it on the ground and goes in to dinner. Dinner is chicken and dumplins, one of them changed-color chickens started out white and ended up blue, yessir, blue as your old daddy's eyes.

She was a total liar. The old man's eyes were murk brown.

Onto the high plains sifted the fine snow, delicately clouding the air, a rare dust, beautiful, he thought, silk gauze, but there was muscle in the wind rocking the heavy car, a great pulsing artery of the jet stream swooping down from the sky to touch the earth. Plumes of smoke rose hundreds of feet into the air, elegant fountains and twisting snow devils, shapes of veiled Arab women and ghost riders dissolving in white fume. The snow snakes writhing across the asphalt straightened into rods. He was driving in a rushing river of cold whiteout foam. He could see nothing, trod on the brake, the wind buffeting the car, a bitter, hard-flung dust hissing over metal and glass. The car shuddered. And as suddenly as it had risen the wind dropped and the road was clear; he could see a long, empty mile.

How do you know when there's enough of anything? What trips the lever that snaps up the STOP sign? What electrical currents fizz and crackle in the brain to shape the decision to quit a place? He had listened to her damn story and the dice had rolled. For years he believed he had left without hard reason and suffered for it. But he'd learned from television nature programs that it had been time for him to find his own territory and his own woman. How many women were out there! He had married three or four of them and sampled plenty.

With the lapping subtlety of incoming tide the shape of the ranch began to gather in his mind; he could recall the intimate fences he'd made, taut wire and perfect corners, the draws and rock outcrops, the watercourse valley steepening, cliffs like bones with shreds of meat on them rising and rising, and the stream plunging suddenly underground, disappearing into subterranean darkness of blind fish, shooting out of the mountain ten miles west on a neighbor's place, but leaving their ranch some badland red country as dry as a cracker, steep canyons with high caves suited to lions. He and Rollo had shot two early in that winter close to the overhang with the painted vulvas. There were good caves up there from a lion's point of view.

He traveled against curdled sky. In the last sixty miles the snow began again. He climbed out of Buffalo. Pallid flakes as distant from each other as galaxies flew past, then more and in ten minutes he was crawling at twenty miles an hour, the windshield wipers thumping like a stick dragged down the stairs.

The light was falling out of the day when he reached the pass, the blunt mountains lost in snow, the greasy hairpin turns ahead. He drove slowly and steadily in a low gear; he had not forgotten how to drive a winter mountain. But the wind was up again, rocking and slapping the car, blotting out all but whipping snow and he was sweating with the anxiety of keeping to the road, dizzy with the altitude. Twelve more miles, sliding and buffeted, before he reached Ten Sleep where streetlights glowed in revolving circles like Van Gogh's sun. There had not been electricity when he left the place. In those days there were seventeen black, lightless miles between the town and the ranch, and now the long arch of years compressed into that distance. His headlights picked up a sign: 20 MILES TO DOWN UNDER WYOMING. Emus and bison leered above the letters.

He turned onto the snowy road marked with a single set of tracks, faint but still discernible, the heater fan whirring, the radio silent, all beyond the headlights blurred. Yet everything was as it had been, the shape of the road achingly familiar, sentinel rocks looming as they had in his youth. There was an eerie dream quality in seeing the deserted Farrier place leaning east as it had leaned sixty years ago, the Banner ranch gate, where the companionable tracks he had been following turned off, the gate ghostly in the snow but still flying its wrought-iron flag, unmarked by the injuries of weather, and the taut five-strand fences and dim shifting forms of cattle. Next would come the road to their ranch, a left-hand turn just over the crest of a rise. He was running now on the unmarked road through great darkness.

Winking at Rollo the girlfriend said, yes, she had said, yes sir, Tin Head eats half his dinner and then he has to take a little nap. After a while he wakes up again and goes outside stretching his arms and yawning, says, guess I'll finish skinning out that steer. But the steer ain't there. It's gone. Only the tongue, laying on the ground all covered with dirt and straw, and the tub of blood and the dog licking at it.

It was her voice that drew you in, that low, twangy voice, wouldn't matter if she was saying the alphabet, what you heard was the rustle of hay. She could make you smell the smoke from an unlit fire.

• • •

How could he not recognize the turnoff to the ranch? It was so clear and sharp in his mind: the dusty crimp of the corner, the low section where the snow drifted, the run where willows slapped the side of the truck. He went a mile, watching for it, but the turn didn't come up, then watched for the Bob Kitchen place two miles beyond, but the distance unrolled and there was nothing. He made a three-point turn and backtracked. Rollo must have given up the old entrance road, for it wasn't there. The Kitchen place was gone to fire or wind. If he didn't find the turn it was no great loss; back to Ten Sleep and scout a motel. But he hated to quit when he was close enough to spit, hated to retrace black miles on a bad night when he was maybe twenty minutes away from the ranch.

He drove very slowly, following his tracks, and the ranch entrance appeared on the right although the gate was gone and the sign down. That was why he'd missed it, that and a clump of sagebrush that obscured the gap.

He turned in, feeling a little triumph. But the road under the snow was rough and got rougher until he was bucking along over boulders and slanted rock and knew wherever he was it was not right.

He couldn't turn around on the narrow track and began backing gingerly, the window down, craning his stiff neck, staring into the redness cast by the taillights. The car's right rear tire rolled up over a boulder, slid and sank into a quaggy hole. The tires spun in the snow, but he got no purchase.

I'll sit here, he said aloud. I'll sit here until it's light and then walk down to the Banner place and ask for a cup of coffee. I'll be cold but I won't freeze to death. It played like a joke the way he imagined it with Bob Banner opening the door and saying, why, it's Mero, come on in and have some java and a hot biscuit, before he remembered that Bob Banner would have to be 120 years old to play that role. He was maybe three miles from Banner's gate, and the Banner ranch house was another seven miles beyond the gate. Say a ten-mile hike at altitude in a snowstorm. On the other hand he had half a tank of gas. He could run the car for a while, then turn it off, start it again all through the night. It was bad luck, but that's all. The trick was patience.

He dozed half an hour in the wind-rocked car, woke shivering and cramped. He wanted to lie down. He thought perhaps he could put a flat rock under the goddamn tire. Never say die, he said, feeling around the passenger-side floor for the flashlight in his emergency bag, then remembering the wrecked car towed away, the flares and car phone and AAA card and flashlight and matches and candle and Power Bars and bottle of water still in it, and probably now in the damn tow-driver's damn wife's car. He might get a good enough look anyway in the snow-reflected light. He put on his gloves and the heavy overcoat, got out and locked the car, sidled around to the rear, bent down. The taillights lit the snow beneath the rear of the car like a fresh bloodstain. There was a cradle-sized depression eaten out by the spinning tire. Two or three flat ones might get him out, or small round ones, he was not going to insist on the perfect stone. The wind tore at him, the snow was certainly drifting up. He began to shuffle on the road, feeling with his feet for rocks he could move, the car's even throbbing promising motion and escape. The wind was sharp and his ears ached. His wool cap was in the damn emergency bag.

My lord, she continued, Tin Head is just startled to pieces when he don't see that steer. He thinks somebody, some neighbor don't like him, plenty of them, come and stole it. He looks around for tire marks or footprints but there's nothing except old cow tracks. He puts his hand up to his eyes and stares away. Nothing in the north, the south, the east, but way over there in the west on the side of the mountain he sees something moving stiff and slow, stumbling along. It looks raw and it's got something bunchy and wet hanging down over its hindquarters. Yah, it was the steer, never making no sound. And just then it stops and it looks back. And all that distance Tin Head can see the raw meat of the head and the shoulder muscles and the empty mouth without no tongue open wide and its red eyes glaring at him, pure teetotal hate like arrows coming at him, and he knows he is done for and all of his kids and their kids is done for, and that his wife is done for and that every one of her blue dishes has got to break, and the dog that licked the blood is done for, and the house where they lived has to blow away or burn up and every fly or mouse in it.

There was a silence and she added, that's it. And it all went against him, too.

That's it? said Rollo. That's all there is to it?

Yet he knew he was on the ranch, he felt it and he knew this road, too. It was not the main ranch road but some lower entrance he could not quite recollect that cut in below the river. Now he remembered that the main entrance gate was on a side road that branched off well before the Banner place. He found a good stone, another, wondering which track this could be; the map of the ranch in his memory was not as bright now, but scuffed and obliterated as though trodden. The remembered gates collapsed, fences wavered, while the badland features swelled into massive prominence. The cliffs bulged into the sky, lions snarled, the river corkscrewed through a stone hole at a tremendous rate and boulders cascaded from the heights. Beyond the barbwire something moved.

He grasped the car door handle. It was locked. Inside, by the dashboard glow, he could see the gleam of the keys in the ignition where he'd left them to keep the car running. It was almost funny. He picked up a big two-handed rock and smashed it on the driver's-side window, slipped his arm in through the hole, into the delicious warmth of the car, a contortionist's reach, twisting behind the steering wheel and down, and had he not kept limber with exercise and nut cutlets and green leafy vegetables he never could have reached the keys. His fingers grazed and then grasped the keys and he had them. This is how they sort the men out from the boys, he said aloud. As his fingers closed on the keys he glanced at the passenger door. The lock button stood high. And even had it been locked as well, why had he strained to reach the keys when he had only to lift the lock button on the driver's side?

Cursing, he pulled out the rubber floor mats and arranged them over the stones, stumbled around the car once more. He was dizzy, tremendously thirsty and hungry, opened his mouth to snowflakes. He had eaten nothing for two days but the burned eggs that morning. He could eat a dozen burned eggs now.

The snow roared through the broken window He put the car in reverse and slowly trod the gas. The car lurched and steadied in the track and once more he was twisting his neck, backing in the red glare, twenty feet, thirty, but slipping and spinning; there was too much snow. He was backing up an incline that had seemed level on the way in but showed itself now as a remorselessly long hill studded with rocks and deep in snow. His incoming tracks twisted like rope. He forced out another twenty feet spinning the tires until they smoked, and the rear wheels slewed sideways off the track and into a two-foot ditch, the engine died and that was it. It was almost a relief to have reached this point where the celestial fingernails were poised to nip his thread. He dismissed the ten-mile distance to the Banner place: it might not be that far, or maybe they had pulled the ranch closer to the main road. A truck might come by. Shoes slipping, coat buttoned awry, he might find the mythical Grand Hotel in the sagebrush.

On the main road his tire tracks showed as a faint pattern in the pearly apricot light from the risen moon, winking behind roiling clouds of snow. His blurred shadow strengthened whenever the wind eased. Then the violent country showed itself, the cliffs rearing at the moon, the snow smoking off the prairie like steam, the white flank of the ranch slashed with fence cuts, the sagebrush glittering and along the creek black tangles of willow bunched like dead hair. There were cattle in the field beside the road, their plumed breaths catching the moony glow like comic strip dialogue balloons.

He walked against the wind, his shoes filled with snow, feeling as easy to tear as a man cut from paper. As he walked he noticed one from the herd inside the fence was keeping pace with him. He walked more slowly and the animal lagged. He stopped and turned. It stopped as well, huffing vapor, regarding him, a strip of snow on its back like a linen runner. It tossed its head and in the howling, wintry light he saw he'd been wrong again, that the half-skinned steer's red eye had been watching for him all this time.

from My Old Man and the Sea
by David Hays and
Daniel Hays

Father-and-son team David (born 1930) and Daniel Hays (born 1960) were the first Americans to round Cape Horn—known for its notorious weather—in a vessel less than 30 feet long. All told, the pair traveled for 317 days and 17,000 miles. This excerpt from their account of the voyage finds them in early December, leaving Easter Island and approaching their first encounter with the Horn.

Dan

Day 153. We are off in light winds. Tiger has grown the hair back on his nose. We don't know why it balded, but he looked like a baboon. Now it's thick, but still short. A crew-cut nose. Dad gives me a haircut and I ask for it shorter and shorter and now it's only a fuzz. He's upset and says I look like Haldeman.

Day 154. We see our first albatross today, bobbing in the water. Our bird book calls it a wandering albatross, and it has a wingspan of ten feet. That's two feet more than *Sparrow*'s width. It flew in, landed near us, and watched us with cold yellow eyes as we sailed slowly by.

Day 156. Tonight's the first night of Chanukah. The ocean is calm— too calm really. We're sort of drifting. Dad yells at the sails, then takes them down. Things clank and we roll. The menorah slides back and forth on the cabin table. We tape it down. We light two candles tonight. The cat walks across and briefly catches fire.

"Dad, do you think my descendants will someday tape the menorah, light the cat, and consider it an ancient ritual, origin lost in history?"

Gifts! Candy. A book of horror stories. Cookies. There will be gifts every night for eight nights. The last night is Christmas, and there are gifts for that too. Julia and Jack have wrapped and labeled each gift. The days are getting longer and soon there'll be only four hours of night and that will be only a sort of protracted dusk-dawn. Our afternoon task is waterproofing mittens. I bought a compound that you squeeze into the seams.

I have no companions to be drunk with and talk to about girls. It's 5:00 a.m. and dads just don't work for every sort of conversation, you know. Fiery red sunrise and no wind, sails swilling about and the cat on his morning space-cadet romp—leaping at nothings and chewing ghosts. Today I pulled out the chart of Port Stanley in the Falklands. We'll be going there once we get around The Horn. It has a beautiful bottleneck harbor, which means it must be a safe anchorage indeed. However, the "sailing directions" caution the tourist about "many thousands of unexploded land mines in the vicinity." They also say that the holding ground (that's the harbor bottom) is so good that boats are often unable to retrieve their anchors.

Day 158. It's pouring rain. We hide below, checking the steering every half-hour or so. We sail 121 miles today.

Day 159. The barometer has fallen from 1026 to 1012 in twenty-four hours. That's bad. The sky is not normal, and the waves are bigger than they should be in this wind. I am eager and afraid. I've never been in what's called a "Roaring Forties" gale. *Sparrow* is jumping along. Dad is asleep below, and I just put on the #2 red jib. I thought of putting up the #1, which is bigger, but am glad I didn't because we are almost rail under. The wind gusts Force 6 and I may soon take in a reef.

Once upon a time sailors could not look at the digital LED readouts in their cockpits or go below to check the wind speed from a dial. Imagine! They relied on what they saw and the pitch of the windsong through the rigging or their hair. So they invented the *Beaufort scale* for clarity. It's not much different than the way Dad and I talk about the weather.

"What's it like out?"

"Windy."

"Extremely windy?"

"Very fucking windy."

The Beaufort scale goes from 0 to 12, with 0 being a calm, smooth, mirror-like sea. These twelve conditions are referred to as "Forces," and a Force 12 is a hurricane. The descriptions are visual, not digital. Force 4 is a "moderate breeze, small waves, becoming longer; fairly frequent white horses." At Force 5, a "fresh breeze" we are told that a "fishing smack . . . shortens sail." (Dad always says that a Force 6 is just a Force 5 blowing against the way you want to go.) Around Force 8 you begin to feel anxious, and "foam is blown in well-defined streaks with the wind." I've never been at sea in anything near Force 10, the official description of which calls for twenty-nine-foot waves where "the tumbling of the sea becomes heavy and shocklike . . . the whole surface of the sea takes a white appearance." In other words, "extremely fucking windy," which sounds like "ydniw gnikcuf ylemertxe" as the words are blown back down your throat.

Day 160. Even floating in this remote part of the earth cut off from input except the news, I am happy to say that "The Larry King Show," whatever that is, thoroughly bores me and I cannot endure it for more than five minutes. I prefer the squeaking of the self-steerer—I could oil it and then there would only be the ripples of the water along the hull and creaking rigging, but I like the squeak. Sure beats Larry.

Day 161. Half the stars fade into haze, which fades into the gray sea, which is illuminated by coin-shaped reflections trailing in the wake.

The wind comes in gentle puffs causing the ghoster to flap, sending vibrations through the mast and then on through the whole boat to the water for any sea creature to feel. I sit crouched in a glow of soft red light from the compass, huddled under a canvas hood, which protects me from the cool gusts of wind. Sometimes they reach me and send chills down my spine. Gently *Sparrow* rocks from side to side, interrupted by soft lurches forward. I am surrounded by time and feel it stretching in all directions.

Day 163. It's Christmas morning now and I can tell I've matured since I was four because I'm letting Dad sleep late, even though I can see the bag of presents stowed forward with the sails. Christmas officially began at midnight when Dad woke me up with burnt popcorn. I have a squirt gun for him. But there isn't really a Christmas spirit. We can stick cloves in an orange and make eggnog, but there are no cars stuck in the snow. We've been at sea ten days and we may have twenty to go. Soon, we'll be in the Roaring Forties (latitudes 40° to 50° south). If you look at a globe you'll see there are no *continents* around the whole world here. The waves tend to get humongous with no beaches to eat them up.

I am eager to get past Cape Horn. It's gotten in the way of thinking of the future, because it seems to me that The Horn's comment on the whole question of my future is, "Maybe not." Dad says I'm going to brag about our passage to everyone; I accuse him of planning to be more sly about it, saving it for casual mentions that produce more effect. I think his ego is larger, but on second thought cannot imagine how it could be. I'm going to accidentally wake him soon, so we can open presents. Should I spill coffee or drop Tiger on him? Things always fall on him anyway, so he won't be suspicious. Books escape from the shelf and hit him, his pants fall off the rack and land on his supper, and once the jam cabinet over his head opened and a pepper shaker hit him on the ear.

Day 164. *Lust.* On the eighth night of Chanukah I got a *Sports Illustrated Bathing Suit Calendar*, which is just one notch below *Playboy*. I looked at each picture twice, then one by one peeled them off and threw them into the sea around latitude 39° 49′ south, longitude 99° 50′ west. Truly I would be a great monk, creating situations over which to suffer and thereby create meaning. (I can't believe I didn't save one page!)

We've been out eleven days now and haven't been in any awful weather. I want to see some *seas!* Yesterday it rained and I took a shower. It was light rain and the wind was cold and I shivered, clinging to the mast, catching each drop that slid down the sail and along the boom toward me. With almost no hair on my head, that part is easy, but as soon as my crotch and armpits got soapy the rain stopped, and I had to wait, trembling, for another spray of precious fresh water. I was cold and very alive, my skin tight and strong. I cuddled into my still-clean sleeping bag (I've been sleeping on top with a blanket) and was ecstatic. My pruned feet dried in their own heat. Then clean clothes and, damn I feel good. My life is ruled by clean clothes—I will be happy for two days and then, as my clothes get clammy again, that will fade.

> Dear Mom,
> Christmas was awful. A big wave disrupted the crèche I'd set up in the fo'c'sle, causing a twelve-foot plaster giraffe to knock over the Virgin and two kings. Dad says the crèche isn't very Jewish, so I shouldn't tell you. Now it's midnight and I'm having my own mass—of course, using the menorah to hold the altar candles. When I get home I may change my name to Winslow III. All we did today was eat sugar: an entire box of cookies, the contents of the socks (ninety-two jelly beans, two chocolate soldiers, and twenty-two sesame-honey things), all eaten. The sugar shock was intense, and we drifted for hours unable to tend the ship.
> Love, Dan

David

The literary news from down under was that at last, after ten or twelve starts that always held me past the "sleep section" but no farther, I finally hooked into *Swann's Way* and was rapturously involved. I knew that someday I'd make it. To amuse ourselves we invented holidays. The first was National Clamp Week. Then it became Rotten Fruit Week.

Of course there were real holidays too. One of the more precious gifts that came with Leonora was a cassette from our dear friends the Bicks and Lorin families. Besides a medley of favorite songs and recorded messages from other friends, there was a long segment of navigation advice by these fellow sailors. The problem was that their atlas had no proper scale, so they could only advise us that the Strait of Magellan was about three and one-half inches down and to the right of Easter Island. Worse, Easter Island's name was on their map but no outline or dot indicated a land mass. Since our cassette player could record, we started a tape to reply to them. Dan began with a report on Easter Island and stated the bad news that indeed there was no land mass, but we were leaving it anyway and you could just see, over the horizon, the tops of the letters *E* and *ST*. Then he described the crèche of full-sized saints and animals, carved in native lava, that we had bought there. The giraffe's neck had already broken, but we were stringing Christmas lights around it. Later, he said, we were pursued by natives in canoes who bartered for the crèche; we sold it just before Christmas, not wanting it to be remaindered. We were happy with the sale because they traded us multicolored beads, lengths of copper wire, and many small mirrors. Anyway, the front, or pointed, end of the boat, where we kept the crèche, had been tipped down about thirty degrees because of the extra weight and therefore we had not been sailing our fastest.

Our tape is full of sea noises—mostly a dull roar, because the sea is noisy. But in our spoof you hear a mad character, Dan, clumping about on deck on his leg. The thump is not too loud because he found a rubber tip for the ivory leg in an old Sperry Top-Sider catalog. He's got a spare, of course. We do a wild New Year's Eve party with hundreds of guests clinking their glasses and blowing horns, but the next morning we report sadly that upon arising and being seated for brunch, a glance toward the back, past the porch and veranda area outside, shows that our most backwards two masts, plus the afterguard and the ship's band, have been swept into the sea. That takes the heart out of our holiday decorating, but we continue—art for art's sake.

The cat was everywhere, and at once. Like the cursor on a computer screen, he showed us where to work. When it was time to reef the mainsail and change jibs, at change of watch, we were *all* on deck— Tiger snug in the dodger, curled around the main halyard winch. "Scat." While Dan was working on that sail I turned to prepare the jib halyard. Tiger had settled into the coils of line. "Off!" Back to the main halyard. "Away!" Then the jib again. "Avast, dammit! " Now to ease the sheet. But why bother to locate the cleat? Just look for the cat. When we went forward while clipped to our lifelines, Tiger was always on the narrow deck, and had to be dribbled forward in soccer style. Coming aft, we'd do arabesques to clear the tether from between our legs, the little ballet ending, with a squeal, on guess who?

So we were crowded with cat. And so was the compass. When a boat is below the equator the compass card, which rotates on a needle-sharp pivot in a glass globe full of fluid, is pulled down and rubs against its bed as the magnet points down *through the earth* toward north. We phoned the manufacturer, Danforth, from Easter Island, and they were surprised that we didn't know all about that, though their literature doesn't mention it, nor do the standard texts I've read over the years. The knowledge just wasn't in our DNA, I suggested. The man, who was kind and patient, explained that our compass was balanced for, well, Connecticut and nearby. We'd have to take it apart and replace the little weights that balance the card. We had two other compasses, but this was the main steering compass, carefully adjusted. Dan set to work on a towel on our tiny table, in the rolly anchorage at Hanga Roa. I played surgical nurse. The trick was to keep all the fluid so that when we reassembled the bowl there wouldn't be an annoying bubble on top. If we lost fluid, we could temporarily supplement it with gin or kerosene, first checking for clotting. But I've seen a compass treated that way by Hum Barton, and the gin ate off the compass paint, and so it snowed like one of those snow-globe souvenirs, a blizzard above a blank card. I believe that there is no word in our language for those Statue of Liberty–type snow globes. The operation succeeded. A sawed-in-half brass washer was glued on to re-weight the delicately suspended card. Hardly a drop of fluid was lost, and after a day of burping the instrument, there was not even the tiniest bubble in the globe. But—and here's what I'm coming at—there was a cat hair in the compass bowl. Long may it float.

Dan

Day 166. We are now in the Roaring Forties. They haven't even hummed yet, but I can feel a certain shiftiness about us like they don't care how much sleep I get. I am still in bare feet though my toes are numb. It would be admitting it's cold if I put on boots. Sailing in "shorts weather" is so easy compared to cold and rain. I always hope the night will be gentle and that I can watch it from the safety of the cockpit. But it is exhilarating to go forward in darkness and know exactly where everything is and how it should be.

I'm scared that when I return all my friends will say, "Dan, Dan who?" It's 0330 and I'm snuggled tight trying to be a ball and save heat. The purpose is to keep the heart beating in the body, on the boat, in the ocean. I like it when things are so miserable that I see that. It is more vital to be concerned about what to do not to die than what to do to "have the best time."

We are trying out a voyaging trick—our cabin floor is a knee-high sea of wadded-up newspaper. It keeps the floor and our feet dry, and when wads get soggy where we come down from deck, we just throw out a few and replace them. It's a snowy landscape and not as ugly as it sounds. Tiger loves it. He burrows and we see wads rippling to trace his course like a mole in a garden. Or he suddenly leaps into sight from nowhere and this is startling. Most of the time he just whacks at the wads from the berths. His head sticks out above the wad level when he squats on his litter pan, and he look silly-dignified as if he were in a bubble bath.

Day 167. First gale—zooming along at six knots under just the storm jib and triple-reefed main. During gusts we take water on the foredeck. It's cool—fifty-five degrees—and clear. The Milky Way is overhead, full of its light dust; all around are pockets of dark clouds reaching down to the water. The stars go *right* down to the horizon where, "snap," they go out, over the edge. You usually don't see that, except perhaps in a desert. Clouds are skittering along quickly—the wind is Force 7 and 8 in gusts. I am eager for dawn, to view the increasing seas. I feel safe and secure tethered to *Sparrow* and in my foul-weather gear.

Day 169.

Dear Mom,
Dad's forgetful. If something is missing, it's under the cat. If something is lost, Dad had it last. He finds his glasses on his head and his socks on his feet but otherwise he doesn't find things at all. I wear a name tag now, "Hello, my name is Daniel," and there's a big sign saying BATHROOM to help him out. The seas got big today and are foam-curled. About every two hours, chance will have it that one breaks on board—a loud crash followed by roaring as the water finds its way off. These waves usually catch one of us who will have peered out at just that particular moment. Dad calls this "Wave-Sailor Syndrome." Sometimes we'll hear the crash, then there will be an orange streak of Tiger shooting below, like a billiard ball. He bounces off two or three surfaces, disappearing in a side locker to emerge cautiously looking like a plucked chicken . . .
Love, Dan

I will describe peeing: first, you're below and it's wet on deck, so you decide to use the toilet, but keep waiting because you've drunk too much coffee and peed just six minutes ago. Finally, you can't wait any longer: you get up, then fall on the sleeping off-watch crew (Dad). You quickly get off and say, "Bad cat!" You stagger forward, accidentally lunging for the towel shelf and pulling all the towels and washcloths to the floor. Fix towel shelf. Say, "Bad cat!" to cover the noise. Now you gotta pee real bad. Brace yourself over the toilet, yank down your foul-weather-gear pants, which pin your legs together so you can't balance, then pick up lid and start peeing. The boat lunges and you fall backward, leaving a stripe of pee (which because of the motion hangs in the air a moment longer than is comprehensible) from the toilet up to the hatch, about three feet, over wall and woodwork. Of course, since you're falling, you can't work your "stop peeing" muscle, so you squeeze the end of your thingy and keep the pee in by sheer pinching pressure. You straighten up and tighten that muscle, which of course builds up just a tad too much pressure as you fall forward, so a thin squirt escapes at an odd angle—you try aiming for the bowl, but the lid just slammed shut, nearly biting off your thing, so you pee on the lid, and maybe put your hand in it to stop yourself from hitting your head on the cabin top (which you do anyway). Of course, which hand did you use? Exactly, so the rest of what's been waiting (between the pinched muscle and the pinched fingertips) dribbles down your leg onto the cat who is, as always, underneath you. Repeat steps 2–6. Dad says I'm so macho that I'll think he's a pervert if he suggests that I could simply sit on the toilet.

It's cold now—we're as far south as the bottom third of Canada is north and to sit on deck you need shirts, a sweater, jacket, foul-weather gear, and gloves because the air is very wet. Big waves seem to acknowledge just how isolated we are. Sixteen days and not a boat, jet trail, or any other sign of *civilization*.

Soon we have to keep an eye out for icebergs. I want to see one, penguin-covered. Seabirds have been with us constantly now, albatross and petrels—it's hard to imagine what a bird is doing a thousand miles out. Could the fishing be better out here? Anyway, they are good company, soaring in long swoops with wings an inch over the waves. Tiger sleeps on my head and I awake as he stretches and claws rows on my scalp. We go "jogging" each morning as the sun rises— we growl at each other and the winner is whoever runs fastest around the "jogging track" to bite the other. At night I write love letters to old, probably married-by-now girlfriends. Being a tragic romantic is great, but it's done alone and I have to remind people about me so they'll worry.

Day 171. Dad wakes long enough to pee in the rubber hot-water bottle and then he puts it down by his feet to keep his toes warm. He learned this when he studied in England. "Very British," he says, then continues snoring.

Day 174. Near gale, I write from inside my shell of plastic, which keeps the heat in. Rain and spray all over. The wind noise is intense, but I find some peace in writing. My hands are lost in big red-and-blue mittens, my body in yellow nylon, and my feet in black rubber. Looking out, my sight is framed by a plastic hood.

> Dear Kim,
> Hi again. It's galing outside and feels especially lonely. It's January 5 and we are about 450 miles from Cape Horn with about 1,000 miles to go before the Falklands. The wind blows the foam off the top of the waves in white streaks. Visibility is only a few feet 'cause of the spray—waves are long and there is a roaring in the rigging. My foul-weather gear leaks, but it keeps the wind out. It's a long watch and I'm tired, wet. I feel like flat soda poured on laundry . . . It's neat looking at the charts and seeing how close we are to The Horn. Finally, we're done with the chart that shows *all* of South America and onto one that is more detailed, more local. Tomorrow, we might even get onto Chart No. 32022

where there are 10 miles to an inch instead of 60. It indicates strong currents—at one point, up to eight knots (9
mph, a lot)—and the chart actually shows a symbol for
tide rip, but at eight knots, I call it a *tide roar*. Can you
imagine a chart with waves drawn permanently on it? First
one I've seen. *Sparrow* has a small flock of birds in tow. . . .
I've been very morbid, death thinking, and am so angry at
Dad who's getting old, and I can't accept it and love him.
Instead, I give him shit. . . . He can give it back, and sometimes that makes me feel better.
"Dad, which comes first, November or October?"
(pause)
"Well, Dan, you'll just have to start with January. Work it
out, dimwit."
"Just testing, Dad."
It's getting worse out, the barometer is falling and it's
raining. Seas are big and scary. The cat is oblivious, cleaning
himself on my chest. He's an excellent cat. Dad quotes his
father's formula for wave height: observed height divided by
two equals exact height.
Love, Dan

Day 175. Dawn, three hundred miles west of Cape Horn. Full moon
and angry oceans. When you think of these waves, imagine a big, green
Mack truck skidding at you sideways, with fifty bathtub loads of
shaving cream on top. *Sparrow* bobs right over them. Last night, in a
three-hour Force 8, a big wave whomped us, filling the cockpit and
finding leaks not yet tested. We've screwed boards over the portholes
and have all sorts of lids, caps, and cloths lashed-to, stuffed-in, and
wadded-around vents, chimneys, and deck fittings.

Icebergs! Hitting an iceberg in a gale is what I fear. One reason Cape
Horn is so feared is that the gales are usually westerly. If you want to
go west, against them, you must fight for every mile. Captain Bligh
spent thirty-one days in a gale, going just eighty-five miles, said, "Forget

this!" turned tall (probably seasick and depressed), and went *all the way around the world* to get to Tahiti. At least we're going east. The gales are with us. Right now the roaring in the rigging is like the soundtrack from a bad dream. Even if you're moving well, it's unsettling. I imagine falling over and freezing. The water temperature is fifty degrees or less, so quickly numbing. You cannot sail to windward in a real blow—right angles to the wind is about the best you can do. I discovered this trying to recover a sail bag. Dad was changing jibs, and before he could smother the empty bag and stuff it below, it filled with wind with a bang like a pistol shot and almost yanked off his arm.

A troop of porpoises—around twenty-five—races with us. From the top of the waves, they leap eight feet in the air. I can see them in the water in the wave crests above us, silhouetted against the sky. They're called Chilean dolphins and are not supposed to be this far offshore.

Sleeping is hard, everything rattles and things fall on you (cats, books, clothes, Dads, pens, toys, flashlights, chopsticks, bowls, crackers—or everything from the spice rack, which escapes together and for no known reason). Exhaustion finally does it, but by then it's time to get up. Dad keeps clothes in the jam cupboard over his head so the jars won't rattle. The weather here is fast to change. I begin my watch at midnight, all bundles with my big furry hat almost covering my eyes, wearing thick mittens and baggy pants. Now it's short sleeves and bright at 0600. Although the temperature range here is like a northern Canadian summer, in the fifties and sixties, the wind is so strong that fifty degrees can feel freezing cold.

David

Sometimes I felt like a marionette badly operated. Around my neck was a loop of string that was pinned to my hat to keep it from blowing away. Another loop kept my reading glasses in place. To keep myself on board I wore a tether harness—a buckle-and-strap affair like a parachute harness—with a metal ring in the middle of my chest. The tether is a strap that attaches to this ring, about eight feet long, with a snap at the end that I could hook on to anything. All the straps and strings snagged on everything. The main difference in my mobility on this voyage compared to my others was my damned glasses. After eight years I still couldn't get used to them and they steamed up or fell off, particularly when I was working on something upside down, which one often does on a boat.

I was never sure if Dan used the tether when he went forward at night. He said he did, but I didn't always hear the metal snap dragging along the deck as he pulled it behind him, clipped to a line that ran along the deck from stern to bow. I would try to avoid imagining coming on deck in the morning to find it empty. What would have happened to him is not the worst of ends, and I've envisioned myself there too, just staying afloat as long as possible, perhaps seeing the boat try to return, but too far off. But if I were on deck, searching the waters for him, those few last hours of my own life are unimaginable. And if I were in the water, seeing the boat at a distance, Dan frantic on the spreaders, would he be shaking uncontrollably too? We've talked about this. Whatever I do, he has promised not to follow me over if I'm lost. (The problem of a two-person voyage: only one witness.) After his dog's death, he spoke of his fear that I would die during the voyage, at sea.

"I see you there, Dad, cold, what do I do?"

"Well, Dan, you take off any clothing that's useful and my wrist-watch and you roll me in and keep sailing and you know that I died doing exactly what I wanted to do and in company I love."

Damn this age business. I believe in fairy tales, and a child's need for the bloody ones too, but I wish the image of parents, like Hansel and Gretel's mother and father, wasn't always white-haired folk bent over with canes. Parents aren't like that anymore. Still, despite his annoyance at my absent-mindedness, Dan had instinctive faith in my constant presence, the knowledge that the father has always been there and will be there. He didn't wake at night in a panic that I might not be on board. For me it was the reverse. He was on this planet because of me, and I was here when he wasn't. I saw the thread broken—I imagined coming on deck and him gone.

My father had his first heart attack when he was fifty-five. My older brother had his two years before our voyage, at fifty-five. Now, at fifty-four, I didn't have the symptoms or conditions they both had. But I ran down that dock in Jamaica and jumped on *Sparrow* and yelled, "I'm safe" because at sea I always feel too alive for any of that.

I recall frightening my father when I was small. We were at a resort. I remember cabins and a lake. I became the companion of an older boy who sported the wisdom and skill of a six-year-old. There was a match-to-a-pile-of-leaves incident that won punishment for him—I was deemed incompetent and earned only a rebuke. But one day we really brought the world down on us. He jumped into a rowboat at the lake's edge, called, "Come on," and in I went. He sat at the oars and pulled manfully away from the sandy edge. I sat in the stern, and soon became aware of shouts on the fading shore. I remember clearly even now how small the people looked. I remember being unable to gather meaning from the shouts, and I waved back. I saw my father run down the beach and dive in. He had a superb physique and had been a competitive swimmer at Columbia. He swam mightily toward us, and as he gained, my captain at the oars pulled harder. Perhaps the race was only a minute, only a hundred feet, but it was miles to me, and I still remember it when I see the Australian crawl done well. Dad came churning on and was within three feet of the boat. I reached out to grasp his hand, happy that he wanted to be with us. He lunged and grabbed the transom with one hand and with the other he swung in a wide arc and slapped me so hard that I flew into the bottom of the boat. Dripping, he stepped over me, brushed aside the other boy, and rowed in. I was too stunned to cry, and lay where I had landed. I remember nothing else about this except a sharp and sudden understanding two or three years later. I was never struck again.

I thought of my father on those long dusks, as we made our southing. At the equator the sun dropped straight down, here it slid and slipped sideways into the sea, and it was never far above or below the horizon. The nights were short, and a few hundred miles south of The Horn, the sun doesn't set at all in the Antarctic summer. But there is a time, sunset, when I believe that fear grips a sailor. Not before sunup, when we are comfortable with the dark, closed in to our little circle, perhaps to the glow of one lamp turned low that keeps the damp from a tight cabin. What chills me, this moment of fear, is the time just after the sun has gone. Ashore it can be soft—"The hour of twilight, when voices bloom," Carson McCullers wrote—but here when the top edge of the friendly sun goes under the clean horizon rim, the scale suddenly shifts. The weather clouds become ominous, and the ocean is achingly vast.

My last sight of my father was near a curiously symmetrical spot on the ocean, latitude 23° 50′ north, longitude 23° 50′ west. I noticed the symmetry when I thumbed through my old sea journals, preparing for this voyage. It's in the North Atlantic, not far from the Canary Islands, and Columbus was near that place when he wrote that he missed the spring in Andalusia and the call of birds. Often, still, I hear my father's voice, but I saw him clearly only that one night, in the spring of 1963, seven months after he died. One of the last times I'd heard his voice, he spoke into my bad ear, and I'd told him crossly to move to the other side. He died in a Connecticut hospital late at night on the last day of September. My brother was there. We were waiting in an alcove painted dull green. The last thing Dad said to me that afternoon was that he was proud of me. He said a few other things that were not clear, but I knew what they were because he'd said them more clearly in his sleep during a week that I'd slept in the room with him at home. It was an apology for a stupid error he'd made during a sailing race that we could have won, and it touches me now because I think I understand that through this trivial means he was trying to say he was sorry for all the wrongs he may have done to his boys. Maybe he felt guilty because we worshiped him as a perfect man.

My father's doctor had gone home. The nurse came into the alcove and whispered something to my brother. He is a physician himself, and walked the way doctors do—he didn't run to the room—and I stood with Leonora outside. We heard the squeakings and plungings and gaspings but the heart didn't restart and after a long time my brother came out and embraced me. We went in and my father's mouth was gaping, open more than in sleep. He didn't look dead to me, he looked beaten, defeated. That was the shock, because in our years he'd never been defeated in all the things he did for us, in getting us all the things we wanted. His head was back on the pillow, his mouth agape, and I asked the nurse to close his mouth and we drove home to get my mother, but when she came into the room with us, it was still open. He was smaller and grayer, but all I really saw was the grotesque open mouth. I remember my mother's hands, with white skeletal knuckles clenched on the railing of the bed, and four days later on the coffin edge until I uncurled her fingers one by one. She said, "Hold on," and then she said, "I can't hold on any longer, can I?" And I said, "No, Mom, not that way."

But my father didn't begin to talk to me again until that next spring when we were lashed out to sea by a gale off Finisterre. My shipmate Marvin March and I sat below, with paperbacks in hand, but our eyes, like those of all sailors in wooden boats, were fixed on the seam between cabin and deck where the sea, hitting like hard-thrown scoops of gravel, might burst in. The wind screamed a full octave that night, and the wedges bracing the mast started to whine in the voice of Dad, speaking in his sleep. He said, only once but clearly, "Relax, boy." Dan was at home then, three years old.

A third crew member, Ed Bigelow, joined us in Vigo and soon we were westing past the Canaries. Before one midnight watch, I knew from a troubled sleep and the way a wooden ship groans that we must take in sail. When I went on deck three combers surged past our beautiful *Rose of York* and swept her forward in a foam of frightening sea white. Stars seemed below us as we flew from wavetop to wavetop. I asked Eddie to keep her steady and went forward to crank down the mainsail, which reefed by being rolled around the boom like a window shade. I braced my feet against a ventilator cowl and worked the handle that rolled the boom. *Rose* started to fly lightly, eased of the labor of carrying too much sail. We would hover a moment and then fall forward in slow motion into troughs too deep and dark to see their bottoms, troughs that brought to mind nightmares of bared rocks at the bottom of black waterless pits. You could imagine plunging down and being shattered into a million bits of wood and steel and bone. We fell and splintered the water into a thousand white birds that burst up like ducks from the water. We rose with my stomach just a notch behind and suddenly the animated face of a drowning man—no, my father's face thrown back hugely on the rounded pillow of the crest—rolling ahead and then under us into the great hollow, and we stood still and then began the great scything curve down. So animated, so alive! The gaping mouth now moving, the eye sockets emptying, trembling. *Dad!* And we fell into the gaping mouth that was tearing into the nostril, and we sliced and shattered the eye into a spray that leaped over us and raced us with the wind and fell salty into my own open mouth.

"Hold on!" It was my mother's voice.

I sprawled on the slippery cabin top. I hadn't ridden the next lifting wave. My legs didn't work and I pulled myself with my hands into the cockpit and put a hand on the tiller. Eddie went to the rail, then said good night and went below. The numbers on the glowing compass card were jiggling and my legs began to shake. The boat shuddered and the stars swept in vibrating lines. *Rose* wallowed and heaved.

"Steady boy, take her down, you're way off course," my father said.

Such were twilight thoughts as *Sparrow* raced to The Horn. The skies were bigger, as they are in the Dutch landscapes with just a strip of land at the bottom of the painting, and that seems like an affectation until you go to Holland and see for yourself that the skies and the clouds *are* bigger. And now the earth was tipped and we slid down to the point of fury at the bottom of the world where the lines of longitude gathered like drawstrings.

Other spirits came to me in those dusks, and the sounds of the curling foam at the wave crests were like whispering—names I didn't imagine had meaning to me, or that I could even remember. Bill Schindler, a one-legged, midget auto-racing driver; Cedarhurst Stadium, 1939 and 1940. Andy Varipapa, a semiprofessional bowler: I set pins for him once in 1942 when I was twelve. I played tapes of Kathleen Ferrier, dead for over thirty years, and that sound brought together the dead and the living in those twilights. A woman once told me that she loved her body's smell because it reminded her that she came from the sea, and I thought then, out there, that we would return to these seas and not to the earth.

On New Year's Eve we blew the uncurling paper whistles that came with our gifts, and there were three party hats. We opened our fortune cookies. Mine: "You are soon to go on a long journey." Dan's: "Watch out for bad companions." Tiger's: "You will be drawn to the glamour of the stage." January 1 was pipe-maintenance day. Then I lost a filling chewing a Christmas caramel, and Dan was desperate to operate and amortize our nineteen-dollar dental emergency kit. No dice. I let him look, but the plastic dental mirror fogged as we laughed. We listened to the water, the *psoosh* of the bow wave, the *hissh* of the water streaming by, white, the *crissch* of the quarter wave starting out from alongside the cockpit, the *fwssh* of wavetops nearby. Four sounds that you learned to hear at the same time, like an orchestra conductor—*Sparrow's* voice.

The cat had magic dewy beads on his fur in the morning. I started a section of my daily journal recording how each spot appeared on my long johns. How could they get so dirty after only a week? There's no air dirt or dust out there. But spill by spill, spot by spot, it added up. Our best surprise meal was when we thought we'd run out of carrots and one rolled out of my berth as I sat to cut the night's vegetables. One evening I was amazed to see Dan crying at the climax of *La Traviata*, but excitement subsided as I saw that he was slicing onions. On my thirtieth wedding anniversary Dan made good biscuits in the pressure cooker. There was a card from Leonora. Good, I was on her list. "I love you, come home soon." We were not to The Horn, but I felt on the way home.

Through all of this the recording barometer was on a long and frightening dive. It inscribes on a roll of paper, and the ink line started at the top of the sheet and descended on a steady slope for ninety-six hours until it was near the bottom. This was like a background of scary anticipatory movie music that went on for days. The temperature was down to forty-three degrees at night. The beauties didn't stop; now we had flocks of exquisite delft-blue whale birds, shaped like small doves. The albatrosses were always with us. They glided, sometimes moving their wings only once every minute and a half, keeping one wing tip an inch from the waves. They must sense exactly that space to the water. The big ones had that quality that bird people call "jizz"—a wonderful word (architects would say "monumental" and performers would say "star quality"). Often, in these steep, short seas of about twelve feet, they would be soaring on the back of a wave and when *Sparrow* lifted to the crest there was a giant bird only a few feet astern, as suddenly revealed as if a magician had dropped a cloth. Dan could make them land in the water by waving his arm. He said it was because they knew man, and the arm motion meant that food was being dropped into the water.

In such waters you can't help wondering at the way following seas approach and then, suddenly and easily, are under you and gone, rolling ahead. It is remarkable how they seem to melt as you rise to them. I believe that this illusion is caused partly by our lack of a firm horizon and the ease with which we come to accept the constant roller coaster. When a boat tilts forward, as the wave starts to lift her stern— and this is the key moment to me—the eye is tilted up as one looks aft, and without the secure horizon reference, the wave is just not there as our eye skims the surface and does not see it square on. Conversely, the eye is tilted down as the stern dips when the crest is past, and so the eye perceives the following mountain of water as higher.

Dan's target was 50° south and 90° degrees west. We would turn eastward then, into the chute of Drake Passage. Our idea was to stay two hundred miles away from land as we angled in, then turn east and go across at the level of The Horn. If we wandered closer, a gale from the southwest could slam us up into the dreaded rocks that curved down the western tip of the continent. Slocum and Darwin spoke of this archipelago of great rocks, and called it the Milky Way of the sea. Now we were leaving all the world I knew—we were south of Africa, south of Australia, south of Tasmania and New Zealand. Only ocean and the one rocky tip remained.

On January 3, still building *Sparrow*, I finished a tiny piece of the bookcase—just a detail to make it pretty. It would have been impossible in heavier weather. Strangely, I was beginning to worry that we wouldn't have any really shocking weather and wouldn't be able to crow about a Horn passage. Dan thought I was crazy and he could have been right. I told him the old joke about the rabbi who became so addicted to golf that at dawn on the morning of the holiest day of the year he was out on the links, hoping no one would see him. He teed off—a hole in one! He fell to his knees and called out, "God! How can you reward such a sinner?" The great voice spoke from the clouds. "And who are you going to tell?" When I told stories like this he'd always remind me that I'd told it before. Now he added, "Dad, you're waning philosophical."

We waited like athletes before the game. We stared at the ceiling. We may not have been in a storm but we were in the great seas, long and gray, and in the grip of the great west wind, of which Conrad said:

> The West Wind is too great a king to be a dissembler: he is no calculator plotting deep schemes in a somber heart; he is too strong for small artifices; there is passion in all his moods, even in the soft mood of his serene days . . . He is all things to all oceans; he is like a poet seated upon a throne—magnificent, simple, barbarous, pensive, generous, impulsive, changeable, unfathomable . . .

When the seas rose, the cat, sitting on the table in a sphinx position, seemed to levitate, become airborne toward my bunk cloth, and slide down into his water bowl without changing his position.

A name kept going through my head incessantly. *Edwige*. Dickens? I spent days digging in my brain. Suddenly I remembered: the costume designer's cat, summer 1954, at Green Mansion Theatre, where I met Leonora.

Under all that stress and movement, something usually needed fixing. The weathercloth, which kept the spray out of the cockpit, split.

I sewed it. Every day I went forward and studied the hardware at our masthead with binoculars. All seemed well, but we were eager to go up the mast as soon as calmer seas made it enjoyable. These were moments to take pleasure from our thoughtful preparations. But I wished Dan would stop yelling, "Where's my crossbow!" every time he saw an albatross.

The most constant sense was that of being so alone. Not a plane, a jet trail, or a piece of floating debris for twenty days. Two thousand miles out of Easter Island, we toasted. I shaved, changed long johns, employed a bit of washrag, and took a quick glance at my skin. Then it was into my last clean *Falklands-or-bust* long johns. There was a tiny toy truck prize in the hot chocolate can we had just opened, and we were delighted. It was on the table and could roll back and forth forever. Swat! It was off, thank you, Tiger. I threw a wad of paper out of the hatch and missed. The paper hit the wooden rim, but I hadn't yet let it go. My bashed fingers ached in the cold, and of course we laughed hysterically about that.

On January 6, we cut to The Horn. At 1145 we passed due south of (and half a world away from) our Manhattan home, and by noon we were south of the East 80s where our friends the Bicks and Lorin families lived. Distances in reference to north are shortened: the lines of longitude gather in, ready to meet at the pole. Soon we'd be south of Montauk Point, the tip of Long Island, and farther east than *Sparrow* had ever gone. We were coming to it. I couldn't write or read. I was stupefied by excitement.

Dan

Day 176. Dawn—Force 6 following wind, first reef and no jib. The barometer is falling fast. Bow foam roars six feet on either side—*Sparrow*'s soft feathers. A few birds. Nervous. We should sight the little southernmost island of Diego Ramirez tonight. The clouds have left a little gap and I can see the sunrise, an awful red. "Red in the morning, sailors take warning . . ."

Now my navigation is critical, and I cannot afford the arrogance and luxury of having a thousand miles on all sides. A landsman might think a five-mile error big, but actually that's not bad—it's usually good enough for a landfall. Yet after twenty-two days of vast ocean I wonder if I've made some tiny error compounded twenty-two times. Then who knows where we'd fetch up? I'm hoping for a couple of good days now—I want to see Horn Island and throw the plaque I made in the Galápagos toward it. How territorial—man and his desire to leave his mark. Maybe I should just empty the trash! If I were to climb Horn Island, what would I do at the top? The same thing any animal would do—pee.

I love the hissing and the chewing cold. I like burning calories just to stay heated. I feel awake and alive.

0600. Seas eight to ten feet, rolling but generally smooth. Trouble with the steering gear with wind building to Force 8. It's a real gale, but pleasant below. Brief galley fire. Pâté, artichoke hearts, crackers, peanut butter, and chicken spread by Dad, à la floor of the cabin, for brunch.

0800–1200. Lively tiller steering—the good old days! Visibility, one-quarter mile; seas, sixteen feet, not so bad. Moving fast under triple-reefed main and full dodger.

Day 177. Barometer easing its angle of dive. Alter course to stay north of Diego Ramirez—can't risk approaching that rock in this visibility. Will go down Drake Passage between it and The Horn, angling up to The Horn. I'm disappointed—Cape Horn is the last land mass of South America, and Diego Ramirez is just a rock, covered by cold waves and the ultimate lonely place before Antartica. Even so, it's land.

Day 178. On January 6, just after I got our noon position and wrote the above, a gale clomped down on us—with Force 8 winds and gusts to Force 9. In the afternoon I came on deck and besides seeing that Dad was working hard at the tiller, the seas and sky looked furious. White streaks were smeared along the waves, the wind almost visible! Seas built and grew until it was necessary for us to look aft and steer down each wave, keeping the stern toward the following seas. Some waves were bigger than others—foaming and looking really mean. Graybeards. The automatic steering wouldn't work—the paddle was spending too much time out of the water. (The whole boat seemed to be spending too much time out of the water.) We took two-hour watches.

It's hard to see a wave (in photos, impossible). You see the mass of it—not much height—then you rise slowly as the water floods beneath you and you're on top. I was at the helm watching this really big one and suddenly I knew *Sparrow* hadn't risen and twenty feet of wave was straight up over us.

We surfed for a moment and fell off it to starboard, flat into the water. The boat didn't seem to tip over but the port rail rose up suddenly above me as I slid down. What I'd been standing on was above my shoulder level. I was in the ocean! The foaming waves I'd been looking at were at my chin. My tether was yanked tight as *Sparrow* came up level, surfed again, and fell over to port, the starboard deck and rail shooting up over my head. I kicked my legs and paddled for a moment in free water, then *Sparrow* righted and I was scooped on deck.

By the time all this happened, it had been thirty-six hours since I'd had a fix on the sun to establish our position. My dead reckoning put us near Diego Ramirez (fifty miles southwest of Cape Horn). But you can't steer accurately in a gale, so I was jumpy.

The gale broke up by 0100 and, with the moon full, there it was: a frozen wave at the end of the continent. A featureless gray hump. The Horn.

David

My Horn passage started at 0700 on January 7. The sunrise had been ominous. The paddle that goes down into the water to work the self-steerer was lumping out as the stern lifted high. I jibed and the main sheet looped under the paddle, threatening to snap it off. I called for Dan and he held me by the heel like Achilles's mother as I went in headfirst for the line and cleared it. Dan was angry because I unclipped my tether, but it didn't stretch that far and I didn't want to take time to reclip it. "But we're not moving, Dan," I said weakly. I was glad he was angry because that meant he'd use the tether himself. We dismantled the Navik and steered by hand for the first time on this passage. Seas and wind built and it was a proper gale, going with us. We took in the jib; she flew with only a spot of mainsail exposed. Slocum's phrase repeated in my head: "Even while the storm raged at its worst, my ship was wholesome and noble." And *Sparrow* was magnificent: delicate but steady, swift and airy on the foam crest, strong and driving through the great valleys. She seemed born for this day.

At noon, Dan shifted course, visibility was down to a few hundred yards. Forget Diego Ramirez. If we didn't hit it we wouldn't see it. And in the slop of this gale we wouldn't see The Horn either. The Horn is three things: the rock itself, Drake Passage (the water in which you sail around it), and the whole idea of the passage. We were in the Passage, and surely we'd survive for the third. I settled for two out of three. At one that afternoon I asked Dan when we'd be off (if not crashed onto) The Horn and he said, "0100 tomorrow morning." The gale picked up and Dan steered, howling "Aaayippeeeeeee!" as we surfed down the long gray waves with their tops torn off and the spray racing us. It was quiet and dry below. I realized that Dan had hardly ever steered by tiller, but his skill was marvelous, undoubtedly honed by hours of handling the joystick in video-game parlors. He looked possessed. Horsemen have their centaurs, why don't we sailors have a name for the half-man, half-boat that Dan was at that moment?

Because we were hand-steering we changed to two-hour stints. During my early-evening watch, the gale started to fly apart, moderating. This is the most dangerous time of a gale, because the puffs can be fierce after random lulls, and the wind can shoot at you suddenly from a different direction. At eight-thirty at night I was below making tea and lighting the evening lamp when *Sparrow* went down hard to starboard. Then bam! down to port. Without a horizon below, hanging on and standing not upright but with the angle of the boat, I only knew that we were down because the water covering the porthole was not wave froth but solid green—I was looking straight down into the ocean. A felt bootliner that was drying knocked the lamp out of my hand and onto the bunk. The water roared, like a train running over us.

"OK, Dan?"

"I'm fine, Dad." His voice sounded subdued.

My eye was taken during this by the blue plastic cat pan, which was secured by cord on two sides. It jumped up, did a 180° turn and landed upside down, then leaped again and did a full 360° flip and landed facedown again. It looked like a little girl in a blue dress, skipping rope. I thought of that calmly. The binoculars were in my berth with the oil lamp; their teak box had broken. It was the only thing we hadn't built ourselves. Everything else was in place. I didn't learn until he told me the next day that Dan had gone overboard.

The gale broke on my ten-to-midnight watch, and the moon, almost full, showed through the racing clouds as they tore apart: a slow film flicker. After my watch I was below, again making tea, and Dan called, "Dad, I think I see The Horn" and I was up on deck at ejection speed and there it was.

"How did you see it, Dan?"

"One wave didn't go down."

I'd never seen it but of course it was The Horn; its form must have been in my genes. The great rock sphinx, the crouching lion at the bottom of the world. The sea and the sky and the faintly outlined huge rock were all the same color—indigo, graded like the first three pulls of the same ink on a Japanese woodblock print. We embraced, then stood entranced. I went below and poured a finger of Kahlua for each of us (I oddly remembered a guest saying, "No, Leonora, the finger is held sideways, not straight down"). We toasted. I was about to say, "To the men who died here," when Dan said, "To the people who died here." It was the only possible thing to say. There was the rock, after 2,500 miles of ocean, our first sighting, the rock itself.

"You said 0100, Dan, and here we are."

"Yes, but I was aiming for ten miles off."

"You can't be less than eight . . ." I was staggered by that. Two hundred and thirty miles in thirty-six hours without sky for sights, only our eyes on the compass and on our wake to judge speed, in full gale, in strong current, and with a course change in the middle, and his error was two miles. The Horn bore north and I stepped behind him. Few had rounded The Horn in a boat this small, and he was ahead of me.

We were in the Atlantic. I had a sudden craving for simple food, and made a plain omelette for us. Three eggs in the pan, one on the floor. Perfectly moist in the middle. Just a sprinkle of dill. It was getting light. Between us and The Horn, thousands of small petrels fluttered and dipped, like a vast spread of brown-and-white lace undulating a foot above the surface.

The Storm

by Sebastian Junger

As many as 10,000 fishermen from a single town—Gloucester, Massachusetts—have died at sea since 1650. Sebastian Junger (born 1962) told the story of six of them in this 1994 article for Outside. *The Piece became the basis for his book,* The Perfect Storm.

G loucester, Massachusetts, a town of 28,000 people, is squeezed between a rocky coast and a huge tract of scrub pine and boulders called Dogtown Common. Local widows used to live in Dogtown, along with the forgotten and the homeless, while the rest of the community spread out along the shore. Today a third of all jobs in Gloucester are fishing related, and the waterfront bars—the Crow's Nest, the Mariners Pub, the Old Timer's Tavern—are dark little places that are unmistakably not for tourists.

One street up from the coastline is Main Street, where the bars tend to have windows and even waitresses, and then there is a rise called Portugee Hill. Halfway up Portugee Hill is Our Lady of Good Voyage Church, a large stucco construction with two bell towers and a statue of the Virgin Mary, who looks down with love and concern at the bundle in her arms. The bundle is a Gloucester fishing schooner.

• • •

September 18, 1991, was a hot day in Gloucester, tourists shuffling down Main Street and sunbathers still crowding the wide expanses of Good Harbor Beach. Day boats bobbed offshore in the heat shimmer, and swells sneaked languorously up against Bass Rocks.

At Gloucester Marine Railways, a haul-out place at the end of the short peninsula, Adam Randall stood contemplating a boat named the *Andrea Gail*. He had come all the way from Florida to go sword-fishing on the boat, and now he stood considering her uneasily. The *Andrea Gail* was a seventy-foot long-liner that was leaving for Canada's Grand Banks within days. He had a place on board if he wanted it. "I just had bad vibes," he would say later. Without quite knowing why, he turned and walked away.

Long-liners are steel-hulled fishing boats that can gross as much as $1 million in a year. Up to half of that can be profit. Swordfish range up and down the coast from Puerto Rico to Newfoundland, and the long-liners trail after them all year like seagulls behind a day trawler. The fish are caught with monofilament lines forty miles long and set with a thousand hooks. For the crew, it's less a job than a four-week jag. They're up at four, work all day, and don't get to bed until mid-night. The trip home takes a week, which is the part of the month when swordfishermen sleep. When they get to port the owner hands each of them several thousand dollars. A certain amount of drinking goes on, and then a week later they return to the boat, load up, and head back out.

"Swordfishing is a young man's game, a single man's game," says the mother of one who died at it. "There aren't a lot of Boy Scouts in the business," another woman says.

Sword boats come from all over the East Coast—Florida, the Car-olinas, New Jersey. Gloucester, which is located near the tip of Cape Ann, a forty-five-minute drive northeast from Boston, is a particularly busy port because it juts so far out toward the summer fishing grounds. Boats load up with fuel, bait, ice, and food and head out to the Grand Banks, about ninety miles southeast from Newfoundland, where warm Gulf Stream water mixes with the cold Labrador current in an area shallow enough—or "shoal" enough, as fishermen say—to be a perfect feeding ground for fish. The North Atlantic weather is so violent, though, that, in the early days, entire fleets would go down at one time, a hundred men lost overnight. Even today, with loran navigation, seven-day forecasts, and satellite tracking, fishermen on the Grand Banks are just rolling the dice come the fall storm season. But swordfish sell for around six dollars a pound, and depending on the size of the boat a good run might take in thirty thousand to forty thousand pounds. Deckhands are paid shares based on the catch and can earn ten thousand dollars in a month. So the tendency among fishermen in early fall is to keep the dice rolling.

The *Andrea Gail* was one of maybe a dozen big commercial boats gearing up in Gloucester in mid-September 1991. She was owned by Bob Brown, a longtime fisherman who was known locally as Suicide Brown because of the risks he'd taken as a young man. He owned a second long-liner, the *Hannah Boden*, and a couple of lobster boats. The *Andrea Gail* and the *Hannah Boden* were Brown's biggest investments, collectively worth well over a million dollars.

The *Andrea Gail*, in the language, was a raked-stem, hard-chined, western-rig boat. That meant that her bow had a lot of angle to it, she had a nearly square cross-section, and her pilothouse was up front rather than in the stern. She was built of welded steel plate, rust-red below the waterline, green above, and she had a white wheelhouse with half-inch-thick safety-glass windows. Fully rigged for a long trip, she carried hundreds of miles of monofilament line, thousands of hooks, and ten thousand pounds of bait fish. There were seven life preservers on board, six survival suits, an emergency position-indicating radio beacon, and one life raft.

The *Andrea Gail* was captained by a local named Frank "Billy" Tyne, a former carpenter and drug counselor who had switched to fishing at age twenty-seven. Tyne had a reputation as a fearless captain, and in his ten years of professional fishing he had made it through several treacherous storms. He had returned from a recent trip with almost forty thousand pounds of swordfish in his hold, close to a quarter of a million dollars' worth. Jobs aboard Tyne's boats were sought after. So it seemed odd, on September 18, when Adam Randall walked back to the dock at Gloucester Marine Railways and returned to town.

Randall's replacement was twenty-eight-year-old David Sullivan, who was mildly famous in town for having saved the lives of his entire crew one bitter January night two years before. When his boat, the *Harmony*, had unexpectedly begun taking on water, Sullivan had pulled himself across a rope to a sister ship and got help just in time to rescue his sinking crew. Along with Sullivan were a young West Indian named Alfred Pierre; thirty year old Bobby Shatford, whose mother, Ethel, tended bar at the Crow's Nest on Main Street; and two men from Brandenton Beach, Florida—Dale Murphy, thirty, and Michael "Bugsy" Moran, thirty-six.

On September 20, Billy Tyne and his crew passed Ten Pound Island, rounded Dogbar Breakwater, and headed northeast on a dead-calm sea.

For several generations after the first British settlers arrived in Gloucester, the main industries on Cape Ann were farming and logging. Then around 1700 the cod market took off, and Gloucester schooners began making runs up to the Grand Banks two or three times a year. French and Basque fishermen had already been working the area since 1510, perhaps earlier. They could fill their holds faster by crossing the Atlantic and fishing the rich waters of the Banks than by plying their own shores.

The Gloucester codfisherman worked from dories and returned to the schooners each night. Payment was reckoned by cutting the tongues out of the cod and adding them up at the end of the trip. When fog rolled in, the dories would drift out of earshot and were often never heard from again. Occasionally, weeks later, a two-man dory crew might be picked up by a schooner bound for say, Pernambuco or Liverpool. The fishermen would make it back to Gloucester several months later, walking up Main Street as if returning from the dead.

The other danger, of course, was storms. Like a war, a big storm might take out all the young men of a single town. In 1862, for example, a winter gale struck seventy schooners fishing the dangerous waters of Georges Bank, east of Cape Cod. The ships tried to ride out fifty-foot seas at anchor. By morning fifteen Gloucester boats had gone down with 125 men.

At least four thousand Gloucestermen have been lost at sea, but some estimates run closer to ten thousand. A bronze sculpture on the waterfront commemorates them: THEY THAT GO DOWN TO THE SEA IN SHIPS 1623–1923. It shows a schooner captain fighting heavy weather, his faced framed by a sou'wester hat.

In the early days, a lot of superstition went into seafaring. Occasionally men stepped off ill-fated boats on a hunch. Captains refused to set sail on Fridays, since that was the day their Lord had been crucified. Boats often had lucky silver coins affixed to the base of their masts, and crew members took care never to tear up a printed page because they never knew—most of them being illiterate—whether it was from the Bible.

The *Andrea Gail* took nearly a week to reach the fishing grounds. The six crewmen watched television, cooked and ate, slept, prepared the fishing gear, talked women, talked money, talked horse racing, talked fish, stared at the sea. Swordfishermen seldom eat swordfish when they're out. Like many ocean fish, it's often full of sea worms, four feet long and thick as pencils, and though the worms are removed prior to market, many of the men who catch swordfish consider it fit only for the landlubbing public. At sea a fisherman will eat steak, spaghetti, chicken, ice cream, anything he wants. On ice in the *Andrea Gail*'s hold was three thousand dollars' worth of groceries.

The boat arrived at the Grand Banks around September 26 and started fishing immediately. On the main deck was a huge pool of six-hundred-pound-test monofilament, the mainline, which passed across a bait table and paid out off the stern. Baiters alternate at the mainline like old-time axmen on a Douglas fir. They are expected to bait a hook with squid or mackerel every fifteen seconds; at this rate it takes two men four hours to set forty miles of line. After they are done they shower and retire to their bunks. Around four in the morning, the crew gets up and starts hauling the line. A hydraulic drum on the wheel-house deck slowly pulls it in, and the crew unclips the leaders as they come. When there's a fish at the end of a leader, deckhands catch it with steel gaffs and drag it, struggling, aboard. They saw the sword off, gut and behead the fish with a knife, and drop it into the hold.

The crew has dinner in midafternoon, baits the line again, and sets it back out. They might then have a couple of beers and go to bed.

The *Andrea Gail* had been out thirty-eight days when the National Weather Service suddenly started issuing fax bulletins about a low-pressure system that was building over southern Quebec and heading out to sea: "DEVELOPING STORM 45N 73W MOVING E 24 KTS. WINDS INCREASING TO 35 KTS AND SEAS BUILDING TO 16 FT." Meanwhile, the Weather Service was keeping a close eye on the mid-Atlantic, where Hurricane Grace, which had developed in the vicinity of Bermuda two days before, was now tracking steadily northwest toward the Carolina coast.

It was Sunday, October 27, very late to be pushing one's luck on the Grand Banks. Most of the fleet was well to the east of Tyne, out on the high seas, but a 150-foot Japanese swordboat named the *Eishan Maru* and the 77-foot *Mary T* were fishing nearby. Tyne told Albert Johnston, the *Mary T*'s captain, that he had forty thousand pounds of fish in his hold—an impressive catch—and now he was heading home.

The question was, could he make it through the Canadian storm that was rapidly coming his way? He would have to cross some very dangerous water while passing Sable Island, a remote spit 120 miles southeast of Nova Scotia, whose shoals are known to fishermen as the Graveyard of the Atlantic. That night Linda Greenlaw, the captain of Bob Brown's other long-liner, the *Hannah Boden*, radioed in and asked Tyne if he'd received the weather chart. "Oh, yeah, I got it," Tyne replied. "Looks like it's gonna be wicked." They set some channels to relay information to Bob Brown and decided to talk the following night.

Though Billy Tyne had no way of knowing it, the heavy weather that

was now brewing in the North Atlantic was an anomaly of historic proportions. Three years later, professional meteorologists still talk ani-
matedly about the storm of '91, debating how it formed and exactly
what role Hurricane Grace played in it all. Generally, hurricanes this
late in the season are anemic events that quickly dissipate over land.
Hurricane Grace, though, never made it to shore; a massive cold front,
called an anticyclone, was blocking the entire eastern seaboard. Well
off the Carolinas, Grace ran up against the cold front and literally
bounced off. She veered back out to sea and, though weakened,
churned northeast along the warm Gulf Stream waters.

At the same time, the low-pressure system that had developed over
Quebec and moved eastward off the Canadian Maritimes was beginning to behave strangely. Normally, low-pressure systems in the region
follow the jet stream offshore and peter out in the North Atlantic, the
usual pattern of the well-known nor'easter storms. But this system did
the opposite: On Monday, October 28, it unexpectedly stalled off the
coast of Nova Scotia and began to grow rapidly, producing record high
seas and gale-force winds. Then it spun around and headed back west,
directly at New England, a reversal known as a retrograde.

Meteorologists still disagree about what caused the storm to grow so
suddenly and then to retrograde. But the best theory offered by the
National Weather Service and its Canadian equivalent, Environment
Canada, is that it was caught between the counterclockwise spin of the
dying hurricane and the clockwise swirl of the anticyclone, creating a
funnel effect that forced it toward the coast at speeds of up to ten knots.
The farther west it tracked, the more it absorbed moisture and energy
from the remnants of Hurricane Grace—and the more ferocious it
became.

The technical name for the new storm was *midlatitude cyclone*. The
people in its path, however, would later call it the No Name Hurricane,
since it had all the force of a hurricane but it was never officially designated as one. And because the brunt of the storm would strike the
eastern seaboard around October 31, it would also acquire another
name: the Halloween Gale.

• • •

Around 6:00 p.m. on Monday, October 28, Tyne told the skipper of a
Gloucester boat named the *Allison* that he was 130 miles north-north-
east of Sable Island and experiencing eighty-knot winds. "She's comin'
on, boys, and she's comin' on strong," he said. According to Tyne, the
conditions had gone from flat calm to fifty knots almost without
warning. The rest of the fleet was farther east and in relative safety, but
the *Andrea Gail* was all alone in the path of the fast-developing storm.
She was probably running with the waves and slightly angled toward
them—"quartering down-sea," as it's called—which is a stable position
for a boat; she'll neither plow her nose into the sea nor roll over broadside. A wave must be bigger than a boat to flip her end over end, and
the *Andrea Gail* was seventy feet long. But by this point, data buoys off
Nova Scotia were measuring waves as high as one hundred feet—
among the highest readings ever recorded. Near Sable Island the
troughs of such monsters would have reached the ocean floor.

Tyne would have radioed for help if trouble had come on slowly—
a leak or a gradual foundering, for example. "Whatever happened, happened quick," a former crew member from the *Hannah Boden* later
said. Tyne didn't even have time to grab the radio and shout.

Waves of unimaginable proportions have been recorded over the years.
When Sir Ernest Shackleton skippered an open sailboat off the South
Georgian Islands on May 1916, he saw a wave so big that he mistook the
foaming crest for a break in the clouds. "It's clearing, boys!" he yelled to
his crew, and then, moments later: "For God's sake, hold on, it's got us!"
By some miracle they managed to survive. In 1933 in the South Pacific
an officer on the USS *Ramapo* looked to stern and saw a wave that was
later calculated to be 112 feet high. In 1984 a three-masted schooner
named the *Marques* was struck by a single wave that sent her down in less
than a minute, taking nineteen people with her. Nine survived, including
a strapping young Virginian who managed to force his way up through
a rising column of water and out an open hatch.

Oceanographers call these "extreme waves" or "rogues." Old-time

Maine fishermen call them "queer ones." They have roared down the stacks of navy destroyers, torn the bows off containerships, and broken cargo vessels in two.

When the rogue hit the *Andrea Gail*, sometime between midnight and dawn on October 29, Tyne would probably have been alone in the wheelhouse and already exhausted after twenty-four hours at the helm. Captains, unwilling to relinquish the wheel to inexperienced crew, have been known to drive for two or even three days straight. The crew would have been below deck, either in the kitchen or in their state-rooms. Once in a while one of the men would have come up to keep Tyne company. In the privacy of the wheelhouse he might have admitted his fears: This is bad, this is the worst I've ever seen. There's no way we could inflate a life raft in these conditions. If a hatch breaks open, if anything lets go . . .

Tyne must have looked back and seen an exceptionally big wave rising up behind him. It would have been at least seventy feet high, maybe a hundred. The stern of the boat would have risen up sicken-ingly and hurled the men from their bunks. The *Andrea Gail* would have flipped end over end and landed hull up, exploding the wheel-house windows. Tyne, upside down in his steel cage, would have drowned without a word. The five men below deck would have landed on the ceiling. The ones who remained conscious would have known that it was impossible to escape through an open hatch and swim out from under the boat. And even if they could, what then? How would they have found their survival suits, the life raft?

The *Andrea Gail* would have rolled drunkenly and started to fill. Water would have sprayed through bursting gaskets and risen in a column from the wheelhouse stairway. It would have reached the men in their staterooms, and it would have been cold enough to take their breath away. At least the end would have come fast.

It wasn't until Tuesday afternoon that the boats on the Grand Banks were able to check in with one another. The *Eishan Maru*, which was closest to Billy Tyne's last known location, reported that she was completely rolled by one huge wave; her wheelhouse windows were blown out, and she was left without rudder or electronics. The *Lori Dawn Eight* had taken so much water down her vents that she lost an engine and headed in. The *Mary T* had fared well but had already taken $165,000 worth of fish in nine days, so she headed in, too, The *Hannah Boden*, the *Allison*, the *Mr. Simon*, and the *Miss Millie* were way to the east and "had beautiful weather," in Albert Johnston's words. That left the *Andrea Gail*.

By Wednesday, October 30, the storm had retrograded so far to the west that conditions at sea were almost tolerable. At that point the worst of it was just hitting Gloucester. The Eastern Point neighborhood, where the town's well-to-do live, had been cut in half. Waves were rolling right through the woods and into some of the nicest living rooms in the state. On the Back Shore, thirty-foot waves were tearing the façades off houses and claiming whole sections of Ocean Drive. The wind, whipping through the power lines, was hitting pitches that no one had ever heard before. Just up the coast in Kennebunkport, some Democrats cheered to see boulders in the family room of President Bush's summer mansion.

"The only light I can shed on the severity of the storm is that until then, we had never—ever—had a lobster trap move offshore," said Bob Brown. "Some were moved thirteen miles to the west It was the worst storm I have ever heard of, or experienced."

By now the storm had engulfed nearly the entire eastern seaboard. Even in protected Boston Harbor, a data buoy measured wave heights of thirty feet. A Delta Airlines pilot at Boston's Logan Airport was surprised to see spray topping two-hundred-foot construction cranes on Deer Island. Sitting on the runway waiting for clearance, his air-speed indicator read eighty miles per hour. Off Cape Cod, a sloop named the *Satori* lost its life raft, radios, and engine. The three people in its crew had resigned themselves to writing good-bye notes when they were finally rescued two hundred miles south of Nantucket by a Coast Guard swimmer who jumped, untethered, from a helicopter into the roiling waves. An Air National Guard helicopter ran out of fuel off

Long Island, and its crew had to jump one at a time through the darkness into the sea. One man was killed; the other four were rescued after drifting throughout the night. All along the coast, waves and storm surge combined to act as "dams" that prevented rivers from flowing into the sea. The Hudson backed up one hundred miles to Albany and caused flooding; so did the Potomac.

Brown tried in vain all day Wednesday to radio Tyne. That evening he finally got through to Linda Greenlaw, who said she'd last heard Billy Tyne talking to other boats on the radio Monday night. "Those men sounded really scared, and we were scared for them," she said later. Later that night Brown finally alerted the U.S. Coast Guard.

"When were they due in?" the dispatcher asked.

"Next Saturday," Brown replied.

The dispatcher refused to initiate a search because the boat wasn't overdue yet. Brown then got the Canadian Coast Guard on the line. "I'm afraid my boat's in trouble, and I fear the worst," he told the dispatcher in Halifax. At dawn Canadian reconnaissance planes, which were already in the area, began sweeping for the *Andrea Gail*.

Two days later, a U.S. Coast Guard cutter and five aircraft were also on the case. But there was no clue about the missing boat until November 5, when the Coast Guard positively identified the *Andrea Gail*'s radio beacon and propane tank, which had washed up on Sable Island. "The recovered debris is loose gear and could have washed overboard during heavy weather," said Petty Officer Elizabeth Brannan. "No debris has been located that indicates the *Andrea Gail* has been sunk."

The search had covered more than sixty-five thousand square miles at that point. In heavy seas it's hard for a pilot to be sure he is seeing everything—one Coast Guard pilot reported spotting a five-hundred-foot ship that he had completely missed on a previous flight—so no one was leaping to any conclusions. Two days and thirty-five thousand square miles later, though, it was hard not to assume the worst: Now the *Andrea Gail*'s emergency position-indicating radio beacon (EPIRB) had been found. It, too, had washed up on the beaches of Sable Island.

An EPIRB is a device about the size of a bowling pin that automatically emits a radio signal if it floats free of its shipboard holster. The signal travels via satellite to onshore listening posts, where Coast Guard operators decode the name of the boat and her location to within two miles. EPIRBs have been required equipment for fishing vessels on the high seas since 1990. The only catch is that the device must be turned on, something captains do automatically when they leave port. ("It's not the sort of thing you forget," says one captain.) Though Bob Brown insists that the *Andrea Gail*'s EPIRB had been turned on when it left port, it was found on Sable Island disarmed.

The Coast Guard called off the search on November 8, eleven days after the *Andrea Gail* had presumably gone down. Search planes had covered 116,000 square miles of ocean. "After taking into account the water temperature and other factors, we felt the probability of survival was minimal," Coast Guard lieutenant Brian Krenzien told reporters at the time. The water temperature was forty-six degrees. When a man falls overboard on the Grand Banks that late in the year, there usually isn't even time to turn the boat around.

"I finally gave up hope after the Coast Guard called the search off," says Ethel Shatford, Bobby Shatford's mother, at the Crow's Nest. "It was very hard, though. You always read stories about people being found floating around in boats. The memorial was on November 16. There were more than a thousand people. This bar and the bar next door were closed, and we had enough food for everyone for three days. Recently we had a service for a New Bedford boat that went down last winter. None of the crew was from here, but they were fishermen."

The Crow's Nest is a low, dark room with wood-veneer paneling and a horseshoe bar where regulars pour their own drinks. On the wall below the television is a photo of Bobby Shatford and another of the *Andrea Gail*, as well as a plaque for the six men who died. Upstairs there are cheap guest rooms where deckhands often stay.

Ethel Shatford is a strong, gray-faced Gloucester native in her late fifties. Three of her own sons have fished, and over the years she has served as den mother to scores of young fishermen on the Gloucester waterfront. Four of the six men who died on the *Andrea Gail* spent their last night onshore in the rooms of the Crow's Nest.

"My youngest graduated high school last June and went fishing right off the b-a-t," she says. "That was what he always wanted to do, fish with his brothers. Bobby's older brother, Rick, used to fish the *Andrea Gail* years ago."

She draws a draft beer for a customer and continues. "The *Andrea Gail* crew left from this bar. They were all standing over there by the pool table saying good-bye. About the only thing different that time was that Billy Tyne let them take our color TV on the boat. He said, 'Ethel, they can take the TV, but if they watch it instead of doing their work, the TV's going overboard.' I said, 'That's fine, Billy, that's fine.'"

That was the last time Shatford ever saw her son. Recently, a young guy drifted into town who looked so much like Bobby that people were stopping and staring on the street. He walked into the Crow's Nest, and another bartender felt it necessary to explain to him why everyone was looking at him. "He went over to the picture of Bobby and says, 'If I sent that picture to my mother, she'd think it was me.'"

Linda Greenlaw still comes into the bar from time to time, between trips, swearing that someday she's going to "meet the right guy and retire to a small island in Maine." Bob Brown settled out of court with several of the dead crewmembers' families after two years of legal wrangles. Adam Randall, the man who had stepped off the *Andrea Gail* at the last minute, went on to crew with Albert Johnston on the *Mary T.* When he found out that the *Andrea Gail* had sunk in the storm, all he could say was, "I was supposed to have been on that boat. That was supposed to have been me."

During the spring of 1993 the *Mary T* was hauled out for repairs, and Randall picked up work on a tuna long-liner, the *Terri Lei*, out of Georgetown, South Carolina. On the evening of April 6, 1993, the crew of the *Terri Lei* set lines. In the early morning, there were reports of gusty winds and extremely choppy seas in the area. At 8:45 a.m. the Coast Guard in Charleston, South Carolina, picked up an EPIRB signal and sent out two aircraft and a cutter to investigate. By then the weather was fair and the seas were moderate. One hundred and thirty-five miles off the coast, they found the EPIRB, some fishing gear, and a self-inflating life raft. The raft had the name *Terri Lei* stenciled on it. There was no one on board.

The Ship That Vanished
by John Vaillant

There's no question that the cruising wind-jammer Fantome *and her crew were in the wrong place at the wrong time. But why? John Vaillant's (born 1962) 1999 story, which first appeared in* The New Yorker, *attempted to reconstruct the worst sailing accident in more than 40 years.*

Windjammer Barefoot Cruises has been a fixture in the Caribbean for nearly half a century. Like most of its younger competitors, Windjammer specializes in water-borne escapes from the developed world. Unlike the clientele of more traditional cruise lines, however, Windjammer's passengers travel under sail in massive pleasure yachts, most of which have been salvaged from the fallen empires of early-twentieth-century industrialists, financiers, and nobility. The Windjammer code on these voyages is informal, fun, and benignly piratical; onboard, bare feet and rum swizzles are the order of the day. The crews are island-born and friendly; when other Windjammer vessels are encountered, mock battles ensue, complete with cannon fire.

Windjammer's founder and sole owner is Michael Burke, who, with the help of his family (he has six children, and they are all in the business) and hundreds of West Indians, purchased, rebuilt, and launched the largest fleet of sailing ships in the postwar world and—most remarkable—made it profitable. During the fifty-odd years he has been sailing in the Caribbean, Captain Burke, who is seventy-five, has emerged as a founding father of the South Florida, sailor-party-animal lifestyle that Jimmy Buffett popularized in his songs. The Captain's current fleet boasts six ships, which sail between the Lesser Antilles and the Yucatán year-round. Last year, some twenty thousand customers booked passage with the company, which is based in Miami Beach. This pattern was interrupted on October 27, 1998, when Hurricane Mitch, the most destructive storm to hit the Caribbean in more than two centuries, overtook the company's flagship, the *Fantome*, resulting in the Atlantic's worst sailing accident in more than forty years.

The *Fantome*, originally commissioned as a destroyer in the Italian Navy, was one of the largest sailing vessels in the world—a two-hundred-and-eighty-two-foot-long four-masted schooner, completed seventy-two years ago in Livorno, Italy. In the late twenties, the Duke of Westminster turned the ship into a pleasure yacht, replete with a ballroom and wood-burning fireplaces; he sailed her throughout the Mediterranean with a full serving staff and even a cow for milk. Arthur Guinness, the British brewing magnate, bought her in the thirties, and gave her the name *Fantome* (French for "ghost"). With the onset of the Second World War, she languished in Seattle until Aristotle Onassis acquired her, in 1956, as a wedding gift for Princess Grace of Monaco. There is a story that Prince Rainier suspected that Onassis wanted a piece of his gaming business, so Onassis never got a wedding invitation—and the Princess never got her yacht. The vessel was left to rust in various ports around Europe until Captain Burke bought her from Onassis, in 1969. Michael Burke loves his fleet, but the *Fantome* was the prize.

As late as four days before Hurricane Mitch struck, ninety-three passengers who had booked for the *Fantome*'s six-day cruise from the Gulf of Honduras to Belize's Turneffe Islands were laying out clothes and shopping for bathing suits. Some of the passengers, including Anthony Moffa, a thirty-six-year-old engineer from Pennsylvania, were watching the Weather Channel, and what Moffa saw—a tropical storm hundreds of miles away, headed toward a place he would not be going—did not concern him much. But early on Saturday, October 24th, Mitch was upgraded to a hurricane; and by Sunday, when many of the passengers were descending from the clouds over the endless banana plantations of Honduras, Mitch was amplifying at an alarming rate. During this twenty-four-hour period, its barometric pressure plunged from nine hundred and seventy-six millibars to nine hundred and twenty-four. Such a precipitate drop is called an explosive deepening; it happens very seldom, but when it does it portends a storm of extraordinary violence. By now, it was common knowledge that Mitch was a monster in the making. Earlier predictions had the storm heading north, but northern cold fronts had moved in, steadily pushing its anticipated trajectory down, like the needle on a compass. Due west would mean a direct hit in the Gulf of Honduras.

Windjammer was aware of this, but once a cruise has been scheduled it is logistically hard to stop. In addition, cancellations are costly, in terms both of lost revenue and of bad PR. During the afternoon and evening of October 25th, passengers were shuttled twenty miles through a driving rain, from the airport in San Pedro Sula, Honduras, to a small wooden dock in Omoa, on the gulf, where launches waited to take them out to the *Fantome*. Moffa, who was on holiday with his girlfriend, Karyn Rutledge, thought that it was just typical rain-forest weather. In fact, it was a rain-bearing outrider generated by Mitch, still more than four hundred miles away. "It was comical, it was raining so hard," Moffa recalls. "You had horizontal rain in sheets. I started singing the theme from 'Gilligan's Island'; it kind of broke the tension. When we saw the ship, it was a beautiful thing—all lit up. We thought, It can't be that bad."

But Guyan March, the English captain, was worried; this was only his second season in the gulf, and over the phone he told his fiancée, Annie Bleasdale, a professional sailor, that he was reluctant to take on passengers. Captain Burke's eldest son, Michael D. Burke, who since 1988 has run International Maritime Resources, Windjammer's ship-operations arm, later told me that he had suggested to Captain March that he drop the passengers in Omoa and get out of there right away.

However, according to the younger Burke, March told him he was going to wait because passengers were still arriving, dinner was being served, and a band was expected. Burke's son then said that there was no further discussion of cancelling the cruise.

Hurricanes are the Atlantic equivalents of typhoons or cyclones, and they are our atmosphere's most violent means of expression. Every year, from June to November, between eighty and a hundred so-called African waves are spawned from a seasonal convergence of high- and low-altitude winds over the mountains of East Africa. Once these rhythmic, westbound pulses of warm air roll across the Sahel and off the coast of Senegal, it takes them around two weeks to cross the Atlantic. Only a fraction ever reach the next level of development, called a tropical depression, a spinning low-pressure system with winds of not more than thirty-eight miles an hour. It was at this stage, while still a harmless disturbance, that the infant Mitch was given a working title: Tropical Depression No. 13.

Once a tropical storm hits seventy-four m.p.h., it becomes a "minimal" hurricane, or a Category 1. At sea, such a storm would be avoided, and, on shore, people living in mobile homes would have cause for concern. However, hurricanes generally don't start doing serious damage until they reach Category 3—about a hundred and twenty m.p.h. This is when objects we think of as being permanent start to fall down, tear loose, and blow away. But, as a wind's speed increases, its destructive power grows dramatically. A Category 5 hurricane can be eight times as destructive as a Category 1. Anything over a hundred and fifty-six m.p.h. is considered a Category 5, a classification the National Weather Service terms "catastrophic." Five is as high as the Saffir-Simpson hurricane-intensity scale goes; it's like a nine on the Richter scale (the Turkish earthquake last month was a 7.4). An Atlantic hurricane of this magnitude doesn't happen very often—the odds of a Category 5 striking a given location, even in the hurricane-prone Gulf of Honduras, are one in every hundred and sixty years—but, when it does, mayhem ensues on a grand scale and pieces of the world are erased. Mobile homes, the canaries in the coal mine of hurricane measurement, are obliterated under these conditions, along with trees, buildings, and even grass. The recent Hurricane Floyd was, briefly, a Category 4 before being downgraded to a destructive tropical storm; Hurricane Andrew, the 1992 hurricane that devastated portions of Florida and Louisiana and became the costliest natural disaster in United States history, was also a Category 4.

According to Anthony Moffa, Mitch was formally acknowledged to the *Fantome*'s passengers on the evening of October 25th. It was also at that point that the ship's itinerary was changed for the first time— from the northern, Turneffe Islands to the more southerly Bay Islands. By this time, Mitch had mutated into a Category 4, and its projected course was now due west. While the passengers slept, still expecting to wake up and go snorkeling, the fate of the *Fantome* was being sealed, and Captain March was probably having the first glimmerings of what was to come. "Karyn heard a loud noise about 2 a.m. and said she felt the ship turn," Moffa remembers. "There were rough seas that night— ten to twelve feet—and twenty-five-knot winds. It was no problem in such a big ship, but, still, there was a pucker factor there."

Moffa is a mechanical engineer, a self-described rationalist, and the "pucker factor" is militarese for fear. Karyn Rutledge's senses had not betrayed her, either. At 9:30 a.m. on Monday, October 26th, Captain Guyan, as March was called onboard, gathered the passengers in the *Fantome*'s saloon, a large, enclosed dining area at the stern of the ship. The morning meeting is a Windjammer tradition; it's called Story Time, and it's when the captain tells the passengers a bit about where they are and what activities will be offered that day. Captain Guyan's story that morning was short and to the point: Hurricane Mitch posed too great a threat to continue the voyage, so they were headed north, for Belize City, where a chartered aircraft would take the passengers back to Miami. Then he apologized for the inconvenience. "There was a pause for a moment," Moffa recalls. "You're thinking, Damn it, my vacation is ruined! Then somebody in the back said, 'Thanks for keeping us safe.' And then everybody started to clap."

• • •

Guyan March grew up in England, racing dinghies off the Cornish coast with his younger brother, Paul, who worked as a relief mate for Windjammer. Their mother, Jennie March, who is the commodore of a sailing club, recalls the pleasure her sons took in "staying out longer than the adults and bashing their heads against the weather." Guyan had a real knack for it, and by the time he was eighteen he was skippering ninety-foot yachts in the Mediterranean; when he heard about Windjammer, through a friend, he was quick to sign on. Many of Windjammer's captains have been from the British Isles, but Guyan was the youngest. At thirty-two, he had already been at the helm of Windjammer ships for ten years. According to one Windjammer veteran, Captain Neil Carmichael, a Scotsman, Guyan "had a gift—he was a natural."

The *Fantome* arrived at Belize City at eleven-thirty Monday morning, and, even as the passengers were getting ready to disembark, the crew was preparing the ship for the worst. "They were tying down the sails," Moffa recalls, "taking down rigging. People were running around with electric drills, screwing down the bench lids on deck. I would guarantee that not one of those guys wanted to be there if he had a choice, but the guys on that ship—I don't think any of them were being held against their will. They were having fun doing their jobs; there was no bitching and moaning, no tension; they were joking."

Specially chartered speedboats arrived, and Captain Guyan stood by the gangway and shook hands with the disembarking passengers, apologizing, again, to each one. Ten "nonessential" crew were also let off at this time, including all the women, but thirty crew members remained on board. As the *Fantome* threaded her way back through the barrier reef toward open water, her former passengers were being hustled through the airport outside Belize City. The spare, gym-size building was now a madhouse, filled with anxious tourists trying to escape what, in a matter of hours, was predicted to be ground zero.

Laurie Fischer, a Canadian and the ship's purser, was one of the last people to get off the ship, and she and Karyn Rutledge sat together on the flight back to Miami. "Laurie and the rest of the crew had been keeping a really brave front up till then," Rutledge told me. "But when I asked her how she thought things looked for the ship she said, 'Just pray. Just pray.' Then she started to cry."

During the previous night, the younger Burke and Captain Guyan had talked by radio and decided to make a run to the north, heading for open water in the Gulf of Mexico, a journey of two and a half days. However, this idea was scrapped in Belize City; when Burke, back in Miami, charted the course, he realized he had underestimated Mitch's reach. The hurricane's feeder bands and their attendant winds were already battering the northern Yucatán coast.

Atlantic hurricanes generally move westward and have a tendency to turn, or "recurve," northward, away from the equator. Because of this and because of the northeast wind's tendency to push you into the leading edge of the storm, sailors refer to the north side of a hurricane as the Dangerous Semicircle. The south side is known as the Navigable Semicircle; here, the winds come from the northwest and west and can help push a vessel out the back of a westward-moving system. However, the fact that Mitch was a slow-moving hurricane negated most of the advantages associated with the Navigable Semicircle and the fact that the *Fantome* was a slow-moving ship meant that outrunning it was out of the question.

But so was staying in Belize City. A ship at the dock, or even at anchor, is a helpless target and runs the risk of getting pounded to pieces. Going to sea in a hurricane is standard procedure for big ships, though it must be said that most vessels the size of the *Fantome* can travel two or three times faster than her maximum speed of seven knots. For a ship with adequate speed and sea room, hurricanes are relatively easy to outmaneuver—not unlike dodging a bulldozer in an empty parking lot.

Twenty-four hours earlier, Captain Guyan had discussed his rapidly dwindling options over the phone with his close friend Captain Ed Snowdon, a former Windjammer skipper, and decided to head a hundred and twenty miles south of Belize City, to the Bahía de Amatique, a shallow bay with a small, naturally enclosed harbor called Puerto Barrios. Captains seeking refuge from storms refer to sheltered places like this as "hurricane holes," but this plan, too, was ultimately rejected; Captain Guyan was leery of boxing himself in. Only one option remained: head southeast for Roatán, the biggest of the Bay Islands, and shelter in its lee while Mitch passed to the north. In theory, the twenty-five-mile-long island would block the heaviest seas and some of the wind and, as the wind swung around, Captain Guyan would move the *Fantome* accordingly, keeping the island between her and the hurricane.

Mitch was now three hundred and fifty miles across, and satellite images were showing a cloud footprint that extended from the Florida Keys to the Pacific Ocean. Because there would have been so much water in the air, being driven so hard by the wind, Captain Stuart Larcombe, a former skipper on the *Fantome*, speculated recently that Guyan and his mates on deck were probably wearing masks and snorkels in order to see and breathe. However, masks and snorkels would not have been much use against Mitch, which by 1 p.m. on Monday, October 26th, had been upgraded to a Category 5. Mitch was now two hundred miles away, with winds in excess of a hundred and eighty m.p.h. When a hurricane grows as powerful as this, it will actually carry tornadoes inside it. These explosions of localized energy cause unlikely juxtapositions of objects to occur: hardwood broom handles are impaled by shards of Plexiglas; trees are pierced, dartlike, by the quills of parrot feathers; a magazine can be left on a table, undisturbed, while the building around it is tossed away like a straw hat. But, mostly, things just fly apart as if they had been caught up in some sort of cataclysmic tantrum.

At 5 a.m. on Tuesday, October 27th, after a rough but manageable crossing, the *Fantome* made the western end of Roatán. She was running her engines and, though her jibs had blown out earlier, she had her forestaysail and mainsail up, as much for power as to hold her steady to the wind in the progressively roughening seas. Throughout the night, the *Fantome* had been in radio contact with the younger

Burke at the Windjammer office, which is housed in a former radio station in Miami Beach. Hurricane-dodging is part of Windjammer's annual routine, so Captain Burke was not involved in the early planning, but that morning Michael Burke called his father at his home, on Biscayne Bay.

The ten-o'clock forecast indicated that Mitch had taken an unexpected turn toward the southeast, almost an about-face from its previous course. This meant that the hurricane was now moving away from the ship, but also that Mitch was a juggernaut capable of anything. The accuracy of the forecast was in doubt, however: that day, the weather satellite that covers the northwest Caribbean was malfunctioning, and the Weather Service had to compensate with a less accurate image from another satellite.

In retrospect, this was a significant moment: the last chance that Windjammer and Captain Guyan had to save the crew. At the west end of Roatán is a deep, narrow anchorage called Dixon Cove; throughout the morning, the *Fantome*, underpowered as she was, still had the mobility to reach it. Had Captain Guyan taken this opportunity, it would have been with the knowledge that he might be sacrificing the ship in order to save the men (though, in the end, Roatán suffered remarkably little damage). However, by 1 p.m. Mitch had turned yet again, this time toward the southwest. It was as if Mitch were scanning the sea with a baleful, Cyclopean eye until it caught sight of the *Fantome*. Its new course was a beeline for the ship, and by midafternoon the *Fantome* was fully in the thrall of Mitch's gigantic eye. A hurricane's strongest winds occur at the edge, or wall, of the eye, and Mitch's eye—twenty-two miles wide and reaching ten miles into the sky—was less than forty miles away. All around it, air and water, gravity and buoyancy, the world and the laws that govern it, were being puréed.

A few miles to the northeast, Mitch had reached the island of Guanaja. Afterward, many of the houses there looked to one Canadian relief worker "as if they had been blown up; they were in pieces all over the place." Half the trees on the island were flattened and the other half were so completely stripped that they looked as though they had been through a forest fire. As Mitch passed over, the air pressure was changing so rapidly it made people's ears pop. Survivors described the sound as a cross between the low rumble of heavy trucks and the shrieking roar of jet engines; it lasted for three days.

By now, Captain Guyan was simply trying to survive. His second mate, Onassis Reyes, a twenty-six-year-old Panamanian, and chief mate, Emmanuel (Brasso) Frederick, a forty-five-year-old Antiguan, were in the pilothouse, at the forward end of the ship. They were steering with an electric joystick connected to the rudder via hydraulic lines, but keeping their footing on a surface that was now rolling through ninety-degree arcs would have taken as much energy as keeping the ship on course. The chief engineer, Constantin Bucur, a Romanian, and his assistants would have been below in the engine room. The rest of the crew would most likely have been aft, holed up in the saloon, behind doors that had been screwed shut from the outside in order to keep them from being blown open by breaking waves forty to fifty feet high. One way to comprehend Mitch's impact on the *Fantome* and her crew that afternoon is to picture the ship—seven hundred tons and almost as long as a football field—being thrown off the roof of a house over and over again.

At four o'clock, Michael Burke called the ship on the satellite phone. Seated at his desk in Windjammer's quiet, air-conditioned offices on Bay Road, he listened while Captain Guyan told him that the *Fantome*'s staysails were ripping away. Burke was the last person to hear Guyan's voice before the phone went dead, at four-thirty that afternoon, probably because the ship's antennae were torn off. "Toward the end, I could hear him kind of gasping," Michael told me months later. He was sitting in his office, on the wall of which hangs a large photograph of the *Fantome* under full sail, looking glorious and unsinkable. He imitated Captain Guyan's gasping sound; it was the sound of great physical effort and, probably, fear. "The last words I can remember him saying were '*Whoo*—that was a big one.'" Michael put his hands to his face and sighed heavily. It was not a sigh of fatigue; it was the kind of breath one takes when overcome by great emotion, or preparing for a long, deep dive. No one knows what happened to the *Fantome* after the satellite phone cut out.

At 4:40 p.m., ten minutes after Windjammer lost contact with *Fantome*, a meteorologist flying in a hurricane-reconnaissance plane registered a gust of two hundred and eight miles an hour—the highest wind speed ever recorded with scientific instruments in a hurricane. Early on the morning of the twenty-eighth, Captain Guyan's fiancée, who was in England, had an unsettling dream. "I knew they'd lost contact with the ship," Annie Bleasdale recalls, "but I didn't think anything of it; that often happens in storms. But early the next morning I dreamed that Guyan was with me in bed. He was dressed in white, and in the dream I knew that he wouldn't be there when I woke up, that this was goodbye." For several nights afterward, Bleasdale says that she awoke to find a hazy presence floating over her bed. Theosophists are familiar with this phenomenon; they describe it as an astral body. "I used to call him Angel," Bleasdale says. "The crew absolutely loved him."

By October 31st, the hurricane had moved on to alter the lives and landscapes of Honduras and Nicaragua. The rain that fell was so torrential it had to be measured in feet. For days afterward, trees, cows, and the roofs of houses were seen drifting throughout the Yucatán Basin, some as much as two hundred miles from land. By then, the former African wave had been a trackable entity for over a month. More than eleven thousand people died.

THE AFTERMATH

The search for the *Fantome* lasted for three weeks and covered more than a hundred and forty thousand square miles. Except for a number of life jackets, life rafts, and fragments of woodwork from the deck, no sign of the ship has been found. Captains and Coast Guard officials familiar with severe storms and missing ships find this "mysterious" and "troubling." Equally puzzling is the fact that the ship's hydrostatic emergency beacon never activated; therefore, one can only guess at her location. She could be lying in a hundred feet of water off the coast of

Honduras, or in four thousand feet of water east of Guanaja. However, given the absence of wreckage or bodies, it is most likely that she sank with great suddenness.

When the search was finally called off, Windjammer experienced a collective emotional collapse. The magnitude of the loss forced this family business, which prefers to handle problems in-house, to seek outside help, including lawyers, publicity experts, and trauma consultants of the sort engaged by airlines after fatal crashes. It is the family atmosphere that draws many employees to the company, and, in a business that requires long separations from home, Windjammer crews tend to function almost like surrogate families. But when the blood families—the mothers, fathers, wives, and children of the crew, who are mostly West Indian and poor—needed Windjammer most, a line was drawn.

In November, Windjammer representatives fanned out across the Caribbean to visit the crew's relatives and try to explain what had happened—in particular, why the crew didn't get off when they still had a chance. What Michael D. Burke and Windjammer's customer service manager, Stehli Newson, couldn't explain was why the company carries no insurance for its crews and why they were offering people who had a negligible understanding of their rights relatively small sums of money—some as low as twenty thousand dollars—to sign papers that would release Windjammer from any future liability.

The Death on the High Seas Act (DOHSA), a United States federal law, requires a shipowner to compensate a dead crewman's family for wages he would have earned had he worked a normal life. Although Windjammer did want to give the families something to live on, it apparently believed that by acting quickly it could avoid more negative publicity and a costly settlement. (The company also wanted to limit its losses; the *Fantome*, which was valued at fifteen million dollars, was not insured.) The strategy backfired when lawyers and investigators showed up, telling the bereaved families that they could win damage awards of a million dollars apiece.

After the *Fantome* went down, Huggett & Scornavacca, a personal-injury law firm, went on Caribbean TV to advertise its services. The Miami firm, which specializes in maritime accidents and whose clients are mostly sailors from the Third World, does not have a particularly good reputation among defendants. William Huggett and his associates have been cited for soliciting clients in hospital rooms. There are judges in Dade County who refuse to hear cases that involve Huggett in any way. Snapshots of Huggett with smiling seamen and their compensation checks, along with photos of sinking and burning ships, line a wall in the waiting room of the firm's offices.

William Huggett himself is a fit and boyish-looking man of fifty. Before going to law school, he served in Vietnam as a lieutenant in the Marines and afterward wrote a novel based on his experiences there. Cruise-ship workers, he told me, are the "modern-day coal miners of the eighteen-nineties." We were talking in his office, whose emptiness is accentuated by a wall-sized plate-glass window overlooking the Dade County courthouse. "Windjammer's done such a bad thing," he went on. "It would be a pleasure to expose them to the public, but I don't think its going to happen." Huggett doesn't like DOHSA, because it allows only for lost wages; he would like to see it expanded to include pain, suffering, and loss of companionship. "I can't use this case to change the law," he said, "because I can't see Congress caring enough . . . . But, if this was thirty-one American seamen, the law would be changed in a minute."

As it happened, there were no Americans aboard the *Fantome* when she went down, and only two white men: Guyan March and Chief Engineer Bucur; in all, the *Fantome*'s crew represented eleven countries. A typical Windjammer deckhand comes from a place like Jamaica, St. Lucia, or Guyana, where unemployment is rampant and opportunities are few. He is on the ship for ten or more months a year and earns about three hundred dollars a month, plus tips. This is better money than he can make elsewhere in the islands, and it is enough to support his family.

The issue of nationality—the company's as well as the crew's—is crucial, because it determines where a case can be heard. Windjammer's ships are registered in Equatorial Guinea; such Third World flags of convenience are common in the cruise-ship industry, because these countries don't tax shipowners very heavily, if at all. What's more, each Windjammer ship is owned by an independent corporation based in Panama. By dividing and subdividing ownership and responsibility for its vessels in this way, a cruise line creates legal fire walls that can help limit liability. It also makes possible the lifestyle Windjammer affords its passengers and its owner.

I telephoned Captain Burke six weeks after the *Fantome* went down. When I told him that I wanted to talk to him about the *Fantome*, he said, cryptically. "I'm feeling some affinity for King Arthur. You're not a Lancelot, are you?" Burke was apparently looking for an ally—someone who would tell the world that it was Mitch, and not Windjammer, that had killed those men. I assured him I wasn't a Lancelot, but I wanted to learn how a big ship could be allowed to sink in such a well-announced storm. Apparently satisfied, Burke invited me to come to Miami for the weekend. If there was enough wind, he said, perhaps we would go for a sail on his ninety-two-foot yacht, *Tondeleyo*, a Polynesian name he translated as "white whore."

A few weeks after that conversation, I went to see Captain Burke. Although his children work for the company, it is the Captain's fantasies and ambitions that Windjammer embodies and supports. It seems appropriate that Burke—Big Daddy, as he is sometimes called—lives in a castle, a walled and moated attempt at medievalism whose squat towers and gargoyled crenellations are defiantly out of place among the Art Deco pastels of Miami Beach. The Captain designed the castle himself, and it is a remarkable combination of Disneyesque grandiosity and homespun invention which reflects Burke's interior mythology as vividly as "The Gates of Hell" reflects Rodin's. In the great hall is a sword in a stone. Just past the servants' quarters, from the mouth of a skull, saltwater gushes on its way into the moat, which is presided over by a life-size bronze statue of Neptune and patrolled by twenty-two live sharks.

Burke lives there with a Jamaican manservant, Gladstone, and a St. Vincentian cabinetmaker named Albert. He is visited regularly by a Salvadoran maid-of-all-work, various masseuses and masseurs, his broker, and members of his family, including his wife, June, from whom he has amicably separated. The Captain is a large, densely packed man with a rugged face, a hard, straight mouth, and tight gray curly hair. I saw traces of a seaman's vitality (he has sailed around the world five times), but he also appeared tired and sad. As it turned out, I arrived in the midst of a surprise fortieth-birthday party for one of Burke's daughters, Susan, the president of Windjammer's cruise business. "You were probably expecting a funeral, not a party," the Captain said when I was introduced to him by a newly hired publicist.

The son of a kosher butcher and a housewife, Burke was born in 1924, three years before the *Fantome* was launched. He grew up during the Depression near Asbury Park, New Jersey, and he spent much of the Second World War in submarines. After he was mustered out, Burke went to the Bahamas, where he found his calling while salvaging a nineteen-foot sloop. He named the vessel *Hangover* and sailed her to Miami. He repeated this procedure with progressively bigger vessels until he had assembled the largest privately owned fleet of tall ships in the world. Burke did for mega-yachting what Ford did for the automobile: he democratized it, bringing a previously inaccessible lifestyle within range of the middle class. Windjammer, which also runs a small freight operation, grosses roughly twenty-five million dollars a year.

Captain Burke's office lies behind a door opened by a ship's wheel that operates like the bolt-throw mechanism on a bank vault. His desk is fashioned from a hundred-and-fifty-gallon fish tank that no longer holds fish. As we ate submarine sandwiches, Burke recalled how, once upon a time, he could handle a seventy-two-foot schooner single-handed. Before a couple of strokes grounded him recently, he also flew an amphibious Grumman Goose, buzzing his fleet as it sailed below. "I had five ships then," he says. "Columbus had only three. I used to race them. I was in my glory; I had more fun than God." He slumped back in his chair. "God, I miss those days." And then, barely audibly, almost to himself, he said, "It's terrible I became a fucking businessman. I feel betrayed. After all these years, God let me down."

The following evening in his pool, surrounded by a menagerie of concrete mermaids and sea monsters, Burke told me, "I'm the mother and the father of these ships. Losing the *Fantome* was like losing a child." Presiding over his private lagoon, with a South Florida sunset flaming behind him across Biscayne Bay, Burke seemed an aging Neptune, unsure if he had the strength, or the heart, to replace what he'd lost. But the moment passed quickly, and he got to the bottom line. "If it wasn't for this lawsuit," he said, "all the money we're spending on lawyers' fees could be going to the families."

Windjammer has long been held in dubious regard by the East Coast's professional sailing community, members of which describe the fleet as haphazardly renovated and poorly maintained. "People in the professional sailing world just cringe at the thought of those vessels out there," Captain Andy Chase, a professor of marine transportation at Maine Maritime Academy, in Castine, told me. Chase represents a relatively recent change in attitude toward ships and risk. "I think going to sea at all costs is an outmoded tactic," he said. "Human life is worth more now than it was fifty years ago."

Yet this view still runs counter to many captains' instincts and training. Captain Burke's son claims that a captain makes the decisions about handling the ship, but Guyan was well aware that for a captain, particularly a young one, to lose his ship and live to tell about it is one of the surest ways to end a sailing career. Guyan March was doubly trapped—first, by a bicentennial storm in a geographic cul-de-sac, and, second, by a nineteenth-century conundrum. "You commit to the sea, and so to the ship," explains Windjammer's Captain Carmichael. "The captain *is* the ship. This may sound a little sick, but a hurricane is a glorious way to go."

Michael D. Burke insists that the decision to go to sea was not made by using nineteenth-century criteria—by weighing the lives of a mostly Third World crew against the prodigious cost of losing the *Fantome*. But in monetary terms the lives of the thirty-one men who died trying to save the *Fantome* will probably be worth only a fraction of what it will cost to replace her. William Huggettt insists that this was the motive for keeping the *Fantome* at sea in the face of a Category 5 hurricane, and his success will depend on whether he can prove that Windjammer acted in a negligent fashion by sending the ship on what he calls a "suicide mission" motivated by "corporate greed."

Andy Chase has spent weeks trying to understand Captain March's last days. "I think his decisions degenerated sequentially," Chase concluded. "Seeking a northern escape route makes no sense in a northwestbound hurricane, and hiding in the lee of Roatán wasn't sustainable." Inspired by Guyan's dilemma, Chase is preparing a paper that revives an old formula for safely anticipating erratic hurricane behavior (a formula that, had it been applied to Mitch, would have indicated, days in advance, that the Fantome had no safe escape route in the Gulf of Honduras). He will present it to the American and International Sail Training Associations' Safety Forum, when it meets in Boston this November.

Despite Mitch's size and ferocity, the *Fantome* was the only ship lost in the gulf; all other ships of similar size had fled the area by October 26th. Michael D. Burke, who had access to better weather information than Captain Guyan did, was relying heavily on an extended forecast predicting a northwesterly course for Mitch. He has been besieged by grieving family members, lawyers, and the media. "My competence is in question," he said, moments after I sat down in his cramped office. "For the forty-eight hours prior, I considered everything—all the options." His voice rose. "I didn't fuck up." Michael was the youngest skipper in the history of Windjammer, commanding his first ship at age twenty. He is smaller than his father, but when I looked at him I was reminded of the sadness in his father's eyes. I asked him why Windjammer tried to pay the crew's families so little.

"I've been demonized in the media by Mr. Huggett," he replied. "We have to remember that we are victims here also. Especially from Captain Burke's perspective, this was an act of God: 'We didn't do anything wrong, so why is it that we have to pay more?' There's a question of whether or not DOHSA even applies. That's going to be a battle that we'll go through with Huggett for the next two years: whether or not U.S. law is even applicable here. It's probably a very uphill battle for us. At the end of the day, DOHSA probably *does* apply."

When he talked about what had happened to the *Fantome* and her crew, his tone changed. "They were working for Windjammer, and they died under our supervision. That's the bottom line for me, anyway." He paused for a moment. "I'm not the owner of this company," he added. "I don't make the final decisions. Captain Burke was in denial. He keeps going back to 'What about me? I'm the one that's hurt. It's the Hurricane Center's fault for having a bad forecast.' Besides, there's survival involved. If it was as easy as getting this out of our lives for three million bucks"—a rough estimate of the compensation, based on DOHSA guidelines—"we would do it. This has been very disruptive. I would love to get it behind us."

As a result of pressure from Huggett, and from inside Windjammer as well, DOHSA has now become the reference point for the company's settlement package, a considerable step up from its initial offers. Michael D. Burke says, "Ideally, we'd like to settle with all the families, but there will probably be some who hold out for a trial." He has been travelling to the islands to negotiate with the families; so far, fourteen families have settled out of court, but it will take years for them to receive all the money. Of the remaining number, ten have committed to Huggett, and the rest have retained separate counsel. Those who decide to sue are gambling on Huggett's success and won't see a verdict or a settlement for quite some time. For some, it is worth the wait. Cansantine Hardware is a Jamaican who once worked for Windjammer; his son, O'Ryan, had been working for Windjammer for only a year. "I don't care about the money," Cansantine told me. "The money won't bring back my boy. I want justice." One parent said flatly, "I would like to crucify Mike Burke—for my son."

Meanwhile, the families who have agreed to settle are being promised awards of between seventy-five thousand and a hundred and seventy-five thousand dollars, depending on the number of children and the crewman's pay scale. This is a paltry sum by American standards, but immense for most of the families involved.

During our last meal together, seated at a table in the castle, the Captain told me of an image that comes to him at night. "I'm in the saloon of the *Fantome*," he said. "She's going down, and I'm trapped inside." The most chilling detail is not the screams of the men around him, or the certainty of death, or the crushing sense of powerlessness. It is that he is alone.

On December 12, 1998, there was a memorial service for the crew, held at Quarantine Point, on the island of Grenada. All the families of the crew were invited, and many came—at Windjammer's expense. Burke was absent; he had sent his children as his proxies. When I watched a videotape of the service, I saw his daughter Susan, a slender, fine-boned woman, and Michael, sitting in the sweltering heat while, all around them, the mothers of Caribbean sons wailed with abandon. After the ceremony (Burke had asked that a favorite passage of his, from Kipling's *Captains Courageous*, be read at the service), the mourners walked out to the end of Quarantine Point, a long, narrow finger of land pointing westward off Grenada's southern coast. Each person held a rose, preparing to throw it into the sea. When that was done, they turned and walked inland, but Annie Bleasdale, who had been Guyan March's fiancée, waited. "I couldn't bear to throw my rose," she told me. "When I finally did, the water suddenly became alive with fish—jumping and dancing on the water for as far as the eye could see. I wasn't the only one who saw it. There were others there, too. The locals said they'd never seen anything like it. I remember somebody saying, 'It's them.'"

from Winterdance: The Fine Madness
of Running the Iditarod
by Gary Paulsen

Gary Paulsen (born 1939) is known to millions of young readers for Hatchet, Dogsong and other books that explore themes such as loss, violence and survival. Paulsen in 1983 ran the Iditarod—the world's most famous dogsled race, which crosses 1,150 miles of Arctic terrain. His book about that experience describes the strangeness and intensity of his encounters with the land, the elements, the dogs and the other sledders.

The beginning of the battle to cross the interior of Alaska by dog starts when you leave McGrath. The distance to be run to reach the Bering coast is something on the order of seven hundred miles—say, from Minneapolis to New Orleans—and the terrain is so varied and difficult that it is well there has been the Burn and crossing the Alaska Range to prepare one.

At first it does not seem such a very bad thing. After leaving McGrath the trail winds on the river and then comes to a bar where wonderful hosts hand out bag lunches and soft—or hard, if you choose—drinks to take us on our way to the last checkpoint before the interior at the town (nearly so) of Ophir.

We hit Ophir after dark and I put the team down for a couple of hours while I worked on their feet. They lay, holding up their feet automatically for ointment, but did not sleep hard and kept fussing so I hooked them up and headed out in darkness.

Because it was not totally pitch I left my headlamp off, and we hadn't gone far before I felt the sled dragging. It kept moving—they could have pulled a Lincoln by this time—but was dragging funny and I stopped to inspect the runners. As I did so I turned my headlamp on and saw that the runner was coated with a full half-inch of dog crap. And more, with the light on I saw that we were running in a three-foot-wide swath of fresh dog shit. I had not seen this before but it would be this way after many of the remaining checkpoints. The dogs are fed heavily in the checkpoints and then rested. As they get more professional about running, they understand the checkpoints and what they mean. They know that when they leave the checkpoint they are going to have to pull for some distance and they do not want to carry any extra weight so they "blow" themselves on their way out. Consequently, there is a sea of fresh dog crap leaving each checkpoint.

I set the hook and flipped the sled on its back and used a pocket knife to scrape the plastic runner shoes clean. This all took some time and dawn came while I was scraping. When I was finished I flipped the sled upright, pulled the snowhook, and looked out over the team at a completely different world.

It was, somehow, almost a different planet—like suddenly being transported to the moon, or Mars. We were on the face of a shallow but very high hill, the sun coming up to the right rear. Out in front and below us lay a huge plain, stretching off to the horizon and beyond. Here and there at vast intervals there were small stands of low brush, and in the distance I could just make out low hills and rolling ground. Other than the odd bits of brush it was treeless and seemed barren. There was very little snow covering the grass—a constant, driving wind blew the snow away—which added to the alien barrenness.

Cookie stopped as if to say, "You can't be serious about wanting to cross *that?* . . ."

And in truth I wasn't thinking anything of the kind. A part of me simply didn't understand the enormity of trying to cross the interior of Alaska by dog team. I could be out there a month, I thought, and never seem to have moved. It . . . was . . . endless.

But in another way I was dazzled by it, and hopelessly drawn to it. Race or no race, life or no life—there was nothing that could keep me out of it, out of the interior.

"Pick it up," I said, to nudge her. "Let's go see it . . ."

She jerked once and started them down the incline and out into Alaska.

The part we were going to see was what I had come to think of as the true north—the tundra sweeps, the Barrens. I had read books about it since I was a child, had felt the lure of it, the northern pull of it.

And now I was going to cross it by team.

Within a few miles I was locked into a mystical dance with the sweeps. I had come to love running dogs as much as I loved the dogs themselves; had come to love the harsh beauty of the woods.

But not like this. Something about this, the tundra, the hugeness of it, went inside me and is there still.

I think now that this was my final break with the normal world. Back there somewhere, back in the real world I had a wife and family, a life. But here, now, was everything I needed, everything I was; the sled, food, fifteen good friends—or fourteen friends and Devil, as it happened—all that I had become. I was complete, and part of that completeness was that we, the team and I, were in some way doing what we were meant to do—heading north into the sweeps.

The breakdown of the run across Alaska to get to the Yukon River was simple in its intent—simple and stark.

Leaving Ophir, we were to run 180 miles to the old ghost town of Iditarod, then another hundred or so over to Shageluk, just before getting on the river ice. The first part, the 180-mile run, is the longest run in the race between checkpoints. It requires carrying extra food and booties and gear in case there is a storm, and therein lies the one true problem of the run across the interior. There is enough time elapsed in the run for weather patterns, for whole climates to change.

The dogs move ten miles an hour (or in my case about seven). For short bursts they can go faster, but not for long. Ten miles an hour for four, five hours, then rest for four or five, then again, and again, around the clock. Climbing slows them drastically, as does deep snow—down to two, three miles an hour. Distance becomes meaningless measured in miles because the speed is so variable. A little thing like dog crap frozen to the runners and not discovered will cut speed by thirty percent. As the time shifts (it really proves to be devastatingly relative in the race) it always seems to slow forward progress.

When we started, the weather was wonderfully clear. The sun rose to our right rear and splashed a new gold light across the barren ground and made it glow. The dogs seemed to like the light and picked up the speed a bit and I thought—foolishly baiting the gods—hell, this won't be so bad.

The sky was clear except for two small wisps of clouds on the far horizon that I chose to ignore and we slid effortlessly on the snow and patchy grass down the long slope.

Until almost exactly midday everything went well.

The two clouds seemed to grow. I noted that as afternoon came. They stretched and smeared themselves across the horizon and then up in the sky. And the wind picked up a bit, but only a little, and I thought about getting ready for fighting wind but decided there would be plenty of time later.

There wasn't.

We dipped into a depression as we moved around a shallow hill on the right and as we came out into the open the wind tore my head off.

It literally worked inside my parka hood and blew it open and back off my face. With the wind came flowing snow, driving needles of ice taken from the ground and turned into projectiles digging into exposed skin.

I was nearly knocked off the sled by the force of it and just before Cookie disappeared behind a wall of blowing snow I could see her blown to the side so hard she had to crouch and dig with her claws to hold position.

I—we—paused. Usually when the wind hits that way it is in a gust and a moment's wait will give relief.

Not this time. It started hard and it just grew worse. I couldn't see anything, had no idea where to go. The wind had come from our left front and I thought we could steer with it, keeping it on my left cheek, until we came to shelter. But it was not to be. The dogs ran with the wind. Cookie tried to hold them and keep a true course, but they were too much for her and I felt them swinging around until the wind was at my rear, where it would be easier running.

"No, damnit—come around!"

But they would not. And worse, I couldn't hold them. The brakes wouldn't grab in the frozen ground and aside from the stubby frozen tundra grass there was nothing to hold the snowhook.

They just kept going. And because we were now moving with the wind it became easier to move and they increased speed to a full lope. I couldn't see any of the dogs, couldn't tell where we were going and they were now running wide open. I was reminded briefly of the military cliché: "Don't know where we are or where we're going but we're making really good time."

But in truth it was a patent recipe for disaster. I could lose the team or they could pile up and get injured. I grabbed the catch rope and tied the sled to my wrist so I could grab at it as a last chance if I fell off (I did this on advice of another musher who spoke to me after he'd finished the Burn; he had lost his team there and had to walk—as he put it—"across north, and I do mean *North* America").

Then I slammed harder on the brake, rode it with both feet, and kept hollering, "Whoa—whoa, damnit."

But it didn't help. They kept moving, running faster and faster. I couldn't see anything by this time—barely to the other end of the sled, none of the dogs—and could do little but hang on and wait for the wreck.

It did not come. The team held the high rate of speed for half an hour or so, then began to slow and, finally, as I felt the sled come to a level area, Cookie stopped them.

When they stopped I jumped on the hook to try to set it in the grass, then tried to turn and was blown completely off my feet. The only reason I wasn't blown away from the team was the catch rope around my wrist. I tried to swear but the words were torn away by the wind.

Seventy, eighty miles an hour, blowing clouds of snow horizontally into and past me—it was a staggering, killing wind.

I knew it was impossible to try and turn the team and run back, impossible to do anything but hunker down and survive.

I crawled hand over hand up the gangline, found each dog already curled into a weatherproof ball, and made my way back to the sled.

It took me only moments to get back to the sled, unzip the sled bag, unroll my sleeping bag inside the sled bag and crawl in. I zipped the sled bag up over my head, bundled up in the sleeping bag, and settled in. There was absolutely nothing else I could do. The weather had taken over.

Outside the wind grew in strength until it shrieked. But the sled bag was tight and the sleeping bag warm—though the temperature was dropping rapidly—and I was comfortable.

My eyes closed, opened, closed again, and I must have slept, although it may have been closer to passing out.

I do not know how long I slept. It was late afternoon when I had crawled into the sled bag. I awakened once and unzipped the bag enough to look out and see that it was dark and the wind was still howling.

The next time I opened my eyes it was silent, absolutely quiet. I heard a strange rasping and realized it was the sound of my breathing inside the confines of the bag, but other than that nothing.

I lay for some time, reluctant to break the warm comfort of the bag. And the truth is I'd probably be there still except that nature called.

I unzipped the bag over my head. It felt strangely heavy and as soon as I unzipped it, a large pile of snow fell in on me, finishing the waking-up process, and I stood to a bright, cold world.

We had moved into a shallow depression, a saucer-shaped bowl perhaps a hundred yards across. The bowl was completely filled with snow, blown level with drifting clouds of it. I was the only thing standing, or showing. The dogs were covered and totally gone. Except for little puffs of steam released up through melted exit holes over each dog's nose where their breath came out, there was no sign of the team, the sled, nothing.

I had to urinate fiercely and I stood to the side of the sled—walking in waist-deep snow—to take care of it. I was not five feet from my sled and fumbling through layers of clothing when suddenly, right where I was going to piss, the snow began moving and a man's head appeared.

"Jesus, it's bright out here, isn't it?"

"Where did you come from?"

He stood and shook the snow off. "Hell, I don't know. We were moving pretty well until the shit hit the fan. Then I couldn't hold them and we wound up here. Must have followed your trail in . . ."

"We? You mean you and the dogs?"

"God, no—we were convoying across the middle. Must have been six, seven teams in our group."

"Where are they?"

He looked around the small basin. "Here."

And they were. Cookie had heard me talking and I saw her head peep out of the snow and swivel around, looking at the day. Devil popped up next, then Max—finally rested enough—and Devil growled at Max and the noise caught other ears and in a second the whole basin exploded in dogs and people standing and shaking off snow, fighting, snarling, pissing, and stretching. Eleven full teams, close to two hundred dogs and ten people had followed us into the small bowl and dug in to ride the windstorm out and I hadn't heard a sound. . . .

from A Wind Storm in the Forest
by John Muir

Most people look for shelter in a storm. John Muir (1838–1914) was more likely to climb a tree for a better view. Muir, best known as a pioneer of the American conservationist movement, led the drive to create Yosemite National Park and founded the Sierra Club. His nature writing is exuberant—even rapturous—as in this description of a powerful wind storm in California's Sierra Nevada Mountains.

One of the most beautiful and exhilarating storms I ever enjoyed in the Sierra occurred in December, 1874, when I happened to be exploring one of the tributary valleys of the Yuba River. The sky and the ground and the trees had been thoroughly rain-washed and were dry again. The day was intensely pure, one of those incomparable bits of California winter, warm and balmy and full of white sparkling sunshine, redolent of all the purest influences of the spring, and at the same time enlivened with one of the most bracing wind-storms conceivable. Instead of camping out, as I usually do, I then chanced to be stopping at the house of a friend. But when the storm began to sound, I lost no time in pushing out into the woods to enjoy it. For on such occasions Nature has always something rare to show us, and the danger to life and limb is hardly greater than one would experience crouching deprecatingly beneath a roof.

It was still early morning when I found myself fairly adrift. Delicious sunshine came pouring over the hills, lighting the tops of the pines, and setting free a stream of summery fragrance that contrasted strangely with the wild tones of the storm. The air was mottled with pine-tassels and bright green plumes, that went flashing past in the sunlight like birds pursued. But there was not the slightest dustiness, nothing less pure than leaves, and ripe pollen, and flecks of withered bracken and moss. I heard trees falling for hours at the rate of one every two or three minutes; some uprooted, partly on account of the loose, water-soaked condition of the ground; others broken straight across, where some weakness caused by fire had determined the spot. The gestures of the various trees made a delightful study. Young Sugar Pines, light and feathery as squirrel-tails, were bowing almost to the ground; while the grand old patriarchs, whose massive boles had been tried in a hundred storms, waved solemnly above them, their long, arching branches streaming fluently on the gale, and every needle thrilling and ringing and shedding off keen lances of light like a diamond. The Douglas Spruces, with long sprays drawn out in level tresses, and needles massed in a gray, shimmering glow, presented a most striking appearance as they stood in bold relief along the hill-tops. The madroños in the dells, with their red bark and large glossy leaves tilted every way, reflected the sunshine in throbbing spangles like those one so often sees on the rippled surface of a glacier lake. But the Silver Pines were now the most impressively beautiful of all. Colossal spires 200 feet in height waved like supple goldenrods chanting and bowing low as if in worship, while the whole mass of their long, tremulous foliage was kindled into one continuous blaze of white sun-fire. The force of the gale was such that the most steadfast monarch of them all rocked down to its roots with a motion plainly perceptible when one leaned against it. Nature was holding high festival, and every fiber of the most rigid giants thrilled with glad excitement.

I drifted on through the midst of this passionate music and motion, across many a glen, from ridge to ridge; often halting in the lee of a rock for shelter, or to gaze and listen. Even when the grand anthem had swelled to its highest pitch, I could distinctly hear the varying tones of individual trees,—Spruce, and Fir, and Pine, and leafless Oak—and even the infinitely gentle rustle of the withered grasses at my feet. Each was expressing itself in its own way—singing its own song, and making its own peculiar gestures—manifesting a richness of variety to be found in no other forest I have yet seen. The coniferous woods of Canada, and the Carolinas, and Florida, are made up of trees that resemble one another about as nearly as blades of grass, and grow close together in much the same way. Coniferous trees, in general, seldom possess individual character, such as is manifest among Oaks and Elms. But the California forests are made up of a greater number of distinct species than any other in the world. And in them we find, not only a marked differentiation into special groups, but also a marked individuality in almost every tree, giving rise to storm effects indescribably glorious.

Toward midday, after a long, tingling scramble through copses of hazel and ceanothus, I gained the summit of the highest ridge in the neighborhood; and then it occurred to me that it would be a fine thing to climb one of the trees to obtain a wider outlook and get my ear close to the Æolian music of its topmost needles. But under the circumstances the choice of a tree was a serious matter. One whose instep was not very strong seemed in danger of being blown down, or of being struck by others in case they should fall; another was branchless to a considerable height above the ground, and at the same time too large to be grasped with arms and legs in climbing; while others were not favorably situated for clear views. After cautiously casting about, I made choice of the tallest of a group of Douglas Spruces that were growing close together like a tuft of grass, no one of which seemed likely to fall unless all the rest fell with it. Though comparatively young, they were about 100 feet high, and their lithe, brushy tops were rocking and swirling in wild ecstasy. Being accustomed to climb trees in making botanical studies, I experienced no difficulty in reaching the top of this one, and never before did I enjoy so noble an exhilaration of motion. The slender tops fairly flapped and swished in the passionate torrent, bending and swirling backward and forward, round and round, tracing indescribable combinations of vertical and horizontal curves, while I clung with muscles firm braced, like a bobolink on a reed.

In its widest sweeps my tree-top described an arc of from twenty to thirty degrees, but I felt sure of its elastic temper, having seen others of the same species still more severely tried—bent almost to the ground indeed, in heavy snows—without breaking a fiber. I was therefore safe, and free to take the wind into my pulses and enjoy the excited forest from my superb outlook. The view from here must be extremely beautiful in any weather. Now my eye roved over the piny hills and dales as over fields of waving grain, and felt the light running in ripples and broad swelling undulations across the valleys from ridge to ridge, as the shining foliage was stirred by corresponding waves of air. Oftentimes these waves of reflected light would break up suddenly into a kind of beaten foam, and again, after chasing one another in regular order, they would seem to bend forward in concentric curves, and disappear on some hillside, like sea-waves on a shelving shore. The quantity of light reflected from the bent needles was so great as to make whole groves appear as if covered with snow, while the black shadows beneath the trees greatly enhanced the effect of the silvery splendor.

Excepting only the shadows there was nothing somber in all this wild sea of pines. On the contrary, notwithstanding this was the winter season, the colors were remarkably beautiful. The shafts of the pine and libocedrus were brown and purple, and most of the foliage was well tinged with yellow; the laurel groves, with the pale undersides of their leaves turned upward, made masses of gray; and then there was many a dash of chocolate color from clumps of manzanita, and jet of vivid crimson from the bark of the madroños, while the ground on the hillsides, appearing here and there through openings between the groves, displayed masses of pale purple and brown.

The sounds of the storm corresponded gloriously with this wild exuberance of light and motion. The profound bass of the naked branches and boles booming like waterfalls; the quick, tense vibrations of the pine-needles, now rising to a shrill, whistling hiss, now falling to a silky murmur; the rustling of laurel groves in the dells, and the keen metallic click of leaf on leaf—all this was heard in easy analysis when the attention was calmly bent.

The varied gestures of the multitude were seen to fine advantage, so that one could recognize the different species at a distance of several miles by this means alone, as well as by their forms and colors, and the way they reflected the light. All seemed strong and comfortable, as if really enjoying the storm, while responding to its most enthusiastic greetings. We hear much nowadays concerning the universal struggle for existence, but no struggle in the common meaning of the word was manifest here; no recognition of danger by any tree; no deprecation; but rather an invincible gladness as remote from exultation as from fear.

I kept my lofty perch for hours, frequently closing my eyes to enjoy the music by itself, or to feast quietly on the delicious fragrance that was streaming past. The fragrance of the woods was less marked than that produced during warm rain, when so many balsamic buds and leaves are steeped like tea; but, from the chafing of resiny branches against each other, and the incessant attrition of myriads of needles, the gale was spiced to a very tonic degree. And besides the fragrance from these local sources there were traces of scents brought from afar. For this wind came first from the sea, rubbing against its fresh, briny waves, then distilled through the redwoods, threading rich ferny gulches, and spreading itself in broad undulating currents over many a flower-enameled ridge of the coast mountains, then across the golden plains, up the purple foot-hills, and into these piny woods with the varied incense gathered by the way.

Winds are advertisements of all they touch, however much or little we may be able to read them; telling their wanderings even by their scents alone. Mariners detect the flowery perfume of land-winds far at sea, and sea-winds carry the fragrance of dulse and tangle far inland, where it is quickly recognized, though mingled with the scents of a thousand landflowers. As an illustration of this, I may tell here that I breathed sea-air on the Firth of Forth, in Scotland, while a boy; then was taken to Wisconsin, where I remained nineteen years; then, without in all this time having breathed one breath of the sea, I walked quietly, alone, from the middle of the Mississippi Valley to the Gulf of Mexico, on a botanical excursion, and while in Florida, far from the coast, my attention wholly bent on the splendid tropical vegetation about me, I suddenly recognized a sea-breeze, as it came sifting through the palmettos and blooming vine-tangles, which at once awakened and set free a thousand dormant associations, and made me a boy again in Scotland, as if all the intervening years had been annihilated.

Most people like to look at mountain rivers, and bear them in mind; but few care to look at the winds, though far more beautiful and sublime, and though they become at times about as visible as flowing water. When the north winds in winter are making upward sweeps over the curving summits of the High Sierra, the fact is sometimes published with flying snow-banners a mile long. Those portions of the winds thus embodied can scarce be wholly invisible, even to the darkest imagination. And when we look around over an agitated forest, we may see something of the wind that stirs it, by its effects upon the trees. Yonder it descends in a rush of water-like ripples, and sweeps over the bending pines from hill to hill. Nearer, we see detached plumes and leaves, now speeding by on level currents, now whirling in eddies, or, escaping over the edges of the whirls, soaring aloft on grand, upswelling domes of air, or tossing on flame-like crests. Smooth, deep currents, cascades, falls, and swirling eddies, sing around every tree and leaf, and over all the varied topography of the region with telling changes of form, like mountain rivers conforming to the features of their channels.

After tracing the Sierra streams from their fountains to the plains, marking where they bloom white in falls, glide in crystal plumes, surge gray and foam-filled in boulder-choked gorges, and slip through the woods in long, tranquil reaches—after thus learning their language and forms in detail, we may at length hear them chanting all together in one grand anthem, and comprehend them all in clear inner vision, covering the range like lace. But even this spectacle is far less sublime and not a whit more substantial than what we may behold of these storm-streams of air in the mountain woods.

We all travel the milky way together, trees and men; but it never occurred to me until this stormday, while swinging in the wind, that trees are travelers, in the ordinary sense. They make many journeys, not extensive ones, it is true; but our own little journeys, away and back again, are only little more than tree-wavings—many of them not so much.

When the storm began to abate, I dismounted and sauntered down through the calming woods. . . .

The Leeward Side
by Whitney Balliett

Whitney Balliett (born 1926) is America's greatest jazz critic. He also is a master of language and a superb essayist on subjects that can range from weather to ghosts. Balliett has written for The New Yorker since 1951. This short piece appeared in the magazine 50 years after the great hurricane of 1938.

I count myself as one of the survivors of the great hurricane of 1938. I was twelve years old, and on that Wednesday my mother drove me to Grand Central Station, from Long Island, where we lived, and deposited me, a homesick wreck, on the noon train to Boston. I was on my way to my first year at the Fessenden School, a day and boarding school in West Newton. The week before (sewing on nametags, packing my trunk, sending it off by Railway Express), the weather had been oppressive and motionless, with low clouds and off-and-on showers, and it was the same on the morning I left New York. The school, in those baronial days, had taken an entire car for its twenty-odd students and some parents. It was a parlor car, the Oriental, and it was the last car on the train. The school had sent as our shepherd Roderick Hagenbuckle, a short, forthright, square-jawed science teacher and football coach.

All I remember about the first couple of hours on the train was trying to make sense of so much strangeness—strange faces, this strange, plushy railroad car, the unbelievable strangeness of leaving home for the first time. But the outer world got through when the train reached New London. It was about three o'clock and was raining hard, and the train had, for some reason, stopped on the railroad bridge over the Thames river. Most of the boys had gathered at the windows on the right side of the car and were watching a huge five-masted sailing ship—its yardarms bare—advance slowly toward the bridge (I found out later that she was a three-hundred-foot barkentine used for training by the American Nautical Academy. She did not hit the bridge, and ended up with her bow tied to one wharf and her stern to another.) When the ship was a hundred yards away, the train began to move. Much of the trackage of what was then the New York, New Haven & Hartford Railroad runs close to the shoreline of Long Island Sound after it leaves New London, but beyond Mystic, which is five or six miles from New London, we entered a kind of sea. There was water on both sides of the train, and, on both sides, islands with occasional houses on them. Above the train, the air had suddenly become gray with flying objects—boards and tree branches and what might have been clothes. By three-thirty, we were on the gravel trestle that crosses a low area just west of the Stonington station. It wasn't a trestle any-more, though; water covered the tracks. The train, barely moving, stopped, then went fifty yards and stopped again. (A woman on the train who was taking her daughter to another school near Boston is quoted in Everett Allen's book *A Wind to Shake the World* as saying, "After the train left New London, we became aware of danger. Trees had been felled along the route and as the train went over a causeway [leading into Stonington] we saw the water pounding angrily on both sides. The train trembled like a bicycle inexpertly ridden.")

Ten minutes later, the Oriental began leaning noticeably to the right. One rumor said a trawler was wedged on the tracks in front of the locomotive; another said a house was. A conductor appeared and told Roderick Hagenbuckle that the train might capsize, and we were to move forward immediately, to the first car. Leave our luggage, he said—it would be sent on later. (I had a small suitcase.) We got through the next two cars, and then, because of the increasing jam-up (there were over two hundred and fifty people on board), someone suggested we get out of the train and walk up the left, or leeward, side to the first car. I went into the open vestibule with half a dozen Fessendens, and we looked out. There was nothing but water and wind and a curious smell, almost a burning smell. Water stretched almost as far as I could see, and scattered houses appeared to float on it. The wind was maniacal. It sounded like unceasing jeering, and it was punctuated with thuds and crashes as debris smashed into the windward side of the train. Everything—homesickness, fear, and chagrin over the prospect of getting my brand-new Rogers Peet clothes *wet*—hit at once, and I started to weep. A lady I have always thought of as being from Texas said some kind words and offered me a sip of Coca-Cola. Two people went down the steps and into the water, awkwardly turned right, and vanished. We followed. Stepping into the chest-deep water was one of the strangest sensations I have known: the water was not cold but it felt icy; it was not turbulent but it felt rough and malevolent. The Texas lady grabbed my right arm and said something, but the wind blew it away. We passed four cars before we reached the first one. The going was slow and clumsy. We were walking on railroad ties and sank almost to our necks whenever we missed one. Whatever had been on the tracks in front of the train had been swept away. Fifteen or twenty people were struggling along a heavy line that had been stretched from the locomotive to a tree or a telephone pole a hundred feet away. I wondered if we would have to do that next. But we were hoisted up the steps at the rear of the first car and pushed inside. Nearly the whole trainload of passengers was in the car, and the din almost shut out the noise of the storm. The rest of the train had been emptied, and after a trainman, working mostly underwater, uncoupled the next car, the locomotive, with barely enough pressure, began to move. A cheer went up, and what was left of the train crept several hundred feet up a gradually curving incline and into the dry, safe Stonington station.

The rest is almost anticlimactic. A third of the Fessenden contingent got off on the right side of the train and ended up for the night in a Catholic school, while the rest of us got off on the left and made our way up a hill to the Stonington town hall. We spent the night on camp chairs in a large gymlike room. My Texas friend cut off my necktie, which had shrunk to the point of strangulation. The next morning broke—as all mornings break after great storms—blue and clear and with that innocent, "What did I do?" look to the sky. The chaos outside was unbelievable: downed elephantine elms, crushed automobiles, askew houses, live wires hanging like snakes from telephone poles. Even more sinister were table-size slates that had blown off the town-hall roof and sliced into the ground around it with decapitating force. We were put on a bus to the Westerly, Rhode Island, train station, and we sat on a motionless train there for four hours. We were then put on another bus, which somehow got through to West Newton. At the school, we were bathed, given shots, and put to bed for two days. Roderick Hargenbuckle, God rest his soul (he ended his days running a sailing camp on Cape Cod) never lost his cool, and had even managed to let the school know we were alive.

The statistics of the storm are still astonishing. With winds clocked at a hundred and eighty-six miles per hour, it hit at high tide without any warning, and almost seven hundred people died. (The weather bureau depended on ships at sea for information about oncoming storms, but, for whatever reason, there were no ships reporting between Cape Hatteras, where the storm had last been sighted, and Long Island. And, of course, everyone in the Northeast had grown lax about hurricanes. None of consequence had hit since 1815.) The property damage was astronomical—twenty thousand houses, two hundred and seventy-five million trees, six thousand boats, twenty-six thousand cars, and on and on.

My suitcase appeared out of the blue the following summer. It had been found in Long Island Sound, and it was swollen and sprung. Inside were an empty toilet kit, a hard-back brush, and leather-bound copies of the Bible and Mary Baker Eddy's *Science and Health*, compliments of my Christian Scientist mother, who never tired of attributing my survival to the presence of the books in my suitcase. Both books were twice their original size and resembled small blimps. On the fly-leaf of the Bible, in barely decipherable water-blurred ink, were my name and address and the customary cosmic tag: "United Sates of America, Western Hemisphere, World, the Universe."

Master and Man

by Leo Tolstoy

*Leo Nikolayevich Tolstoy (1828–1910) yearned
and even fought to live a life of spiritual purity,
as though the world to which he so powerfully
bore witness had somehow come between him
and God. Yet his work in stories like "Master and
Man" has reminded generations of readers that
grace knows where to find us.*

It happened in the seventies, in winter, on the day after St. Nicholas's day. There was a holiday in the parish, and the village innkeeper and second-guild merchant, Vasily Andreyevich Brekhunov, could not go away, as he had to attend church (he was a church warden), and go receive and entertain friends and acquaintances at home. But at last all the guests were gone, and Vasily Andreyevich began preparations for a drive over to a neighboring landowner to buy from him the forest for which they had been bargaining this long while. He was very anxious to go, so as to forestall the town merchants, who might snatch away this profitable purchase. The youthful landowner only asked ten thousand rubles for the forest, while Vasily Andreyevich offered seven thousand. In reality, seven thousand was but a third of the real worth of the property. Vasily Andreyevich might, perhaps, be able to drive the better bargain, because the forest stood in his district, and by an old-standing agreement between him and the other village-merchants, no one of them competed in another's territory. But Vasily Andreyevich had learned that the timber merchants from the capital town of the province intended to bid for the Gory-achkin forest, and he decided to go at once and conclude the bargain. Accordingly, as soon as the feast was over, he took seven hundred rubles of his own from the strongbox, added to them twenty-three hundred belonging to the church, and after carefully counting the whole, he put the money in his pocketbook and made haste to be gone. Nikita, the laborer, the only one of Vasily Andreyevich's men who was not drunk that day, ran to harness the horse. He was not drunk on this occasion because he was a drunkard; since the last day before the fast, when he spent his coat and boots in drink, he had forsworn his debauchery and kept sober for a month. He was not drinking even now, in spite of the temptation arising from the universal absorption of alcohol during the first two days of the holiday.

Nikita was a fifty-year-old muzhik from the neighboring village; an "unreliable" man, as folk called him, "one who lived most of his life with other people" and not at his own home. He was esteemed everywhere for his industry, quickness, and strength, and still more for his kindliness and pleasantness. But he could never live long in one place because about twice a year, or even more often he gave way to drink; and at such times, besides spending all he had, he became turbulent and quarrelsome. Vasily Andreyevich had dismissed him several times, and afterward engaged him again, valuing his honesty and kindness to animals, but chiefly his cheapness. The merchant did not pay Nikita eighty rubles, the worth of such a man, but forty; and even that he paid without regular account, in small installments, and mostly not in cash, but in high-priced goods from his own shop.

Nikita's wife, Martha, a vigorous and once-beautiful woman, carried on the home, with a boy and two girls. She never pressed Nikita to live at home; first, because she had lived for about twenty years with a cooper, a muzhik from another village, who lodged with them; and second, because, although she treated her husband as she pleased when he was sober, she feared him like fire when he was drinking. Once, when drunk at home, Nikita, perhaps to counterbalance his sober humility, broke open his wife's box, took her best clothes, and seizing an ax, cut to shreds all her gala dress and garments. The whole wages that Nikita earned went to his wife, without objection from him. It was in pursuance of this arrangement that Martha, two days before the holiday, came to Vasily Andreyevich, and got from him wheat flour, tea, sugar, with a pint of vodka—about three rubles worth in all—and five rubles in cash; for which she gave thanks as for a great and special favor, when in fact, and at the lowest figure, the merchant owed twenty rubles.

"What agreement did I make with you?" said Vasily Andreyevich to Nikita. "If you want anything, take it; you will work it out. I am not like other folks, with their putting off, and accounts, and fines. We are dealing straightforwardly. You work for me, and I stand by you. What you need, I give it to you."

Talking in this way, the merchant was honestly convinced of his beneficence to Nikita; and he spoke with such assertion that everyone, beginning with Nikita, confirmed him in this conviction.

"I understand, Vasily Andreyevich, I do my best, I try to do as I would for my own father. I understand all right," answered Nikita, understanding very well that he is cheated, but at the same time feeling that it is useless to try to get the accounts cleared up. While there is nowhere else to go, he must stay where he is, and take what he can get.

When Nikita was told by his master to put the horse in, willingly and cheerfully as always, and with a firm and easy stride, he stepped to the cart shed, took down from the nail the heavy, tasseled leather bridle, and jingling the rings of the bit, went to the stable where stood the horse that Vasily Andreyevich had bidden to be harnessed.

"Well, silly, are you tired, tired?" said Nikita, in answer to the soft whinny that greeted him from the stallion, a fairly good dark bay of medium height, with sloping quarters, who stood solitary in his stall. "Quiet, quiet, there's plenty of time! Let me give you a drink first," he went on to the horse, as though speaking to a creature with reason. With the skirt of his coat he swept down the horse's broad, double-ridged back, roughed and dusty as it was; then he put the bridle on the handsome young head, arranged his ears and mane, and led him away to drink. Picking his way out of the dung-strewn stable, the dark bay began to plunge, making play with his hind foot, as though to kick Nikita, who was hurrying him to the well.

"Now, then, now, then, you rogue," said Nikita, knowing Moukhorta was careful that the hind foot went no farther than his fur coat, doing no hurt, and knowing how the horse liked this play.

After the cold water, the horse stood awhile, breathing, and moving his wet, strong lips, from which transparent drops fell into the trough; then he sniffed.

"If you want no more, you needn't take it. Well, let it be at that; but don't ask again for more," said Nikita, quite seriously emphasizing to Moukhorta the consequences of his behavior. Then he briskly led him back to the shed, pulling the rein on the young horse, who lashed out all the way along the yard.

No other men were about, except a stranger to the place, the husband of the cook, who had come for a holiday.

"Go and ask, there's a good fellow, which sleigh is wanted, the wide one or the little one," said Nikita to him.

The cook's husband went away, and soon returned with the answer, that the small one was ordered. By this time, Nikita had harnessed the horse, fixed the brass-studded saddle, and carrying in one hand the light-painted yoke, with the other hand he led the horse toward the two sleighs that stood under the shed.

"All right, let us have the small one," said he, backing the intelligent horse (which all the time pretended to bite at him) into the shafts; and with the help of the cook's husband, he began to harness.

When all was nearly ready, and only the reins needed fixing, Nikita sent the cook's husband to the shed for straw, and to the storehouse for the rug.

"That's nice. Don't, don't don't bristle up!" said Nikita, squeezing into the sleigh the freshly thrashed oat straw that the cook's husband had brought. "Now give me the sacking, while we spread it out, and put the rug over it. That's all right, just the thing, comfortable to sit on," said he, doing that which he was talking about, and making the rug tight over the straw all around.

"Thanks, my dear fellow," said Nikita to the cook's husband. "When two work, it's done quicker." Then, disentangling the leather reins, the ends of which were brought together and tied on a ring, he took the driver's seat on the sleigh and shook up the good horse, who stirred himself, eager to make across the frozen refuse that littered the yard, toward the gate.

"Uncle Mikit, eh, Uncle!" came a shout behind him from a seven-year-old boy in black fur cloak, new white felt boots, and warm cap, who slammed the door as he hurried from the entrance hall toward the yard. "Put me in!" he asked, in a shrill voice, buttoning his cloak as he ran.

"All right, come, my dove," said Nikita; and stopping the sleigh, he put in the master's son, full of joy, and drove out into the road.

It was three o'clock, and cold (about ten degrees of frost), gloomy, and windy. In the yard it seemed quiet, but in the street a strong breeze blew. The snow showered down from the roof of the barn close by and, at the corner by the baths, flew whirling around. Nikita had scarcely driven out and turned around by the front door when Vasily Andreyevich, too, with a cigarette in his mouth, wearing a sheepskin overcoat tightly fastened by a girdle placed low, came out from the entrance hall. He strode down the trampled snow of the steps, which creaked under his boots, and stopped to turn in the corners of his overcoat collar on both sides of his ruddy face (clean-shaven, except for a mustache), so as to keep the fur clear from the moisture of his breath.

"See there! What a manager! Here he is!" said he, smiling and showing his white teeth, on catching sight of his little son on the sleigh. Vasily Andreyevich was excited by the wine he had taken with his guests, and was therefore more than usually pleased with everything that belonged to him, or that was of his doing. His wife, a pale and meager woman, about to become a mother, stood behind him in the entrance hall, with a woolen plaid so wrapped about her head and shoulders that only her eyes could be seen.

"Would it not be better to take Nikita with you?" she asked, timidly, stepping out from the door. Vasily Andreyevich answered nothing, but spat. "You have money with you," the wife continued, in the same plaintive voice. "What if the weather gets worse. Be careful, for God's sake."

"Do you think I don't know the road, that I need a guide?" retorted Vasily Andreyevich, with that affected compression of the lips that he used when speaking among dealers in the market, as though he valued his own speech.

"Really, do take him, I ask you, for God's sake!" repeated his wife, folding her plaid closer.

"Just listen! She sticks to it like a leaf in the bath! Why, where must I take him to?"

"Well, Vasily Andreyevich, I'm ready," said Nikita cheerfully. "If I'm away, there are only the horses to be fed," he added, turning to his mistress.

"I'll look after that, Nikitushka; I'll tell Simon," answered the mistress.

"Shall I come, Vasily Andreyevich?" asked Nikita, waiting.

"It seems we must consider the old woman. But if you come, go and put on something warmer," said Vasily Andreyevich, smiling once more, and winking at Nikita's fur coat, which was very old, torn under the arms and down the back, and soiled and crease-worn around the skirts.

"Hey, friend, come and hold the horse awhile!" shouted Nikita to the cook's husband in the yard.

"I'll hold him myself," said the little boy, taking his cold red hands out of his pockets and seizing the cold leather reins.

"Only don't be too long putting your best coat on! Be quick!" shouted Vasily Andreyevich jestingly to Nikita.

"In a breath, good master Vasily Andreyevich!" said Nikita, and he ran down the yard to the laborers' quarters.

"Now, Arinushka, give me my overcoat off the oven, I have to go with the master!" said Nikita, hastening into the room and taking his girdle down from the nail.

The cook, who had just finished her after-dinner nap, and was about to get ready the samovar for her husband, turned to Nikita merrily, and catching his haste, moved about quickly, took the worn-out woolen overcoat off the oven where it was drying, and shook and rubbed it.

"How comfortable you must be, with your husband here," said Nikita to the cook, always, as part of his good-natured politeness, ready to say something to anyone whom he came across. Then putting around himself the narrow and worn girdle, he drew in his breath and tightened it about his spare body.

"There," he said, afterward, addressing himself not to the cook but to the girdle, while tucking the ends under his belt. "This way you won't jump out." Then working his shoulders up and down to get his arms loose, he put on the overcoat, again stretching his back to free his arms; and that done, he took his mittens from the shelf. "Now we're all right."

"You ought to change your boots," said the cook, "those boots are very bad."

Nikita stopped, as if remembering something.

"Yes, I ought . . . . But it will be all right; it's not far." And he ran out into the yard.

"Won't you be cold, Nikitushka?" said his mistress, as he came up to the sleigh.

"Why should I be cold? It is quite warm," answered Nikita, arranging the straw in the forepart of the sleigh, so as to bring it over the feet, and stowing under it the whip that a good horse would not need.

Vasily Andreyevich was already in the sleigh, almost filling up the whole of the curved back with the bulk of his body wrapped in two great fur coats; and taking up the reins, he started at once. Nikita jumped in, seating himself in front to the left and hanging one leg over the side.

The good stallion sped the sleigh along at a brisk pace over the trodden and frozen road, the runners creaking faintly as they went.

"Look at him there, hanging on! Give me the whip, Nikita," shouted Vasily Andreyevich, evidently enjoying the sight of his boy holding to the sleigh runners behind. "I'll give it to you! Run to your mother, you young dog!"

The boy jumped off. The dark bay began to amble, and then, getting his breath, broke into a trot.

Kresty, the village where the home of Vasily Andreyevich stood, consisted of six houses. Scarcely had they passed the blacksmith's house when they suddenly felt the wind to be stronger than they had thought. The road was no longer visible. The tracks of the sleigh as they were left behind were instantly covered with snow, and the road was only to be distinguished by its rise above the land on either side. The snow swept over the plain like thick smoke, and the horizon disappeared. The Telyatin forest, always particularly visible, loomed dimly through the driving snow dust. The wind came from the left hand, persistently blowing aside the mane on Moukhorta's lofty neck, turning away even his knotted tail, and pressing the deep collar of Nikita's overcoat (he sat on the windward side) against his face and nose.

"There is no chance of his showing speed with this snow," said Vasily Andreyevich, proud of his horse. "I once went to Pashutino with him, and we got there in half an hour."

"What?"

"Pashutino, I said, and he did it in half an hour."

"A good horse that, no question," said Nikita.

They became silent. But Vasily Andreyevich wanted to talk.

"Now I think of it, did you tell your good woman not to give any drink to the cooper?" asked the merchant, who was wholly of opinion that Nikita must feel flattered, talking with such an important and sensible man as himself. He was so pleased with this, his own jest, that it never entered his head that the subject might be unpleasant to Nikita.

Again the man failed to catch his master's words, the voice being carried away by the wind.

Vasily Andreyevich, in his clear and loud voice, repeated the jest about the cooper.

"God help them, master, I don't think about the matter. I only watch that she does no harm to the boy; if she does—then God help her!"

"That is right," said Vasily Andreyevich. "Well, are you going to buy a horse in the spring?" Thus he began a new topic of conversation.

"I must buy one," answered Nikita, turning aside the collar of his coat and leaning toward his master. The conversation had become interesting to him, and he did not wish to lose a word.

"My lad is grown up, and it is time he plowed for himself and gave up hiring out," said he.

"Well, then, take that horse with the thin loins; the price will not be high," shouted Vasily Andreyevich, eagerly entering into his favorite business of horse dealing, to which he gave all his powers.

"You had better give me fifteen rubles, and I'll buy in the market," said Nikita, who knew that at the highest price, the horse with the thin loins that his master wanted to sell to him was not worth more than seven rubles, but would cost him, at his master's hands, twenty-five; and that meant half a year's wages gone.

"The horse is a good one. I treat you as I would myself. Honestly. Brekhunov injures no man. Let me stand the loss, and me only. Honestly," he shouted in the voice that he used in cheating his customers, "a genuine horse."

"As you think," said Nikita, sighing, sure that it was useless to listen further; and he again drew the collar over his ear and face.

They drove in silence for about half an hour. The wind cut sharply into Nikita's side and arm, where his coat was torn. He huddled himself up and breathed in his coat collar, which covered his mouth, and breathing this way seemed to make him warmer.

"What do you think, shall we go through Karamyshevo, or keep the straight road?" said Vasily Andreyevich.

The road through Karamyshevo was more frequented, and staked on both sides, but it was longer. The straight road was nearer, but it was little used, and the stakes, now snow-covered, marked it out but badly.

Nikita thought awhile.

"Through Karamyshevo is farther, but it is better going," he said.

"But straight on, we have only to be careful in passing the little valley, and then the way is fairly good," said Vasily Andreyevich, who favored the direct road.

"As you say," replied Nikita.

So the merchant went his own way. After driving about half a verst, passing a waymark, a long branch of oak, which shook in the wind and on which a dry leaf hung here and there, he turned to the left.

Upon turning, the wind blew almost directly against them, and the snow showered from on high. Vasily Andreyevich stirred up the horse and inflated his cheeks, blowing his breath upon his mustache. Nikita dozed.

They drove thus silently for about ten minutes. Then the merchant began to say something.

"What?" asked Nikita, opening his eyes.

Vasily Andreyevich did not answer, but bent himself about, looking behind them, and then ahead of the horse. The sweat had curled the animal's coat on the groin and neck, and he was going at a walk.

"I say, what's the matter?" repeated Nikita.

"What is the matter?" mocked Vasily Andreyevich, irritated. "I see no waymarks. We must be off the road."

"Well, pull up, then, and I will find the road," said Nikita, and lightly jumping down, he drew out the whip from the straw and struck out to the left from his own side of the sleigh.

The snow was not deep that season, but in places it was up to one's knee, and Nikita got it into his boots. He walked about, feeling with his feet and the whip, but could nowhere find the road.

"Well?" said the merchant when Nikita returned to the sleigh.

"There is no road on this side. I must try the other."

"What is that dark thing in front? Go and see," said Vasily Andreyevich.

Nikita walked ahead, got near the dark patch, and found it was black earth that the wind had strewn over the snow from some fields of winter wheat. After searching to the right also, he returned to the sleigh, shook the snow off himself, cleared his boots, and took his seat.

"We must go to the right," he said decidedly. "The wind was on our left before, now it is straight ahead. To the right," he repeated, with the same decision.

Vasily Andreyevich turned accordingly. But yet no road was found. He drove on for some time. The wind kept up, and the snow still fell.

"We seem to be astray altogether, Vasily Andreyevich," said Nikita suddenly, and as pleasantly as possible. "What is that?" he said, pointing to some black potato leaves that thrust themselves through the snow.

Vasily Andreyevich stopped the horse, which by this time was in heavy perspiration and stood with its deep sides heaving. "What can it mean?" asked he.

"It means that we are on the Zakharian lands. Why, we are ever so far astray!"

"Bosh!" remarked Vasily Andreyevich, who now spoke quite otherwise than when at home, in an unconstrained and vulgar tone.

"I am telling you no lie; it is true," said Nikita. "You can feel that the sleigh is moving over a potato field, and there are the heaps of old leaves. It is the Zakharian factory land."

"What a long way we are off!" said the other. "What are we to do?"

"Go straight ahead, that's all. We shall reach someplace," said Nikita. "If we do not get to Zakharovka, we shall come out at the owner's farm.'"

Vasily Andreyevich, assented and let the horse go as Nikita had said. They drove in this way for a long while. At times they passed winter wheat fields, where the wind had turned up and blown loose soil over the snow-covered dikes and the snowdrifts. Sometimes they passed a stubble field, sometimes a cornfield, where they could see the upstanding wormwood and straw beaten by the wind; sometimes they saw on all sides deep white snow, with nothing above it. The snow whirled down from on high, and up from below. Now they seemed to be going downhill, and now uphill; then they seemed as though standing still, while the snowfield ran past them. Both were silent. The horse was evidently tiring; his coat grow crisp and white with frost, and he no better than walked. Suddenly he stumbled in some ditch or watercourse and went down. Vasily Andreyevich wanted to halt, but Nikita opposed him.

"Why should we stop? We have gone astray, and we must find our road. Hey, old fellow, hey," he shouted in an encouraging voice to the horse; and he jumped from the sleigh, sinking into the ditch. The horse dashed forward and quickly landed upon a frozen heap. Obviously it was a made ditch.

"Where are we, then?" said Vasily Andreyevich.

"We shall see," answered Nikita. "Go ahead, we shall get to somewhere."

"Is not that the Goryachkin forest?" asked the merchant, pointing out a dark mass that showed across the snow in front of them.

"When we get nearer, we shall see what forest it is," said Nikita.

He noticed that from the side of the dark mass long dry willow leaves were fluttering toward them; and he knew thereby that it was no forest, but houses; yet he chose not to say so. And in fact they had scarcely gone twenty-five yards when they distinctly made out the trees and heard a new and melancholy sound. Nikita was right; they had come upon not a forest but a row of tall willow trees, whereon a few scattered leaves still shivered. The willows were evidently ranged along the ditch and around a barn. Coming up to the trees, through which the wind moaned and sighed, the horse suddenly planted his forefeet above the height of the sleigh, then drew up his hind legs after him, and they were out of the snow and on the road.

"Here we are," said Nikita, "but we don't know where."

The horse went right away along the snow-covered road, and they had not gone many yards when they saw a fence around a barn, from which the snow was flying in the wind. Passing the barn the road turned in the direction of the wind and brought them upon a snow-drift. But ahead of them was a passage between two houses; the drift was merely blown across the road, and must be crossed. Indeed, after passing the drift, they found a village street. In front of the end house of the village, the wind was shaking desperately the frozen linen that hung there: shirts, one red, one white, some leg cloths, and a skirt. The white shirt especially shook frantically, tugging at the sleeves.

"Look there, either a lazy woman, or a dead one, left her linen out over the holiday," said Nikita, seeing the fluttering shirts.

At the beginning of the street the wind was still felt and the road was snow-covered. But well within the village there was shelter, more warmth, and life. At one house a dog barked; at another, a woman, with her husband's coat over her head, came running from within and stopped at the door to see who was driving past. In the middle of the village could be heard the sound of girls singing. Here the wind, the snow, the frost, seemed subdued.

"Why, this is Grishkino," said Vasily Andreyevich.

"It is," said Nikita.

Grishkino it was. It turned out they had strayed eight versts to the left, out of their proper direction; still, they had gotten somewhat nearer to their destination. From Grishkino to Goryachkino was about five vesrts more.

In the middle of the village they almost ran into a tall man walking in the center of the road.

"Who is driving?" said this man, and he held the horse. Then, recognizing Vasily Andreyevich, he took hold of the shaft and leaped up to the sleigh, where he sat himself on the driver's seat.

It was the muzhik Isai, well-known to the merchant, and known through the district as a first-rate horsethief.

"Ah, Vasily Andreyevich, where is God sending you?" said Isai, from whom Nikita caught the smell of vodka.

"We are going to Goryachkino."

"You've come a long way around! You had better have gone through Malakhovo."

"Yes, but we got astray," said Vasily Andreyevich, pulling up.

"A good horse," said Isai, examining him and dexterously tightening the loosened knot in his tail. "Are you going to stay the night here?"

"No, friend, we must go on."

"Your business must be pressing. And who is that? Ah, Nikita Stepanovich!"

"Who else?" answered Nikita. "Look here, good friend, can you tell us how not to miss the road again?"

"How can you possibly miss it? Just turn back straight along the street, and then, outside the houses, keep straight ahead. Don't go to the left until you reach the high road, then turn to the left."

"And which turning do we take out of the high road? The summer or the winter road?" asked Nikita.

"The winter road. As soon as you get clear of the village there are some bushes, and opposite them is a waymark, an oaken one, all branches. There is the road."

Vasily Andreyevich turned the horse back and drove through the village.

"You had better stay the night," Isai shouted after them. But the merchant did not answer; five versts of smooth road, two versts of it through the forest, was easy enough to drive over, especially as the wind seemed quieter and the snow seemed to have ceased.

After passing along the street, darkened and trodden with fresh horse tracks, and after passing the house where the linen was hung out (a sleeve of the white shirt was by this time torn off, and the garment hung by one frozen sleeve), they came to the weirdly moaning and sighing willows, and then were again in the open country. Not only was the snowstorm still raging, but it seemed to have gained strength. The whole road was under snow, and only the stakes, the waymarks, proved that they were keeping right. But even these signs of the road were difficult to make out, for the wind blew right in their faces.

Vasily Andreyevich screwed up his eyes and bent his head, examining the marks; but for the most part he left the horse alone, trusting to his sagacity. And, in fact, the creature went correctly, turning now to the left, now to the right, along the windings of the road which he sensed under his feet. So that in spite of the thickening snow and strengthening wind, the waymarks were still to be seen, now on the left, now on the right.

They had driven thus for ten minutes when suddenly, straight in front of their horse, a black object sprang up, moving through the snow. Moukhorta had caught up to a sleigh containing other travelers, and he struck his forefeet against it.

"Drive around! Go ahead!" cried these others.

Vasily Andreyevich shaped to go around them. In the sleigh were four peasants, three men and a woman, evidently returning from a feast. One of the men whipped the quarters of their poor horse with a switch, while two of them, waving their arms from the fore part of the sleigh, shouted out something. The woman, muffled up and covered with snow, sat quiet and rigid at the back.

"Who are you?" asked Vasily Andreyevich.

"A-a-a!" was all that could be heard.

"I say, who are you?"

"A-a-a!" shouted one of the peasants with all his strength; but nevertheless it was impossible to make out the name.

"Go on! Don't give up!"

"You have been enjoying yourselves."

"Get on! Get on! Up, Semka! Step out! Up, up!"

The sleighs struck together, almost locked their sides, then fell apart, and the peasants' sleigh began to drop behind. The shaggy, snow-covered, big-bellied pony, obviously distressed, was making his last efforts with his short legs to struggle along through the deep snow, which he trod down with labor. For a moment, with distended nostrils and ears set back in distress, he kept his muzzle, which was that of a young horse, near Nikita's shoulder; then he began to fall still farther behind.

"See what drink does," said Nikita. "They have tired that horse to death. What heathens!"

For a few minutes the pantings of the tired-out horse could be heard, with the drunken shouts of the peasants. Then the pantings become inaudible, and the shouts, also. Again all was silent, except for the whistling wind and the occasional scrape of the sleigh runners upon a bare spot of road.

This encounter livened up and encouraged Vasily Andreyevich, who drove more boldly, not examining the waymarks, and again trusting to his horse.

Nikita had nothing to occupy him, and dozed. Suddenly the horse stopped, and Nikita was jerked forward, knocking his nose against the front.

"It seems we are going wrong again," said Vasily Andreyevich.

"What is the matter?"

"The waymarks are not to be seen. We must be out of the road."

"Well, if so, let us look for the road," said Nikita laconically, and he got out again to explore the snow. He walked for a long time, now out of sight, now reappearing, then disappearing; at last he returned.

"There is no road here; it may be farther on," said he, sitting down in the sleigh.

It began to grow dark. The storm neither increased nor diminished.

"I should like to meet those peasants again," said Vasily Andreyevich.

"Yes, but they won't pass near us; we must be a good distance off the road. Maybe they are astray, too," said Nikita.

"Where shall we make for, then?"

"Leave the horse to himself. He will find his way. Give me the reins."

The merchant handed over the reins, the more willingly that his hands, in spite of his warm gloves, felt the frost.

Nikita took the reins and held them lightly, trying to give no pressure; he was glad to prove the good sense of his favorite. The intelligent horse, turning one ear and then the other, first in this, then in that direction, presently began to wheel around.

"He only stops short of speaking," said Nikita. "Look how he manages it! Go on, go on, that's good."

The wind was now at their backs; they were warmer.

"Is he not wise?" continued Nikita, delighted with his horse. "A Kirghiz beast is strong, but stupid. But this one—look what he is after with his ears. There is no need of a telegraph wire; he can feel through a mile."

Hardly half an hour had gone when a forest, or a village, or something loomed up in front; and to their right, the waymarks again showed. Evidently they were upon the road again.

"We are back at Grishkino, are we not?" exclaimed Nikita suddenly.

Indeed, on the left hand rose the same barn, with the snow flying from it; and farther on was the same line with the frozen shirts and drawers, so fiercely shaken by the wind.

Again they drove through the street, again felt the quiet and shelter, again saw the road with the horse tracks, heard voices, songs, the barking of a dog. It was now so dark that a few windows were lighted.

Halfway down the street, Vasily Andreyevich turned around the horse toward a large house and stopped at the yard pit.

"Call out Taras," he ordered Nikita.

Nikita went up to the snow-dimmed window, in the light from which glittered the flitting flakes, and knocked with the handle of the whip.

"Who is there?" a voice answered to his knock.

"The Brekhunovs, from Kresty, my good man," answered Nikita. "Come out for a minute."

Someone moved from the window, and in about two minutes the door in the entrance hall was heard to open, the latch of the front door clicked, and holding the door against the wind, there peeped out an old, white-bearded man, who wore a high cap and a fur coat over a white holiday shirt. Behind him was a young fellow in a red shirt and leather boots.

"Glad to see you," said the old man.

"We have lost our road, friend," said Vasily Andreyevich. "We set out for Goryachkino and found ourselves here. Then we went on, but lost the road again."

"I see; what a wandering!" answered the old man. "Petrushka, come, open the gates," he said to the young man in the red shirt.

"Of course I will," said the young fellow cheerfully as he ran off through the entrance hall.

"We are not stopping for the night, friend," said Vasily Andreyevich.

"Where can you go in darkness? You had better stop."

"Should be very glad to, but I must go on."

"Well, then, at least warm yourself a little; the samovar is just ready," said the old man.

"Warm ourselves? We can do that," said Vasily Andreyevich. "It cannot get darker, and when the moon is up, it will be still lighter. Come, Nikita, let us go in and warm up a bit."

"I don't object; yes, let us warm ourselves," said Nikita, who was very cold, and whose one desire was to warm his benumbed limbs over the oven.

Vasily Andreyevich went with the old man into the house. Nikita drove through the gate that Petrushka opened, and by the latter's advice, stood the horse under a shed, the floor of which was strewn with stable litter. The high bow over the horse caught the roof beam, and the hens and a cock perched up there began to cackle and scratch on the wood. Some startled sheep, pattering their feet on the frozen floor, huddled themselves out of the way. A dog, evidently a young one, yelped desperately in fright and barked fiercely at the stranger.

Nikita held conversation with them all. He begged pardon from the fowls, and calmed them with assurances that he would give them no more trouble; he reproved the sheep for being needlessly frightened; and while fastening up the horse, he kept on exhorting the little dog.

"That will do," said he, shaking the snow from himself. "Hear how he is barking!" added he, for the dog's benefit. "That's quite enough for you, quite enough, stupid! That will do! Why do you bother yourself? There are no thieves or strangers about."

"It is like the tale of the Three Domestic Counselors," said the young man, thrusting the sleigh under the shed with his strong arm.

"What counselors?"

"The tale is in P'uls'n. A thief sneaks up to a house; the dog barks— that means 'Don't idle, take care'; the cock crows—that means 'Get up'; the cat washes itself—that means 'A welcome guest is coming, be ready for him,'" said the young man, with a broad smile.

Petrushka could read and write, and knew almost by heart the only book he possessed, which was Paulsen's primer; and he liked, especially when, as now, he had a little too much to drink, to quote from the book some saying that seemed appropriate to the occasion.

"Quite true," said Nikita.

"I suppose you are cold, uncle," said Petrushka.

"Yes, something that way," said Nikita. They both crossed the yard and entered the house.

• • •

The house at which Vasily Andreyevich had drawn up was one of the richest in the village. The family had five fields, and besides these, hired others outside. Their belongings included six horses, three cows, two heifers, and a score of sheep. In the house lived twenty-two souls; four married sons, six grandchildren (of whom one, Petrushka, was married), two great-grandchildren, three orphans, and four daughters-in-law with their children. It was one of the few families that maintain their unity; yet even here was beginning that indefinable interior discord—as usual, among the women—that must soon bring about separation. Two sons were water carriers in Moscow; one was in the army. At present, those at home were the old man, his wife, one son who was head of the house, another son who came from Moscow on a holiday, and all the women and children. Besides the family there was a guest, a neighbor, who was the elder of the village.

In the house there hung over the table a shaded lamp, which threw a bright light down upon the tea service, a bottle of vodka, and some eatables, and upon the brick wall of the corner where hung the holy images with pictures on each side of them. At the head of the table sat Vasily Andreyevich in his black fur cost, sucking his frozen mustache and scrutinizing the people and the room with his eyes of a hawk. Beside him at the table sat the white-bearded bald old father of the house, in a white homespun shirt; by him, wearing a thin cotton shirt, sat a son with sturdy beck and shoulders, the one who was holiday-making from Moscow; then the other son, the strapping eldest brother who acted as head of the house; then the village elder, a lean and red-haired muzhik.

The muzhiks, having drunk and eaten, prepared to take tea; the samovar already boiled, standing on the floor near the oven. The children were in evidence about the oven and the sleeping shelves. On the bench along the wall sat a woman with a cradle beside her. The aged mother of the house, whose face was wrinkled all over, even to the lips, waited on Vasily Andreyevich. As Nikita entered the room, she filled up a coarse glass with vodka and handed it to Vasily Andreyevich.

"No harm done, Vasily Andreyevich, but you must drink our good health," said the old man.

The sight and smell of vodka, especially in his cold and tired condition, greatly disturbed Nikita's mind. He became gloomy, and after shaking the snow from his coat and list, stood before the holy images; without noticing the others, he made the sign of the cross thrice, and bowed to the images; then, turning to the old man, he bowed to him first, afterward to all who sat at the table, and again to the women beside the oven, saying, "Good fortune to your feast." Without looking at the table, he began to take off his overcoat.

"Why, you are all over frost, uncle," said the eldest brother, looking at the rime on Nikita's face, eyes, and beard.

Nikita got his coat off, shook it, hung it near the oven, and came to the table. They offered him vodka also. There was a moment's bitter struggle; he wavered on the point of taking the glass and pouring the fragrant, transparent liquid into his mouth. But he looked at Vasily Andreyevich, remembered his vow, remembered the lost boots, the cooper, his son for whom he had promised to buy a horse when the spring came; he sighed, and refused.

"I don't drink, thank you humbly," he said gloomily, and sat down on the bench near the second window.

"Why not?" asked the eldest brother.

"I don't drink, that's all," said Nikita, not daring to raise his eyes, and looking at the thawing icicles in his beard and mustache.

"It is not good for him," said Vasily Andreyevich, munching a biscuit after emptying his glass.

"Then have some tea," said the kindly old woman. "I daresay you are quite benumbed, good soul. What a while you women are with the samovar."

"It is ready," answered the youngest, and wiping around the samovar with an apron, she bore it heavily to the table and set it down with a thud.

Meanwhile, Vasily Andreyevich told how they had gone astray and worked their way back twice to the same village, what mistakes they had made, and how they had met the drunken peasants. Their hosts expressed surprise, showed why and where they had missed the road, told them the names of the revelers they had met, and made plain how they ought to go.

"From here to Molchanovka, a child might go; the only thing is to make sure where to turn out of the high road, just beside the bushes. But yet you did not get there," said the village elder.

"You ought to stop here. The women will make up a bed," said the old woman persuasively.

"You would make a better start in the morning; much pleasanter, that," said the old man, affirming what his wife had said.

"Impossible, friend! Business!" said Vasily Andreyevich. "If you let an hour go, you may not be able to make it up in a year," added he, remembering the forest and the dealers who were likely to compete with him. "By all means, let us stretch out," he said, turning to Nikita.

"We may lose ourselves again," said Nikita moodily. He was gloomy because of the intense longing he felt for the vodka; and the tea, the only thing that could quench that longing, had not yet been offered to him.

"We have only to reach the turning, and there is no more danger of losing the road, as it goes straight through the forest," said Vasily Andreyevich.

"Just as you say, Vasily Andreyevich; if you want to go, let us go," said, Nikita, taking the glass of tea offered to him.

"Well, let us drink up our tea, and then march!"

Nikita said nothing, but shook his head, and carefully pouring the tea into the saucer, began to warm his hands over the steam. Then, taking a small bite of sugar in his mouth, he turned to their hosts, said "Your health," and drank down the warming liquid.

"Could anyone come with us to the turning?" asked Vasily Andreyevich.

"Why not? Certainly," said the eldest son. "Petrushka will put in the horse and go with you as far as the turning."

"Then put in your horse, and I shall be in your debt."

"My dear man," said the kindly old woman, "we are right glad to do it."

"Petrushka, go and put in the mare," said the eldest son.

"All right," said Petrushka, with his broad smile; and taking his cap from the nail, he hurried away to harness the horse.

While the harnessing was in progress, the talk turned back to the point where it stood when Vasily Andreyevich arrived. The old man had complained to the village elder about the conduct of his third son, who had sent him no present this holiday time, though he had sent a French shawl to his wife.

"These young folk are getting worse and worse," said the old nun.

"Very much worse!" said the village elder. "They are unmanageable. They know too much. There's Demochkin, now, who broke his father's arm. It all comes from too much learning."

Nikita listened, watched the faces, seeming as though he, too, would like to have a share in the conversation, were he not so busy with his tea; as it was, he only nodded his head approvingly. He emptied glass after glass, growing warmer and more and more comfortable. The talk kept on in the one strain, all about the harm that comes from family division; clearly, no theoretical discussion, but concerned with a rupture in this very house, arising through the second son, who sat there in his place, morosely silent. The question was a painful one, and absorbed the whole family; but in politeness they refrained from discussing their private affairs before strangers. At last, however, the old man could endure no longer. In a tearful voice, he began to say that there should be no breakup of the family while he lived, that the house had much to thank God for, but if they fell apart—they must become beggars.

"Just like the Matvayeffs," said the village elder. "There was plenty among them all, but when they broke up the family, there was nothing for any of them."

"That's just what you want to do," said the old man to his son.

The son answered nothing, and there was a painful pause. Petrushka broke the silence, having by this time harnessed the horse and returned to the room, where he had been standing for a few minutes, smiling all the time.

"There is a tale in P'uls'n, just like this," said he. "A father gave his sons a besom to break. They could not break it while it was bound together, but they broke it easily by taking every switch by itself. That's the way here," he said, with his broad smile. "All's ready!" he added.

"Well, if we're ready, let us start," said Vasily Andreyevich. "As to this quarrel, don't you give in, grandfather. You got everything together, and you are the master. Apply to the magistrate; he will show you how to keep your authority."

"And he gives himself such airs, such airs," the old man continued to complain, appealingly. "There is no ordering him! It is as though Satan lived in him."

Meanwhile, Nikita, having drunk his fifth glass of tea, did not stand it upside down, in sign that he had finished, but laid it by his side, hoping they might fill it a sixth time. But as the samovar had run dry the hostess did not fill up for him again; and then Vasily Andreyevich began to put on his things. There was no help; Nikita, too, rose, put back his nibbled little cake of sugar into the sugar basin, wiped the moisture from his face with the skirt of his coat, and moved to put on his overcoat.

After getting into the garment, he sighed heavily, then, having thanked their hosts and said good-bye, he went out from the warm, bright room and through the dark, cold entrance hall, where the wind creaked the doors and drove the snow in at the chinks, into the dark yard. Petrushka, in his fur coat, stood in the center of the yard with the horse, and smiling as ever, recited a verse from 'P'uls'n":

> The storm covers the heaven with darkness,
> Whirling the driven snow,
> Now, howling like a wild beast,
> Now, crying like a child.

Nikita nodded appreciatively, and arranged the reins.

The old man, coming out with Vasily Andreyevich, brought a

lantern, wishing to show the way; but the wind put it out at once. Even in the enclosed yard, one could see that the storm had risen greatly.

"What weather!" thought Vasily Andreyevich. "I'm afraid we shall not get there. But it must be! Business! And then, I have put our friend to the trouble of harnessing his horse, God helping, we'll get there."

Their aged host also thought it better not to go; but he had offered his arguments already, and they had not been listened to. "Maybe it is old age makes me overcautious; they will get there all right," thought he. "And we can all go to bed at the proper time. It will be less bother."

Petrushka likewise saw danger in going, and felt uneasy; but he would not let anyone see it, and put on a bold front, as though he had not a fear; the lines about "whirling the driven snow" encouraged him, because they were a quite true description of what was going on out in the street. As to Nikita, he had no wish to go at all; but he was long used to following other people's wishes, and to give up his own. Therefore nobody withheld the travelers.

Vasily Andreyevich went over to the sleighs, found them with some groping through the darkness, got in, and took the reins.

"Go ahead!" he shouted. Petrushka, kneeling in his sleigh, started the horse. The dark bay, who had before been whinnying, aware of the mare's nearness, now dashed after her, and they drove out into the street. They rode once more through the village, down the same road, past the space where the frozen linen had hung, but hung no longer; past the same barn, now snowed-up almost as high as the roof, from which the snow flew incessantly; past the moaning, whistling, and bending willows. And again they came to where the sea of snow raged from above and below. The wind had such power that, taking the travelers sideways when they were crossing its direction, it heeled the sleigh over so that the horse was pushed aside. Petrushka drove his good mare in front, at an easy trot, giving her an occasional lively shout of encouragement. The dark bay pressed after her.

After driving thus for about ten minutes, Petrushka turned around and called out something. But neither Vasily Andreyevich nor Nikita could hear for the wind, but they guessed that they had reached the turning. In fact, Petrushka had turned to the right; the wind came in their front, and to the right, through the snow, loomed something black. It was the bush beside the turning.

"Well, good-bye to you!"

"Thanks, Petrushka!"

"'The storm covers the heaven with darkness!'" shouted Petrushka, and disappeared.

"Quite a poet," said Vasily Andreyevich, and shook the reins.

"Yes, a fine young man, a genuine fellow," said Nikita.

They drove on. Nikita sank and pressed his head between his shoulders, so that his short beard covered up his throat. He sat silent, trying to keep the warmth that the tea had given him. Before him he saw the straight lines of the shafts, which to his eyes looked like the ruts of the road; he saw the shifting quarters of the horse, with the knotted tail swayed in the wind; beyond, he saw the high bow between the shafts, and the horses rocking head and neck, with the floating mane. From time to time he noticed waymarks, and knew that, thus far, they had kept right, and he need not concern himself.

Vasily Andreyevich drove on, trusting to the horse to keep to the road. But Moukhorta, although he had picked himself up a little in the village, went unwillingly, and seemed to shirk from the road, so that Vasily Andreyevich had to press him at times.

"Here is a waymark on the right, here's another, and there's a third," reckoned Vasily Andreyevich, "and here, in front, is the forest," he thought, examining a dark patch ahead. But that which he took for a forest was only a bush. They passed the bush, drove about fifty yards farther, and there was neither the fourth waymark nor the forest.

"We must reach the forest soon," thought Vasily Andreyevich; and buoyed up by the vodka and the tea, he shook the reins. The good, obedient animal responded, and now at an amble, now at an easy trot, made in the direction he was sent, although he knew it was not the way in which he should have been going. Ten minutes went by, but no forest.

"I'm afraid we are lost again!" said Vasily Andreyevich, pulling up.

Nikita silently got out from the sleigh, and holding with his hand the flaps of his coat, which pressed against him or flew from him as he stood and turned in the wind, began to tread the snow, first to one side, then to the other. About three times he went out of sight altogether. At last he returned and took the reins from the hands of Vasily Andreyevich.

"We must go to the right," he said sternly and peremptorily; and he turned the horse.

"Well, if it must be to the right, let us go to the right," said Vasily Andreyevich, passing over the reins and thrusting his hands into his sleeves. "I should be glad to be back at Grishkino, anyway," he said.

Nikita did not answer.

"Now, then, old fellow, stir yourself," he called to the horse; but the latter, in spite of the shake of the reins, went on only slowly. In places the snow was knee-deep, and the sleigh jerked at every movement of the horse.

Nikita took the whip, which hung in front of the sleigh, and struck once. The good creature, unused to the lash, sprang forward at a trot, but soon fell again to a slow amble. Thus they went for five minutes. All was so dark, and so blurred with snow from above and below, that sometimes they could not make out the bow between the shafts. At times it seemed as though the sleigh was standing, and the ground running back. Suddenly the horse stopped, feeling something wrong in front of him. Nikita once more lightly jumped out, throwing down the reins, and went in front to find out what was the matter. But hardly had he taken a pace clear ahead, when his feet slipped and he fell down some steep place.

"Whoa, whoa!" he said to himself, trying to stop his fall, and falling. There was nothing to seize hold of, and he only brought up when his feet plunged into a thick bed of snow that lay in the ravine. The fringe of snow that hung on the edge of the ravine, disturbed by Nikita's fall, showered upon him, and got into his coat collar.

"That's bad treatment!" said Nikita, reproaching the snow and the ravine, as he cleared out his coat collar.

"Mikit, ha, Mikit," shouted Vasily Andreyevich, from above. But

Nikita did not answer. He was too much occupied in shaking away the snow, then in looking for the whip, which he lost in rolling down the bank. Having found the whip, he started to climb up the bank, but failed, rolling back every time, so that he was compelled to go along the foot of the bank to find a way up. About ten yards from the place where he fell, he managed to struggle up again, and turn back along the bank toward where the horse should have been. He could not see horse nor sleigh; but by going over in the direction to which the wind was blowing, he heard the voice of Vasily Andreyevich and the whinny of Moukhorta calling him, before he saw them.

"I'm coming. Don't make a noise for nothing," he said.

Only when quite near the sleigh could he make out the horse and Vasily Andreyevich, who stood close by, and looked gigantic.

"Where the devil have you gotten lost? We've got to drive back. We must get back to Grishkino anyway," the master began to rebuke him angrily.

"I should be glad to get there, Vasily Andreyevich, but how are we to do it? Here is a ravine where if we once get in, we shall never come out. I pitched in there in such a way that I could hardly get out."

"Well, surely we can't stay here; we must go somewhere," said Vasily Andreyevich.

Nikita made no answer. He sat down on the sleigh with his back to the wind, took off his boots and emptied them of snow, then, with a little straw that he took from the sleigh, he stopped from the inside a gap in the left boot.

Vasily Andreyevich was silent, as though leaving everything to Nikita alone. Having put on his boots, Nikita drew his feet into the sleigh, took the reins, and turned the horse along the ravine. But they had not driven a hundred paces when the horse stopped again. Another ditch confronted him.

Nikita got out again and began to explore the snow. He was afoot a long while. At last he reappeared on the side opposite to that from which he started.

"Vasily Andreyevich, are you alive?" he called.

"Here! What is the matter?"

"I can't make anything out, it is too dark; except some ditches. We must drive to windward again."

They set off once more; Nikita explored again, stumbling in the snow, or resting on the sleigh; at last, falling dawn, he was out of breath, and stopped beside the sleigh.

"How now?" asked Vasily Andreyevich.

"Well, I'm quite tired out. And the horse is done up."

"What are we to do?"

"Wait a minute." Nikita moved off again, and soon returned.

"Follow me," he said, going in front of the horse.

Vasily Andreyevich gave orders no more, but implicitly did what Nikita told him.

"Here, this way," shouted Nikita, stepping quickly to the right. Seizing Moukhorta's head, he turned him toward a snowdrift. At first the horse resisted, then dashed forward, hoping to leap the drift, but failed and sank in snow up to the hams.

"Get out!" called Nikita to Vasily Andreyevich, who sat in the sleigh; and taking hold of a shaft, he began to push the sleigh after the horse.

"It's a hard job, friend," he said to Moukhorta, "but it can't be helped. Stir yourself! Once more! Ah-oo-oo! Just a little!" he called out. The horse leaped forward, once, twice, but failed to clear himself, and sank again. He pricked his ears and sniffed at the snow, putting his head down to it as if thinking out something.

"Well, friend, this is no good," urged Nikita to Moukhorta. "A-ah, just a little more!" Nikita pulled on the shaft again; Vasily Andreyevich did the same on the opposite side. The horse lifted his head and made a sudden dash.

"A-ah, A-ah, don't be afraid, you won't sink," shouted Nikita. One plunge, a second, a third, and at last the horse was out from the snow-drift and stood still, breathing heavily and shaking himself clear. Nikita wanted to lead him on farther; but Vasily Andreyevich, in his two fur coats, had so lost his breath that he could walk no more, and dropped into the sleigh.

"Let me get my breath a little," he said, unbinding the handkerchief that tied the collar of his coat.

"We are all right here, you might as well lie down," said Nikita. "I'll lead him along"; and with Vasily Andreyevich in the sleigh, he led the horse by the head, about ten paces faster, then up a slight rise, and stopped.

The place where Nikita drew up was not in a hollow, where the snow might gather, but was sheltered from the wind by rising ground. At moments the wind, outside this protection, seemed to become quieter; but these intervals did not last long, and after them the storm, as if to compensate itself, rushed on with tenfold vigor, and tore and whirled the more. Such a gust of wind swept past as Vasily Andreyevich, with recovered breath, got out of the sleigh and went up to Nikita to talk over the situation. They both instinctively bowed themselves, and waited until the stress should be over. Moukhorta laid back his ears and shook himself discontentedly. When the blast had abated a little, Nikita took off his mittens, stuck them in his girdle, and having breathed a little on his hands, began to undo the strap from the bow over the shafts.

"'Why are you doing that?" asked Vasily Andreyevich.

"I'm taking out the horse. What else can we do? I'm worn out," said Nikita, as though apologizing.

"But we could drive out to somewhere."

"No, we could not. We should only do harm to the horse. The poor beast is worn out," said Nikita, pointing to the creature, who stood there, awaiting the next move with heavily heaving sides. "We must put up for the night," he repeated, as though they were at their inn. He began to undo the collar straps, and detached the collar.

"But we shall be frozen?" queried Vasily Andreyevich.

"Well, if we are, we cannot help it," said Nikita.

In his two fur coats, Vasily Andreyevich was quite warm, especially after the exertion in the snowdrift. But a cold shiver ran down his back when he learned that they must stay where they were the night long. To calm himself, he sat down in the sleigh and got out his cigarettes and matches.

Meanwhile, Nikita continued to take out the horse. He undid the belly band, took away the reins and collar strap, and laid the bow aside from the shafts, continuing to encourage Moukhorta by speaking to him.

"Now, come out, come out," he said, leading the horse clear of the shafts. "We must tie you here. I'll put a bit of straw for you, and take off your bridle," he went on, doing as he said. "After a bite, you'll feel ever so much better."

But Moukhorta was not calmed by Nikita's words; uneasily he shifted his feet, pressed against the sleigh, turned his back to the wind, and rubbed his head on Nikita's sleeve.

As if not wholly to reject the treat of straw that Nikita put under his nose, Moukhorta just once seized a wisp out of the sleigh, but quickly deciding that there was more important business than to eat straw, he threw it down again, and the wind instantly tore it away and hid it in the snow.

"Now we must make a signal," said Nikita, turning the front of the sleigh against the wind; and having tied the shafts together with a strap, he set them on end in the front of the sleigh. "If the snow covers us, the good folk will see the shafts and dig us up," said Nikita. "That's what old hands advise."

Vasily Andreyevich had meanwhile opened his fur coat, and making a shelter with its folds, he rubbed match after match on the box. But his hands trembled, and the kindled matches were blown out by the wind, one after another, some when just struck, others when he thrust them to the cigarette. At last one match burned fully and lighted up for a moment the fur of his coat, his hand with the gold ring on the bent forefinger, and the snow-sprinkled straw that stuck out from under the sacking. The cigarette took light. Twice he eagerly whiffed the smoke, draw it in, blew it through his mustache, and would have gone on, but the wind tore away the burning tobacco. Even these few whiffs of tobacco smoke cheered up Vasily Andreyevich.

"Well, we will stop here," he said authoritatively.

Looking at the raised shafts, he thought to make a still better signal, and to give Nikita a lesson.

"Wait a minute, and I'll make a flag," he said picking up the handkerchief that he had taken from around his collar and put down in the sleigh. Drawing off his gloves and reaching up, he tied the handkerchief tightly to the strap that held the shafts together. The handkerchief at once began to beat about wildly, now clinging around a shaft, now streaming out, and cracking like a whip.

"That's fine," said Vasily Andreyevich, pleased with his work, and getting into the sleigh. "We should be warmer together, but there's not room for two," he said.

"I can find room," said Nikita, "but the horse must be covered; he's sweating, the good fellow. Excuse me," he added, going to the sleigh and drawing the sacking from under Vasily Andreyevich. This he folded, and after taking off the saddle and breeching, covered the dark bay with it.

"Anyway, it will be a bit warmer, silly," he said, putting the saddle and heavy breeching over the sacking.

"Can you spare the rug? and give me a little straw?" said Nikita, after finishing with the horse.

Taking these from under Vasily Andreyevich, he went behind the sleigh, dug there a hole in the snow, put in the straw, and pulling his hat over his eyes and covering himself with the rug, sat down on the straw, with his back against the bark matting of the back of the sleigh, which kept off the wind and snow

Vasily Andreyevich, seeing what Nikita was doing, shook his head disapprovingly, in the way he usually did over the signs of peasant folks' ignorance and denseness; and he began to make arrangements for the night.

He smoothed the remaining straw, heaped it more thickly under his side, thrust his hands into his sleeves, and adjusted his head in the corner of the sleigh in front, where he was sheltered from the wind. He did not wish to sleep. He lay down and thought; about one thing only, which was the aim, reason, pleasure, and pride of his life; about the money he had made, and might make, the amount his neighbors had, and the means whereby they gained it and were gaining it; and how he, like them, could gain a great deal more.

"The oak can be sold for sleigh runners. And certainly, the trees for building. And there are a hundred feet of firewood to the acre"—so he estimated the forest, which he had seen in the autumn, and which he was going to buy. "But for all that, I won't pay ten thousand; say eight thousand; and besides, in allowing for the bare spaces, I'll oil the surveyor—a hundred rubles will do it—a hundred and fifty, if necessary, and get him to take about thirteen acres out of the forest. He is sure to sell for eight; three thousand down. Yes, sure, he will weaken at that," he thought, pressing his forearm on the pocketbook beneath. "And how we've gotten astray, God knows! The forest and the keeper's hut should be just by. I should like to hear the dogs, but they never bark when they're wanted, the cursed brutes." He opened his collar a little to look and listen; there was only the dark head of the horse, and his back, on which the sackcloth fluttered; theft was only the same whistle of the wind, the flapping and cracking of the handkerchief on the shafts, and the lashing of the snow on the bark matting of the sleigh. He covered himself again. "If one had only known this beforehand, we had better have stayed where we were. But no matter, tomorrow will be time enough. It is only a day later. In this weather, the other fellows won't dare to go." Then he remembered that on the ninth he had to receive the price of some cattle from the butcher. He wanted to do the business himself, for his wife had no experience, and was not competent in such matters. "She never knows what to do," he continued to reflect, remembering how she had failed in her behavior toward the commissary of police when he visited them yesterday at the feast. "Just a woman, of course. What has she ever seen? In my father's and mother's time, what sort of a house had we? Nothing out of the way; a well-to-do countryman's; a barn, and an inn, and that was the whole property. And now what a change I've made, these fifteen years! A general store, two taverns, a flour mill, a stock of grain, two farms rented, a house and warehouse all iron-roofed," he remembered proudly. "Not like in the old people's time! Who is known over the whole place? Brekhunov.

"And why is all this? Because I stick to business, I look after things; not like others, who idle, or waste their time in foolishness. I give up sleep at night. Storm or no storm, I go. And of course, the thing is done. They think money is made easily, by just playing. Not at all; it's work and trouble. They think luck makes men. Look at the Mironovs, who have their millions, now. Why? They worked. Then God gives. If God only grants us health!" And the idea that he, also, might become a millionaire like Mironov, who began with nothing, so excited Vasily Andreyevich that he suddenly felt a need to talk to someone. But there was nobody. If he could only have reached Goryachkino, he might have talked with the landowner, and got around him.

"What a gale! It will snow us in so that we can't get out in the morning," he thought, listening to the sound of the wind, which blew against the front of the sleigh and lashed the snow against the bark matting.

"And I did as Nikita said, all for nothing," he thought. "We ought to have driven on, and gotten to somewhere. We might have gone back to Grishkino and stayed at Taras's. Now we must sit here all night. Well, what was I thinking about? Yes, that God gives to the industrious, and not to the lazy, loafers, and fools. It's time for a smoke, too." He sat up, got his cigarette case, and stretched himself flat on his stomach, to protect the light from the wind with the flaps of his coat; but the wind got in and put out match after match. At least he managed to get a cigarette lit. It began to burn, and the achievement of his object greatly delighted him. Although the wind had more of his cigarette than he himself, nevertheless he got about three puffs, and felt better. He again threw himself back in the sleigh, wrapped himself up, and returned to his recollections and dreams; he fell asleep. But suddenly something pushed and awoke him. Was it the dark bay pulling the straw from under him, or some fancy of his own? At all events he awoke, and his heart began to beat so quickly and strongly that the sleigh seemed to be shaking under him. He opened his eyes. Everything around was the same as before; but it seemed a shade brighter. "The morning," he thought, "it can't be far from morning." But he suddenly remembered that the light was only due to the rising of the moon. He lifted himself, and looked first at the horse. Moukhorta stood with his back to the wind and shivered all over. The sacking, snow-covered and turned up at one corner; the breeching, which had slipped aside; the snowy head and fluttering mane; all was now more clearly visible. Vasily Andreyevich bent over the back of the sleigh and looked behind. Nikita sat in his old position. The rug and his feet were covered with snow. "I'm afraid he will be frozen, his clothes are so bad. I might be held responsible. He is tired out, and, has not much resisting power," reflected Vasily Andreyevich; and he thought of taking the sacking from the horse, to put over Nikita; but it was cold to disturb himself, and besides, he did not want the horse frozen. "What was the use of bringing him? It is all her stupidity!" thought Vasily Andreyevich, remembering the unloved wife; and he turned again to his former place in the front of the sleigh. "My uncle once sat in snow all night like this," he reflected, "and no harm came of it. And Sebastian also was dug out," he went on, remembering another case, "but he was dead, stiff like a frozen carcass.

"It would have been all right if we had stopped at Grishkino." Carefully covering himself, not to waste the warmth of the fur, and so as to protect his neck, knees, and the soles of his feet, he shut his eyes, trying to sleep. But however much he tried, no sleep came; on the contrary, he felt alert and excited. He began again to count his gains and the debts due to him; again he began to boast to himself, and to feel proud of himself and his position; but he was all the while disturbed by a lurking fear, and by the unpleasant reflection that he had not stopped at Grishkino. He changed his attitude several times; he lay down and tried to find a better position, more sheltered from wind and snow, but failed; he rose again and changed his position, crossed his feet, shut his eyes, and lay silent; but either his crossed feet, in their high felt boots, began to ache, or the wind blew in somewhere. Thus lying for a short time, he again began the disagreeable reflection, how comfortably he would have lain in the warm house at Grishkino. Again he rose, changed his position, wrapped himself up, and again lay down.

Once Vasily Andreyevich fancied he heard a distant cock crow. He brightened up and began to listen with all his might; but however he strained his ear, he heard nothing but the sound of the wind whistling against the shafts, and the snow lashing the bark matting of the sleigh. Nikita had been motionless all the time, not even answering Vasily Andreyevich, who spoke to him twice.

"He doesn't worry; he seems to be asleep," Vasily Andreyevich thought angrily, looking behind the sleigh at the snow-covered Nikita.

Twenty times Vasily Andreyevich thus rose and lay down. It seemed to him this night would never end. "It must be near morning now," he thought once, rising and looking around him. "Let me see my watch. It is cold to unbutton oneself; but if I only knew it was near morning, it would be better. Then we might begin to harness the horse." At the bottom of his mind, Vasily Andreyevich knew that the dawn could be nowhere near; but he began to feel more and more afraid, and he chose both to deceive himself and to find himself out. He began cautiously to undo the hooks of the inside fur coat, then putting his hands in at the bosom, he felt about until he got at the vest. With great trouble, he drew out his silver, flower-enameled watch, and began to examine it. Without a light, he could make out nothing. Again he lay down flat, as when he lit the cigarette, got the matches, and began to strike. This time he was particularly careful, and selecting a match with most phosphorous on, at one attempt lit it. Lighting up the face of the watch, he could not believe his eyes. It was not later than ten minutes past twelve. The whole night was yet before him.

"Oh, what a weary night!" thought Vasily Andreyevich, a cold shiver running down his back; and buttoning up again, he hugged himself close in the corner of the sleigh. Suddenly, through the monotonous wail of the wind, he distinctly heard a new and a living sound. It grew gradually louder and became quite clear, then began to die away. There could be no doubt; it was a wolf. And this wolf's howl was so near that down the wind one could hear how he changed his cry by the movement of his jaws. Vasily Andreyevich turned back his collar and listened attentively. Moukhorta listened likewise, pricking up his ears, and when the wolf had ceased howling, he shifted his feet and sniffed warningly. After this Vasily Andreyevich not only was unable to sleep, but even to keep calm. The more he tried to think of his accounts, of his business, reputation, importance, and property, more and more fear grew upon him; and above all his thoughts, one thought stood out predominantly and penetratingly: the thought of his rashness in not stopping at Grishkino.

"The forest—what do I care about the forest? There is plenty of business without that, thank God! Ah, why did I not stay the night?" said he to himself. "They say people who drink are soon frozen," he thought, "and I have had some drink." Then testing his own sensations, he felt that he began to shiver, not knowing whether from cold or fear. He tried to wrap himself up and to lie down as before; but he could not. He was unable to rest, wanted to rise, to do something to suppress gathering fears, against which he felt helpless. Again he got his cigarettes and matches; but only three of the latter remained, and these were bad ones. All three rubbed away without lighting.

"To the devil, curse it, to—!" he broke out, himself not knowing why, and he threw away the cigarette, broken. He was about to throw away the matchbox, but stayed his hand, and thrust it in his pocket instead. He was so agitated that he could no longer remain in one place. He got out of the sleigh, and standing with his back to the wind, set his girdle again, tightly and low down.

"What is the use of lying down; it is only waiting for death, much better mount the horse and get away!" The thought suddenly flashed into his mind. "The horse will not stand still with someone on his back. He"—thinking of Nikita—"must die anyway. What sort of a life has he? He does not care much even about his life, but as for me—thank God, I have something to live for!"

Untying the horse from the sleigh, he threw the reins over his neck and tried to mount, but failed. Then he clambered on the sleigh, and tried to mount from that; but the sleigh tilted under his weight, and he failed again. At last, on a third attempt, he backed the horse to the sleigh, and cautiously balancing on the edge, got his body across the horse. Lying thus for a moment, he pushed himself once, twice, and finally threw one leg over and seated himself, supporting his feet on the breeching in place of stirrups. The shaking of the sleigh roused Nikita, and he got up; Vasily Andreyevich thought he was speaking.

"Listen to you, fool? What, must I die in this way, for nothing?" exclaimed Vasily Andreyevich. Tucking under his knees the loose skirts of his far coat, he turned the horse around and rode away from the sleigh in the direction where he expected to find the forest and the keeper's hut.

Nikita had not stirred since, covered by the rug, he took his seat behind the sleigh. Like all people who live with nature, and endure much, he was patient and could wait for hours, even days, without growing restless or irritated. When his master called to him, he heard, but made no answer, because he did not wish to stir. The thought that he might, and very likely must, die that night came to him at the moment he was taking his seat behind the sleigh. Although he still felt the warmth from the tea he had taken, and from the exercise of struggling through the snowdrift, he knew the warmth would not last long, and that he could not warm himself again by moving about, for he was exhausted and felt as a horse may when it stops and must have food before it can work again. Besides, his foot, the one in the torn boot, was numbed, and already he could not feel the great toe. And the cold began to creep all over his body.

The thought that he would die that night came upon him, seeming not very unpleasant, nor very awful. Not unpleasant, because his life had been no unbroken feast, but rather an incessant round of toil of which he began to weary. And not awful, because, beyond the masters whom he served here, like Vasily Andreyevich, he felt himself dependent upon the Great Master; upon Him who had sent him into this life. And he knew that even after death he must remain in the power of that Master, who would not treat him badly. "Is it a pity to leave what you are practiced in and used to? Well, what's to be done? You must get used to fresh things as well.

"Sins?" he thought, and recollected his drunkenness, the money wasted in drink, his ill treatment of his wife, neglect of church and of the fasts, and all things for which the priest reprimanded him at the confessional. "Of course, these are sins. But then, did I bring them on me myself? Whatever I am, I suppose God made me so. Well, and about these sins? How can one help it?"

So he thought, concerning what might happen to him that night, and having reached his conclusion, he gave himself up to the thoughts and recollections that ran through his mind of themselves. He remembered the visit of his wife, Martha; the drunkenness among the peasants, and his own abstinence from drink; the beginning of their journey; Tarass's house, and the talk about the breakup of the family; his own lad; Moukhorta, with the sacking over him for warmth; and his master, rolling around in the sleigh and making it creak. "He is uneasy," thought Nikita, "most likely because a life like his makes one want not to die; different from people of my kind." And all these recollections and thoughts interwove and jumbled themselves in his brain, until he fell asleep.

When Vasily Andreyevich mounted the horse, he twisted aside the sleigh, and the back of it slid away from behind Nikita, who was struck by one of the runner ends. Nikita awoke, thus compelled to move. Straightening his legs with difficulty, and throwing off the snow that covered them, he got up. Instantly an agony of cold penetrated his whole frame. On making out what was happening, he wanted Vasily Andreyevich to leave him the sacking that lay over the horse, which was no longer needed there, so that he might put it around himself. But Vasily Andreyevich did not wait, and disappeared in the midst of snow. Thus left alone, Nikita considered what he had better do. He felt unable to move off in search of some house; and it was already impossible for him to sit down in the place he had occupied, for it was already covered with snow; and he knew he could not get warm in the sleigh, having nothing to cover him. He felt as cold as though he stood in his shirt; there seemed no warmth at all from his coat and overcoat. For a moment he pondered, then sighed, and keeping the rug over his head, he threw himself into the sleigh, in the place where his master had lain. He huddled himself up into the smallest space, but still got no warmth. Thus he lay for about five minutes, shivering through his whole body; then the shivering ceased, and he began to lose consciousness, little by little. Whether he was dying or falling asleep, he knew not; but he was as ready for the one as for the other. If God should bid him get up again, still alive in the world, to go on with his laborer's life, to care for other men's horses, to carry other men's grain to the mill, to again start drinking and renouncing drink, to continue the money supply to his wife and that same cooper, to watch his lad growing up—well, so be His holy will. Should God bid him arise in another world, where all would be as fresh and bright as this world was in his young childhood, with the caresses of his mother, the games among the children, the fields, forests, skating in winter—arise to a life quite out of the common—then, so be His holy will. And Nikita wholly lost consciousness.

During this while, Vasily Andreyevich, guiding with his feet and the gathered reins, rode the horse in the direction where he, for some cause, expected to find the forest and the forester's hut. The snow blinded him, and the wind, it seemed, was bent on staying him; but with head bent forward, and continually pulling up his fur coat between him and the cold, nail-studded pad on which he could not settle himself, he urged on the horse. The dark bay, though with difficulty, obediently ambled on in the direction to which he was turned.

For some minutes he rode on—as it seemed to him, in a straight line—seeing nothing but the horse's head and the white waste, and hearing only the whistling of the wind about the horse's ears and his own coat collar.

Suddenly a dark patch showed in front of him. His heart began to beat with joy, and he rode on toward the object, already seeing in it the house walls of a village. But the dark patch was not stationary, it moved. It was not a village, but a ridge, covered with tall mugwort, which rose up through the snow, and bent to one side under the force of the wind. The sight of the high grass, tormented by the pitiless wind, somehow made Vasily Andreyevich tremble, and he started to ride away hastily, not perceiving that in approaching the place, he had quite turned out of his first direction, and that now he was heading the opposite way. He was still confident that he rode toward where the forester's hut should be. But the horse seemed always to make toward the right, and Vasily Andreyevich had to guide it toward the left.

Again a dark patch appeared before him; again he rejoiced, believing that now surely he saw a village. But once more it was the ridge, covered with high grass, shaking ominously, and as before, frightening Vasily Andreyevich. But it was not the same ridge of grass, for near it was horse track, now disappointing in the snow. Vasily Andreyevich stopped, bent down, and looked carefully: a horse track, not yet snow-covered; it could only be the hoofprints of his own horse. He was evidently moving in a small circle. "And I am perishing in this way," he thought. To repress his terror, he urged on the horse still more, peering into the mist of snow, in which he saw nothing but flitting and fitful points of light. Once he thought he heard either the barking of dogs or the howling of wolves, but the sounds were so faint and indistinct that he could not be sure whether he had heard them or imagined them; and he stopped to strain his ears and listen.

Suddenly a terrible, deafening cry beat upon his ears, and everything began to tremble and quake about him. Vasily Andreyevich seized the horse's neck, but that also shook, and the terrible cry rose still more frightfully. For some moments Vasily Andreyevich was beside himself and could not understand what had happened. It was only this: Moukhorta, whether to encourage himself or to call for help, had neighed, loudly and resonantly.

"The devil! How that cursed horse frightened me!" said Vasily Andreyevich to himself. But even when he understood the cause of his terror, he could not shake it off.

"I must bethink myself, steady myself," he went on, even while, unable to regain his self-control, he urged forward the horse without noting that he was now going with the wind instead of against it. His body, especially where his fur coat did not protect it against the pad, was freezing, shivering and aching all over. He forgot all about the forester's hut and desired one thing only—to get back to the sleigh, that he might not perish alone, like that mugwort in the midst of the terrible waste of snow.

Without warning, the horse suddenly stumbled under him, caught in a snowdrift, began to plunge, and fell on his side. Vasily Andreyevich jumped off, dragged down the breeching with his foot, and turned the pad around by holding to it as he jumped. As soon as he was clear, the horse righted itself, plunged forward one leap and then another, and neighing again, with the sacking and breeching trailed after him, disappeared, leaving Vasily Andreyevich alone in the snowdrift. The latter pressed on after the horse, but the snow was so deep, and his fur coat so heavy, that, sinking over the knee at each step, he was out of breath after not more than twenty paces, and stopped. "The forest, the sheep, the farms, the shop, the taverns," thought he, "how can I leave them? What is really the matter? This is impossible!" surged through his head. And he had a strange recollection of the wind-shaken mugwort that he had ridden past twice, and such a terror seized him that he lost all sense of the reality of what was happening. He thought, "Is not this all a dream?"—and tried to wake himself. But there was no awakening. The snow was real, lashing his face and covering him; and it was a real desert in which he was now alone, like that mugwort, waiting for inevitable, speedy, and incomprehensible death.

"Queen in heaven, Nicholas the miracle doer, sustainer of the faithful!"—He recalled yesterday's Te Deums; the shrine with the black image in a golden chasuble; the tapers that he sold for the shrine, and that, as they were at once returned to him, he used to put back in the store chest hardly touched by the flame. And he began to implore that same Nicholas—the miracle doer—to save him, vowing to the saint a Te Deums and tapers. But in some way, here, he clearly and without a doubt realized that the image, chasuble, tapers, priests, thanksgivings, and so forth, while very important and necessary in their place, in the church, were of no service to him now; and that between those tapers and Te Deums, and his own disastrous plight, there could be no possible relation.

"I must not give up; I must follow the horse's tracks, or they, too, will be snowed over." The thought struck him, and he made on. But despite his resolution to walk quietly, he found himself running, falling down every minute, rising and falling again. The hoofprints were already almost indistinguishable where the snow was shallow. "I am lost!" thought Vasily Andreyevich, "I shall lose this track as well!" But at that instant, casting a glance in front, he saw something dark. It was the horse, and not him alone, but the sleigh, the shafts. Moukhorta, with the pad twisted around and the trailed breeching and sacking, was standing, not in his former place, but nearer to the shafts, and was shaking his head, drawn down by the reins beneath his feet. It appeared that Vasily Andreyevich had stuck in the same ravine into which they had, with Nikita, previously plunged, that the horse had led him back to the sleigh, and that he had dismounted at not more than fifty paces from the place where the sleigh lay.

When Vasily Andreyevich, with great difficulty, regained the sleigh, he seized upon it and stood motionless for a long time, trying to calm himself and to take breath. Nikita was not in his old place, but something was lying in the sleigh, something already covered with snow; and Vasily Andreyevich guessed it to be Nikita. His terror had now quite left him; if he felt any fear, it was lest that terror should return upon him in the way he had experienced it when on the horse, and especially when he was alone in the snowdrift. By any and every means, he must keep away that terror; to do that, he must forget himself, think about something else; something must be done. Accordingly, the first thing he did was to turn his back to the wind and throw open his fur cloak. As soon as he felt a little refreshed, he shook out the snow from his boots and gloves, bound up his girdle again, tight and low down, as though making ready for work, as he did when going out to buy grain from the peasants' carts. The first step to take, it appeared to him, was to free the horse's legs. And he did this; then clearing the rein, he tied Moukhorta to the iron cramp in front of the sleigh, as before, and walking around the horse's quarters, he adjusted the pad, breeching, and sacking. But as he did this, he perceived a movement in the sleigh; and Nikita's head rose out of the snow that was about it. With obvious great difficulty, the peasant rose and sat up; and in a strange fashion, as though he were driving away flies, waved his hand before his face, saying something which Vasily Andreyevich interpreted as a call to himself.

Vasily Andreyevich left the sack unadjusted and went to the sleigh.

"What is the matter with you?" he asked. "What are you saying?"

"I am dy-y-ing, that's what's the matter," said Nikita brokenly, struggling for speech. "Give what I have earned to the lad. Or to the wife; it's all the same."

"What, are you really frozen?" asked Vasily Andreyevich.

"I can feel I've got my death. Forgiveness . . . for Christ's sake . . .," said Nikita in a sobbing voice, continuing to wave his hand before his face, as if driving away flies.

Vasily Andreyevich stood for half a minute quiet and still; then suddenly, with the same resolution with which he used to strike hands over a good bargain, he took a step back, turned up the sleeves of his fur coat, and using both hands, began to rake the snow from off Nikita and the sleigh. That done, Vasily Andreyevich quickly took off his belt, made ready the fur coat, and moving Nikita with a push, he lay down on him, covering him not only with the fur coat, but with the full length of his own body, which glowed with warmth.

Adjusting with his hands the skirts of his coat, so as to come between Nikita and the bark matting of the sleigh, and tucking the tail of the coat between his knees, Vasily Andreyevich lay flat, with his head against the bark matting in the sleigh front. He no longer could hear, either the stirring of the horse or the wind's whistling; he had ears only for the breathing of Nikita. At first, and for a long time, Nikita lay without a sign; then he sighed deeply, and moved, evidently with returning warmth.

"Ah, there you are! And yet you say 'die.' Lie still, get warm, and we shall . . .," began Vasily Andreyevich. But to his own surprise, he could not speak: because his eyes were filled with tears, and his lower jaw began to quiver strongly. He said no more; only swallowed down the risings in his throat.

"I have been frightened, that is clear, and have lost my nerve," he thought of himself. But this weakness came not as an unpleasant sensation; rather as a notable, and hitherto unknown, delight.

"That's what we are!" he said to himself, with a strange, tender, and tranquil sense of victory. He lay quiet for some time, wiping his eyes with the fur of his coat, and returning the right skirt under his knees as the wind continually turned it up.

He felt a passionate desire to let someone else know of his happy condition.

"Nikita!" he said.

"It's comfortable," came an answer from below.

"So it is, friend! I was nearly lost. And you would have been frozen, and I should . . ."

But here again his face began to quiver, and eyes his once more filled with tears; he could say no more.

"Well, never mind," he thought, "I know well enough myself what I know," and he kept quiet.

Several times he looked at the horse, and saw that his back was uncovered and the sacking and breeching were hanging down nearly to the snow. He ought to get up and cover the horse; but he could not bring himself to leave Nikita for even a moment and so disturb that happy situation in which he felt himself; for he had no fear now.

Nikita warmed him from below, and the fur coat warmed him from above; but his hands, with which he held the coat skirts down on both sides of Nikita, and his feet, from which the wind continually lifted the coat, began to freeze. But he did not think of them. He thought only of how to restore the man who lay beneath him.

"No fear, he will not escape," he said to himself as Nikita grew warmer; and he said this boastingly, in the way he used to speak of his buying and selling.

Then he lay for a long while. At first his thoughts were filled with impressions of the snowstorm, the shafts of the sleigh, the horse under the sleigh bow, all jostling before his eyes; he recollected Nikita, lying under him, then upon these impressions rose others, of the feast, his wife, the commissary of police, the taper box; then again of Nikita, this time lying under the taper box. Then came apparitions of peasants at their trafficking, and white walls, and iron-roofed houses, with Nikita stretched out beneath; then all was confused, one thing running into another; like the colors in the rainbow, which blend into one whiteness, all the different impressions fused into one nothing; and he fell asleep. For a long time he slept dreamlessly; but before daybreak dreams visited him again. He was once more standing beside the taper box, and Tikhon's wife asked him for a five-kopeck taper, for the feast; he wanted to take the taper and give it to her, but he could not move his hands, which hung down, thrust tightly into his pockets. He wanted to walk around the box; but his feet would not move; his galoshes, new and shiny, had grown to the stone floor, and he could neither move them nor take out his feet. All at once the box ceased to be a taper box, and turned in to a bed; and Vasily Andreyevich saw himself lying, face downward, on the taper box, which was his own bed at home. Thus lying, he was unable to get up; and yet he must get up, because Ivan Matveich, the commissary of police, would soon call upon him, and with Ivan Matveich he must either bargain for the forest or set the breeching right on Moukhorta. He asked his wife, "Well, has he not come?" "No," she said, "he has not." He heard someone drive up to the front door. It must be he. No, whoever it was, he has gone past. "Mikolayevna, Mikolayevna! What, has he come yet?" No. And he lay on the bed, still unable to rise, and still waiting, a waiting that was painful, and yet pleasant. All at once, his joy was fulfilled; the expected one came; not Ivan Matveich, the commissary of police, but another; and yet the one for whom he had waited. He came, and called to him; and he that called was he who had bidden him lie down upon Nikita. Vasily Andreyevich was glad because that one had visited him. "I am coming," he cried joyfully. And the cry awoke him.

He wakes, but wakes in quite another state that when he fell asleep. He wants to rise, and cannot; to move his arm, and cannot—his leg, and he cannot do that. He wants to turn his head, and cannot do even so much. He is surprised, but not at all disturbed by this. He divines that this is death, and is not at all disturbed even by that. And he remembers that Nikita is lying under him, and that he has gotten warm and is alive; and it seems to him that he is Nikita, and Nikita is he, that his life is not in himself, but in Nikita. He makes an effort to listen, and hears the breathing, even the slight snoring, of Nikka. "Nikita is alive, and therefore I also am alive!" he says to himself triumphantly. And something quite new, such as he had never known in all his life, is stealing down upon him.

He remembers his money, the shop, the house, the buying and selling, the Mironovs' millions; and he really cannot understand why that man, called Vasily Brekhunov, had troubled with all those things with which he had troubled himself. "Well, he did not know what it was all about," he thinks, concerning this Vasily Brekhunov. "He did not know, but now I know. No mistake this time; now I know." And again he hears the summons of that one who had before called him. "I am coming, I am coming," all his being speaks joyfully and tenderly. And he feels himself free; with nothing to encumber him more. And nothing more, in this world, saw, heard, or felt Vasily.

Around about, all was as before. The same whirling snow, driving upon the fur coat of the dead Vasily Andreyevich, upon Moukhorta, whose whole body shivered, and upon the sleigh now hardly to be seen, with Nikita lying in the bottom of it, kept warm beneath his now dead master.

• • •

Toward daybreak, Nikita awoke. The cold roused him, again creeping along his back. He had dreamed that he was driving from the mill with a cartload of his master's flour, and that near Liapin's, in turning at the bridge end, he got the cart stuck. And he saw that he went beneath the cart, and lifted it with his back, adjusting his strength to it. But, wonderful!—the cart did not stir, it stuck to his back, so that he could neither lift nor get from under. It crushed his back. And how cold it was! He must get away somehow.

"That's enough," he cried to whoever, or whatever, it was that pressed his back with the cart. "Take the sacks out!" But the cart still pressed him, always colder and colder; and suddenly a peculiar knocking awoke him completely, and he remembered all. The cold cart—that was his dead and frozen master, lying upon him. The knocking was from Moukhorta, who struck twice on the sleigh with his hooves.

"Andreyevich, eh, Andreyevich!" says Nikita inquiringly, straightening his back and already guessing the truth. But Andreyevich does not answer, and his body and legs are hard, and cold, and heavy, like iron weights.

"He must have died. May his be the kingdom of heaven!" thinks Nikita. He turns his head, digs with his hand through the snow about him, and opens his eyes. It is daylight. The wind still whistles through the shafts, and the snow is still falling, but with a difference, not lashing upon the bark matting as before, but silently covering the sleigh and horse, even deeper and deeper; and the horse's breathing and stirring are no more to be heard. "He must be frozen too," thinks Nikita. And in fact, those hoof strokes upon the sleigh were the last struggles of Moukhorta, by that time quite benumbed, to feel his legs.

"God, Father, it seems thou callest me as well," says Nikita to himself. "Let Thy holy will be done. But it is . . . Still, one cannot die twice, and must die once. If it would only come quicker! . . ." And he draws in his arm again, shutting his eyes; and he loses consciousness, with the conviction that this time he is really going to die altogether.

About dinnertime on the next day, the peasants with their shovels dug out Vasily Andreyevich and Nikita, only seventy yards from the road, and half a mile from the village. The wind had hidden the sleigh in snow, but the shafts and the handkerchief were still visible. Moukhorta, over his belly in snow, with the breeching and sacking trailing from his back, stood all whitened, his dead head pressed in upon the apple of his throat; his nostrils were fringed with icicles, his eyes filled with rime and frozen around as with tears. In that one night he had become so thin that he was nothing but skin and bone. Vasily Andreyevich was stiffened like a frozen carcass, and he lay with his legs spread apart, just as he was when they rolled him off Nikita. His prominent hawk eyes were shriveled up, and his open mouth under his clipped mustache was filled with snow. But Nikita, though chilled through, was alive. When he was roused, he imagined he was already dead and that the happenings about him were by this time not in this world, but in another. When he heard the shouts of the peasants, who were digging him out and rolling the frozen Vasily Andreyevich from him, he was surprised at first to think that in the other world, also, peasants should be making noise. But when he understood that he was still here, in this world, he was rather sorry than glad, especially when he realized that the toes of both his feet were frozen.

Nikita lay in the hospital for two months. They cut off three toes from him, and the others recovered, so that he was able to work. For twenty years more, he went on living, first as a farm laborer, lately as a watchman. He died at home, just as he wished, only this year; laid under the holy images, with a lighted taper in his hands. Before his death, he asked forgiveness from his old wife, and forgave her for the cooper; he took leave of his son and the grandchildren went away, truly pleased that, in dying, he released his son and daughter-in-law from the added burden of his keep, and that he himself was, this time really, going out of a life grown wearisome to him, into that other one which with every passing year had grown clearer and more desirable to him. Is he better off, or worse off, there in the place where he awoke after that real death? Is he disappointed? Or has he found things there to be such as he expected? That we shall all of us soon learn.

acknowledgments

Many people made this anthology.

At Thunder's Mouth Press and Avalon Publishing Group:
Neil Ortenberg and Susan Reich continued to offer vital support and expertise. Dan O'Connor, Ghadah Alrawi and Matthew Trokenheim also were indispensable.

At Balliett & Fitzgerald Inc.:
Tom Dyja and f-stop Fitzgerald lent intellectual and moral support. Sue Canavan created the book's look. Maria Fernandez oversaw production with scrupulous care and attention with help from Paul Paddock.

At the Portland Public Library in Portland, Maine:
The librarians cheerfully worked to locate and borrow books from across the country.

At Shawneric.com:
Shawneric Hachey handled permissions, found photographs and scanned copy—all with his usual aplomb.

At the Writing Company:
Nate Hardcastle and Nat May played vital roles in finding the selections for this book. John Bishop provided research assistance and helped coordinate the final stages of the book's production. Taylor Smith, Mark Klimek and Deborah Satter also helped with the book, and took up slack on other projects.

Among friends and family:
Jennifer Willis lent me her judgement—again.
Will Balliett made it a pleasure—again.

Finally, I am grateful to the writers whose work appears in this book.

We gratefully acknowledge all those who gave permission for written material to appear in this book. We have made every effort to trace and contact copyright holders. If an error or omission is brought to our notice we will be pleased to correct the situation in future editions of this book. For further information, please contact the publisher.

Excerpt from *Dark Wind* by Gordon Chaplin. Copyright © 1999 by Gordon Chaplin. Used by permission of Grove/Atlantic. ❖ Excerpt from *Sheer Will* by Michael Groom. Copyright © 1997 by Michael Groom. Used by permission of Random House Australia. ❖ "The Hermit's Story" by Rick Bass. Copyright © 1998 by Rick Bass. Reprinted by permission of the author. First published in *The Paris Review*, Summer 1998. ❖ "In the Storm" by James LeMoyne. © 1992 by James LeMoyne. Reprinted by permission of the author. First appeared in *The New Yorker*, October 5, 1992.❖ "Storm Over the Amazon" by Edward O. Wilson. © 1992 by Edward O. Wilson. Reprinted by permission of the author. ❖ Excerpt from *Alone* by Richard E. Byrd. Copyright © 1938 by Richard E. Byrd. Reprinted by permission of Island Press. ❖ Excerpt from *Song of the Sirens* by Ernest K. Gann. Copyright © 1961 by Ernest K. Gann. Reprinted by permission of Simon & Schuster. ❖ Excerpt from *Arctic Dreams* by Barry Holstun Lopez. Copyright © 1986 by Barry Holstun Lopez. Reprinted by permission of Sterling Lord Literistic. ❖ Excerpt from "Genesis" by Earle Wallace Stegner. Copyright © 1990 by Earle Wallace Stegner. Reprinted by permission of Random House, Inc. ❖ "The Half-Skinned Steer" from *Close Range: Wyoming Stories* by Annie Proulx. Copyright © 1999 by Annie Proulx. Reprinted by permission of Scribner, a Division of Simon & Schuster. ❖ Excerpt from *My Old Man and the Sea* by David Hays and Daniel Hays. Copyright © 1995 by the authors. Reprinted by permission of Algonquin Books of Chapel Hill, a division of Workman Publishing. ❖ "The Storm" by Sebastian Junger. Copyright © 1997 by Sebastian Junger. Used by permission of the Stuart Krichevsky Literary Agency, Inc. ❖ "The Ship that Vanished" by John Vaillant. Copyright © 1999 by John Vaillant. Used by permission of the Stuart Krichevsky Literary Agency, Inc. First appeared in *The New*

bibliography

The selections used in this anthology were taken from the editions listed below. In some cases, other editions may be easier to find. Hard-to-find or out-of-print titles often are available through inter-library loan services or through Internet booksellers.

Best American Short Stories. New York: Houghton Mifflin, 1999. (For "The Hermit's Story" by Rick Bass.)

Best of Outside: The First Twenty Years. New York: Villard Books, 1997. (For "The Storm" by Sebastian Junger.)

Byrd, Richard E. *Alone*. New York: G.P. Putnam's Sons, 1938.

Chaplin, Gordon. *Dark Wind: A Survivor's Tale of Love and Loss*. New York: Atlantic Monthly Press, 1999.

Gann, Ernest K. *Song of the Sirens*. New York: Simon & Schuster, 1968.

Groom, Michael. *Sheer Will*. Milsons Point, NSW, Australia: Random House Australia, 1997.

Hays, Daniel and David Hays. *My Old Man and the Sea*. Chapel Hill, NC: Algonquin Books of Chapel Hill, 1995.

London, Jack. *South Sea Tales*. Honolulu: Mutual Publishing, 1998.

Lopez, Barry. *Arctic Dreams*. New York: Bantam Books, 1986.

Nature Reader, The. Edited by D. Halpern and D. Frank. Hopewell, NJ: The Ecco Press, 1996. (For "Storm Over the Amazon" by Edward O. Wilson.)

New Yorker, The. September 19, 1988. (For "The Leeward Side" by Whitney Balliett. Originally published as "Fiftieth.")

New Yorker, The. October 11, 1999. (For "The Ship That Vanished" by John Vaillant.)

New Yorker, The. October 5, 1992. (For "In the Storm" by James LeMoyne.)

Norton Book of Nature Writing, The Edited by Robert Finch and John Elder. New York: W.W. Norton & Company, Inc., 1990. (For "A Wind-Storm in the Forests" by John Muir.)

Paulsen, Gary. *Winterdance: The Fine Madness of Running the Iditarod*. Orlando, Florida: Harcourt Brace & Company, 1994.

Proulx, Annie. *Close Range: Wyoming Stories*. New York: Scribner, 2000.

Stegner, Wallace. *Collected Stories of Wallace Stegner*. New York: Random House, Inc., 1990.

Tolstoy, Leo. *Master and Man*. New York: Penguin Books, 1995.

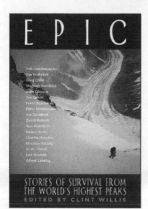

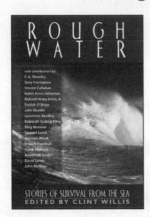
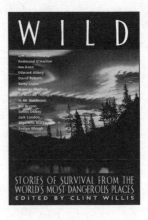

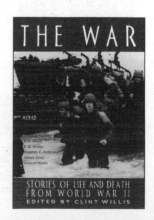